QUEEN OF THE
BLACK BLACK

Megan Kelso

QUEEN
OF THE
BLACK
BLACK

Fantagraphics Books

Fantagraphics Books, 7563 Lake City Way NE, Seattle, Washington 98115 | Editor: Gary Groth; Designer: Alexa Koenings; Publishers: Gary Groth and Kim Thompson; Associate Publisher: Eric Reynolds | *Queen of the Black Black* is copyright © 2011 Megan Kelso. All rights reserved. No part of this book (except small portions for review purposes) may be reproduced in any form or by any electronic or mechanical means without the written permission of the author or the publisher. | Distributed in the U.S. by W.W. Norton and Company, Inc. (800-233-4830); Distributed in Canada by Canadian Manda Group (888-452-6642 x862); Distributed in the U.K, by Turnaround Distribution (44 020 8829-3002); Distributed to comic stores by Diamond Comics Distributors (800-452-6642 x215) | ISBN: 978-1-60699-497-7 | First Fantagraphics printing: July 2011 | Printed in China

FOREWORD

Cartooning is art's most spectacular calling. It's hard enough to learn to write a good story, but to have to figure out how to draw well too requires a kind of freakish ambidexterity. Most cartoonists are either better artists than they are writers, or the other way around, but on the first page of *Queen of the Black Black*, Megan Kelso announces her intention to belong to that rare tribe who masters both. In the twelve years since that bold assertion, she has become one of the most adventurous, intelligent, and graceful cartoonists around.

If this collection is your introduction to Megan Kelso, these stories will whet your appetite for the later work that awaits you. If you're already a Kelso fan, this book provides the most satisfying of prequels, the origin stories of a cartoonist hell-bent on developing her craft, her mind, her eye, and her understanding of the human condition. Here, on display, is the dedication and rigor of a young cartoonist fearlessly flexing her muscles. The work is young in all the best ways—it's hungry, intrepid, and uncompromising— while also defying youthful stereotypes with its surprising empathy. Somehow, in her twenties, Kelso not only already understands the emotional complexity of a deceptively simple moment, but she can wordlessly com-municate this in a single panel—whether it's the deep disappointment of a little girl who has to return a box of cereal to the grocery shelf in the "The Daddy Mask" or the omnivorous, naïve intensity of pre-pubescent sexuality in "In Zanana."

All Kelso's touchstones are present in this first collection. In the book's title story, her use of gouache presages her gorgeous color work. "The Daddy Mask" and "Reunion" document the beginning of her fascination with family and her unerring eye for its complex inter-dynamics. Stories like "Pennyroyal Tea" and "Successful Business Girl" provide glimpses into her singular imagination and her passion for history.

The last page of this book proclaims, "I am not satisfied!" This is the best artistic credo I can think of, and particularly fitting for the restless, vibrant stories featured here. Megan has dedicated herself to rendering the invisible visible, whether it's music or desire, love or disenchantment. In that perpetual pursuit, her dissatisfaction is our gain.

MYLA GOLDBERG
September, 2010

Between 1993 and 1997 I self-published six issues of a comic book called *Girlhero* in which I serialized a long epic story called "Bottlecap" and filled up the extra pages with short stories. Surprise, surprise! The short stories turned out a lot better than the epic.

Since this book encompasses the first five years of my work in comics, it necessarily shows a pretty wide range of ability, documenting my first rocky steps on the path I still tread towards mastery. But I didn't put the stories in chronological order; instead I arranged them in a way that I hope will provide a lively read.

So let me just say this. I plan to be drawing comics when I am an old, old, woman, barring early death or a freak accident. Maybe I'll own a skating rink or maybe I'll be living on catfood omelettes in a damp basement apartment, but I WILL be making comics. Bear this in mind when you finish this book and put it back on the shelf. Forget about it. Then, a few decades from now, pick it up again, read it, and you will say, "Ahhh... so this is where she began."

MEGAN KELSO
Seattle, Washington
May, 1998

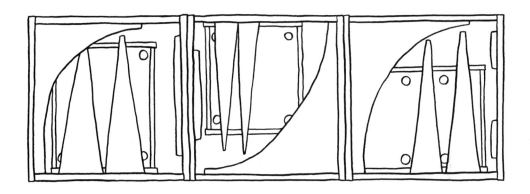

THE DADDY MASK

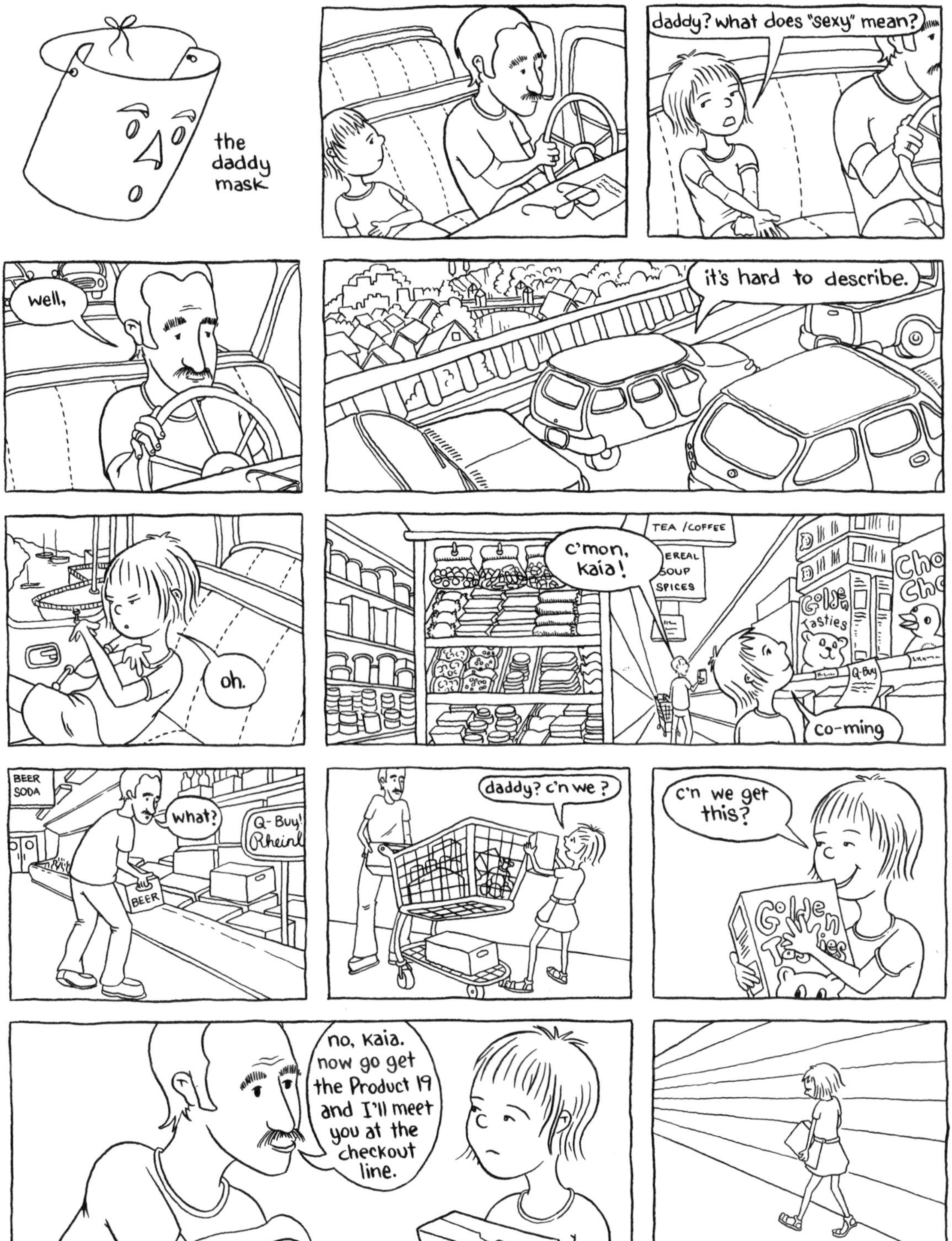
the daddy mask
daddy? what does "sexy" mean?
well,
it's hard to describe.
oh.
TEA / COFFEE
EREAL
SOUP
SPICES
c'mon, kaia!
Golden Tasties
Q-Buy
co-ming
BEER
SODA
what?
Q-Buy!
BEER
daddy? c'n we ?
c'n we get this?
Golden Tasties
no, kaia. now go get the Product 19 and I'll meet you at the checkout line.

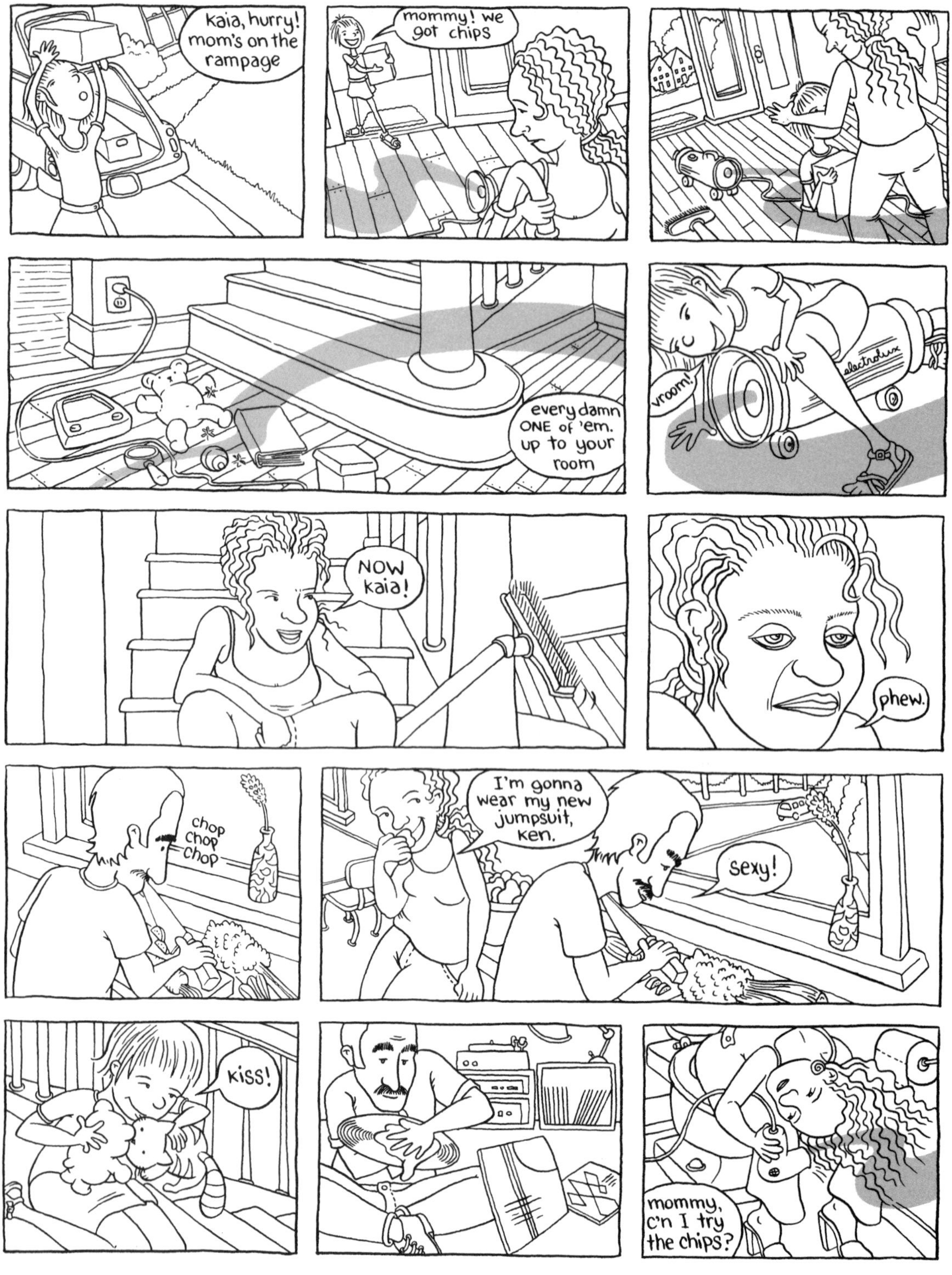
kaia, hurry! mom's on the rampage
mommy! we got chips
every damn ONE of 'em. up to your room
vroom!
electrolux
NOW kaia!
phew.
chop chop chop
I'm gonna wear my new jumpsuit, ken.
sexy!
kiss!
mommy, c'n I try the chips?

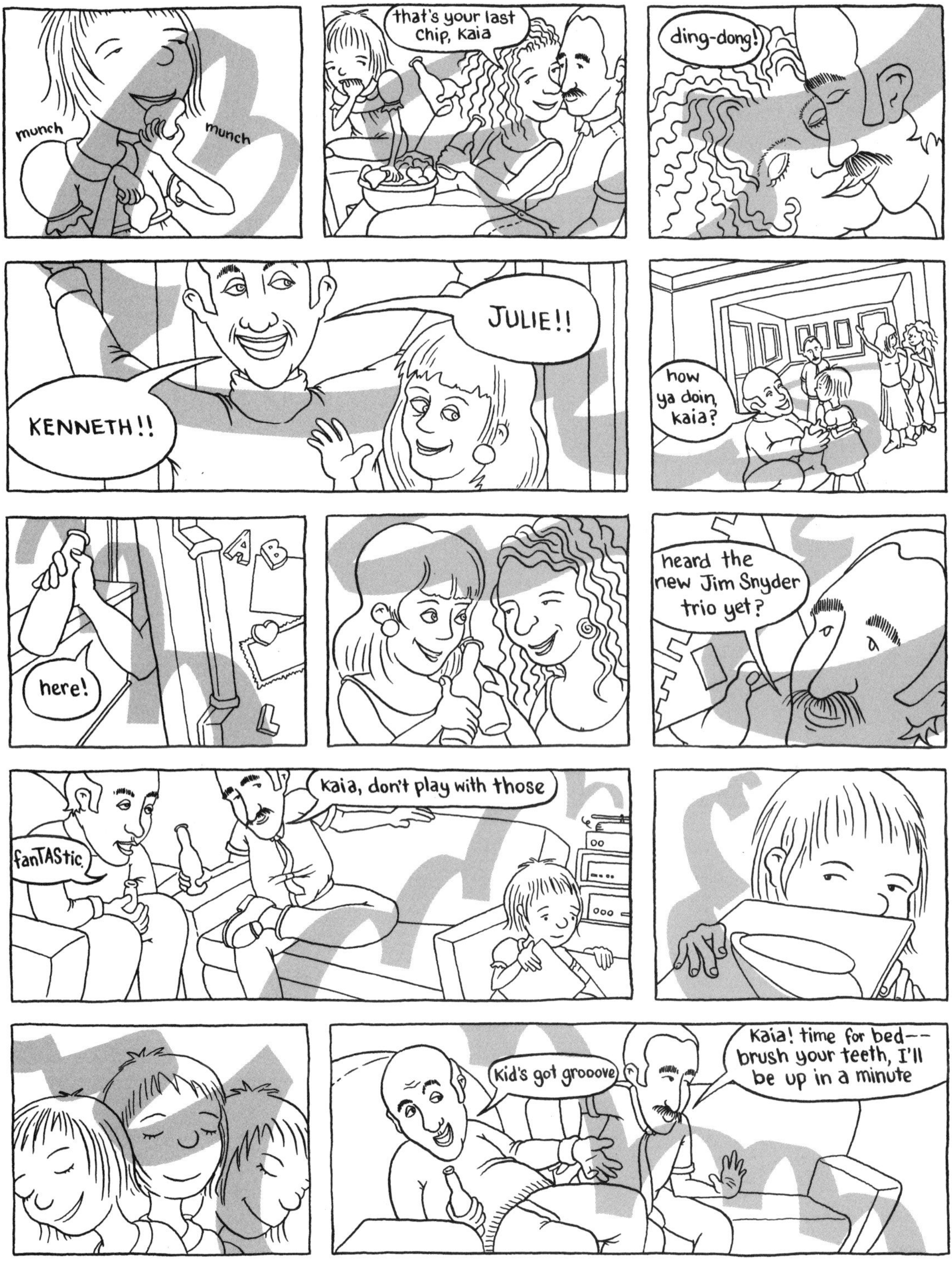
munch
munch
that's your last chip, kaia
ding-dong!
KENNETH!!
JULIE!!
how ya doin, kaia?
here!
heard the new Jim Snyder trio yet?
kaia, don't play with those
fanTAStic.
Kid's got grooove
Kaia! time for bed-- brush your teeth, I'll be up in a minute

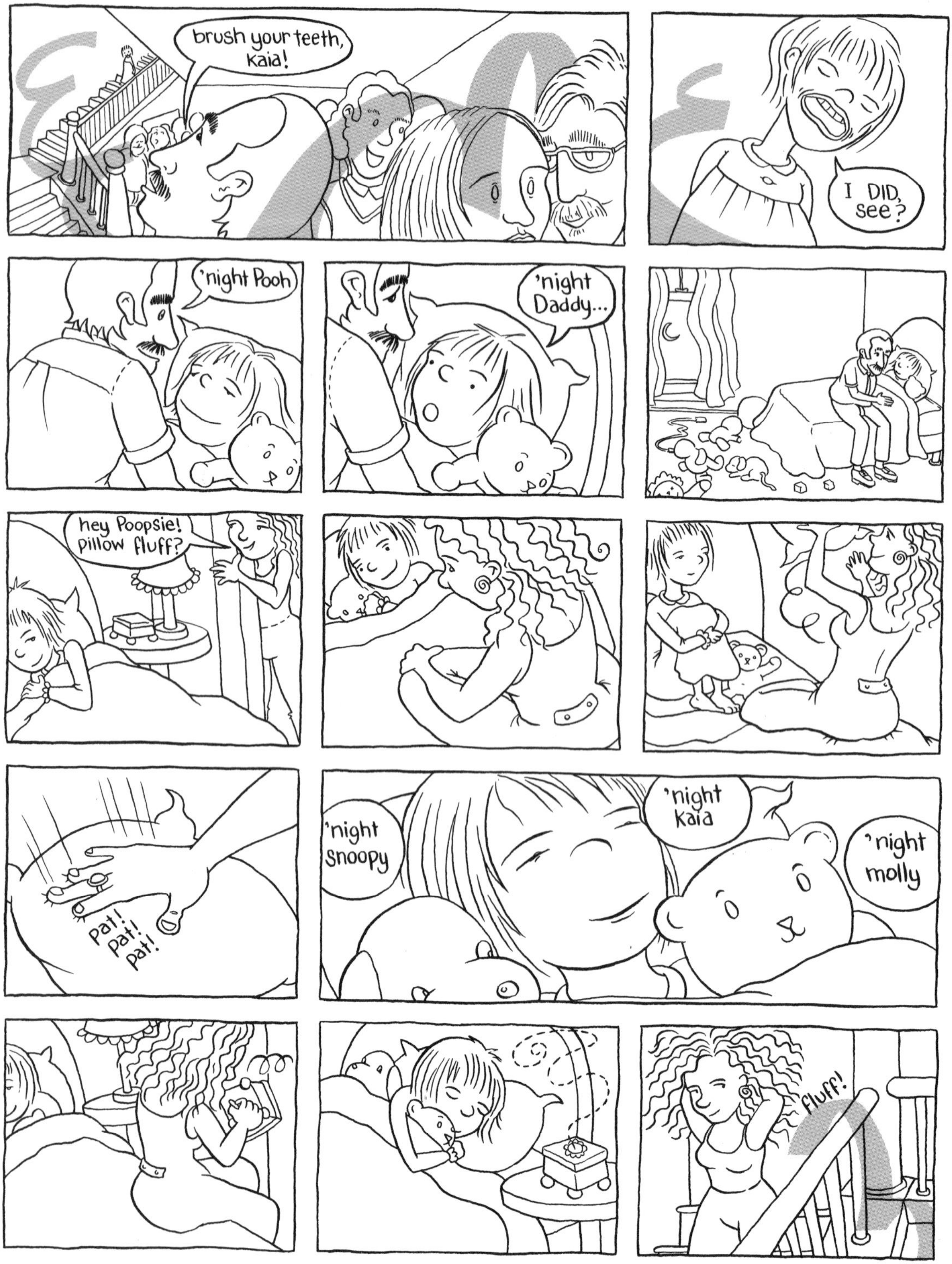
brush your teeth, kaia!
I DID, see?
'night Pooh
'night Daddy...
hey Poopsie! pillow fluff?
pat! pat! pat!
'night snoopy
'night kaia
'night molly
fluff!

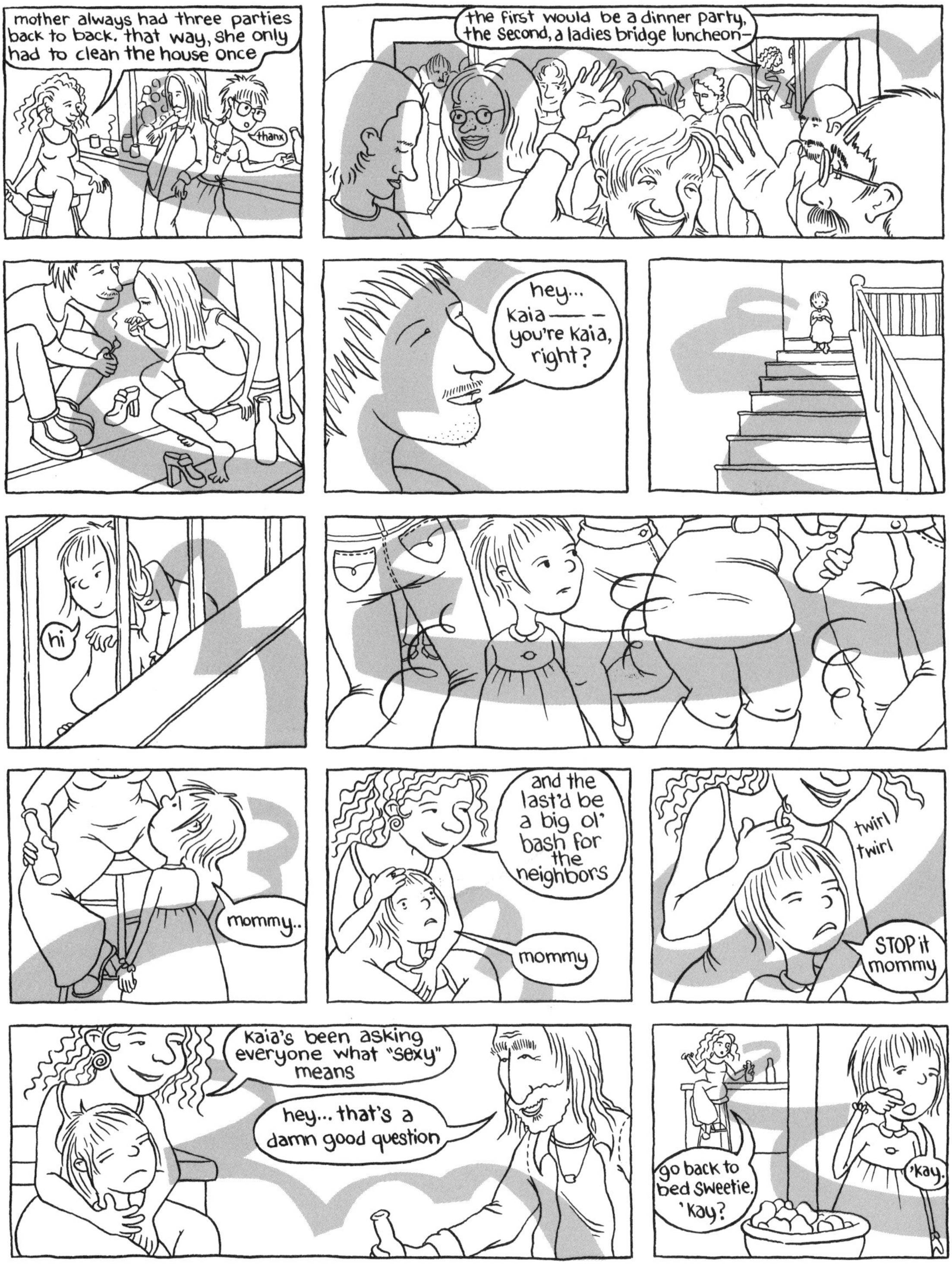
mother always had three parties back to back. that way, she only had to clean the house once
thanx
the first would be a dinner party, the second, a ladies bridge luncheon—
hey... kaia—— — you're kaia, right?
hi
and the last'd be a big ol' bash for the neighbors
mommy..
mommy
twirl twirl
STOP it mommy
kaia's been asking everyone what "sexy" means
hey... that's a damn good question
go back to bed sweetie, 'kay?
'kay.

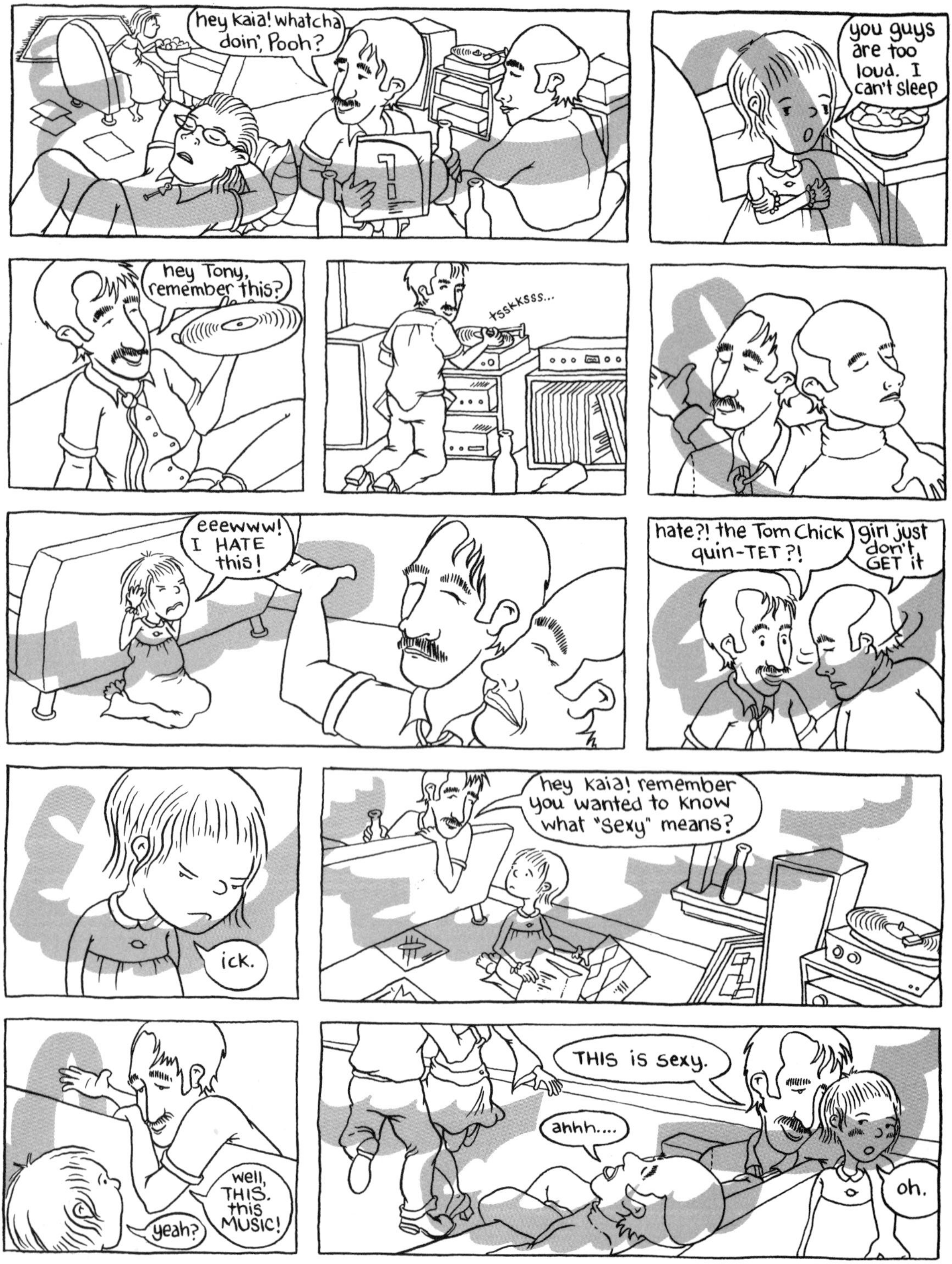
hey kaia! whatcha doin', Pooh?
you guys are too loud. I can't sleep
hey Tony, remember this?
tsskksss...
eeewww! I HATE this!
hate?! the Tom Chick quin-TET?!
girl just don't GET it
ick.
hey kaia! remember you wanted to know what "sexy" means?
yeah?
well, THIS. this MUSIC!
THIS is sexy.
ahhh....
oh.

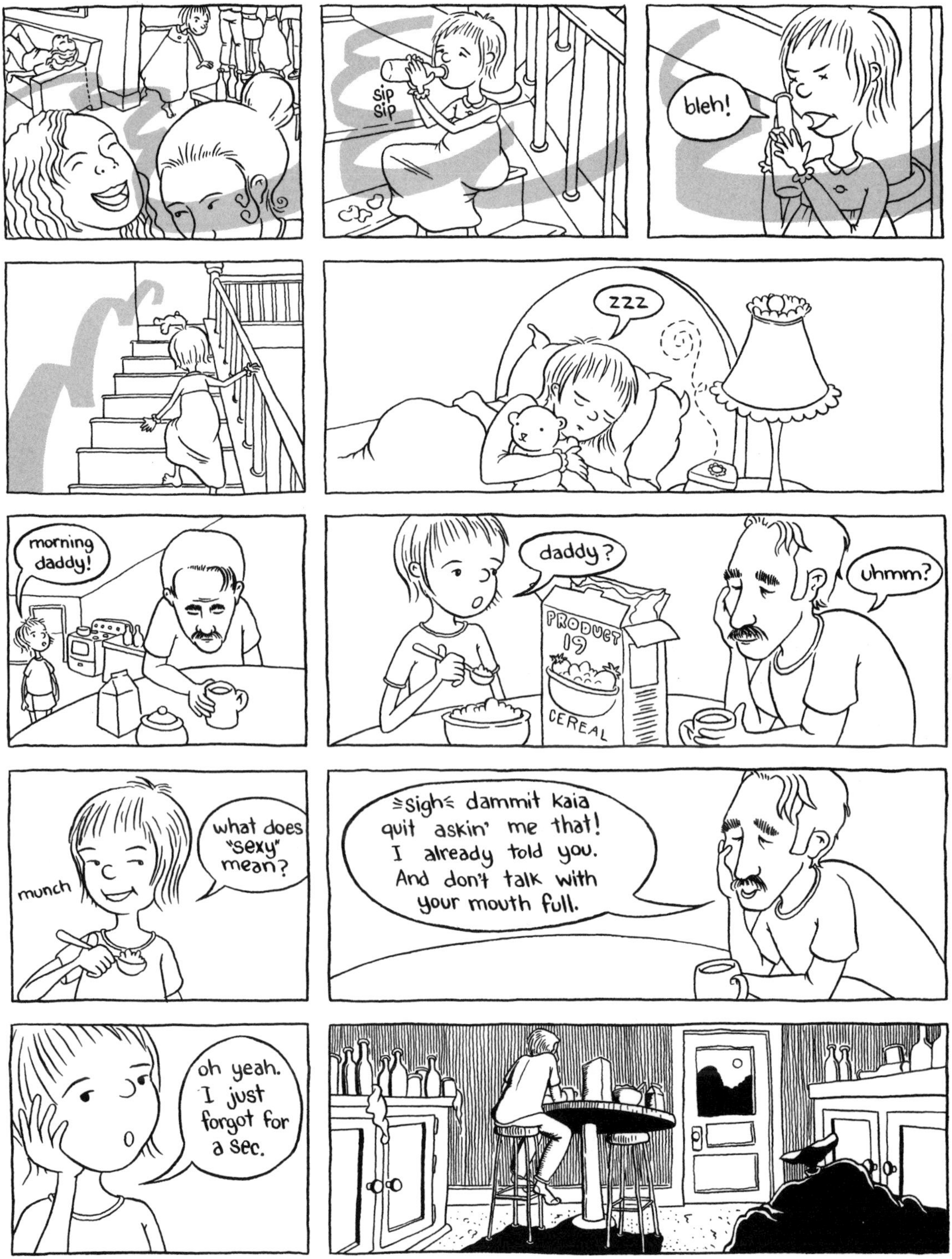
sip
sip
bleh!
zzz
morning daddy!
daddy?
PRODUCT 19
CEREAL
uhmm?
munch
what does "sexy" mean?
≶sigh≷ dammit kaia quit askin' me that! I already told you. And don't talk with your mouth full.
oh yeah. I just forgot for a sec.

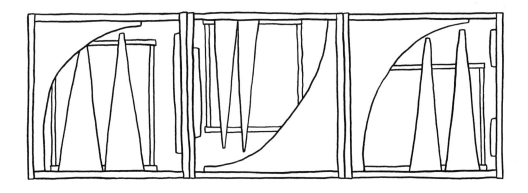

IN ZANANA

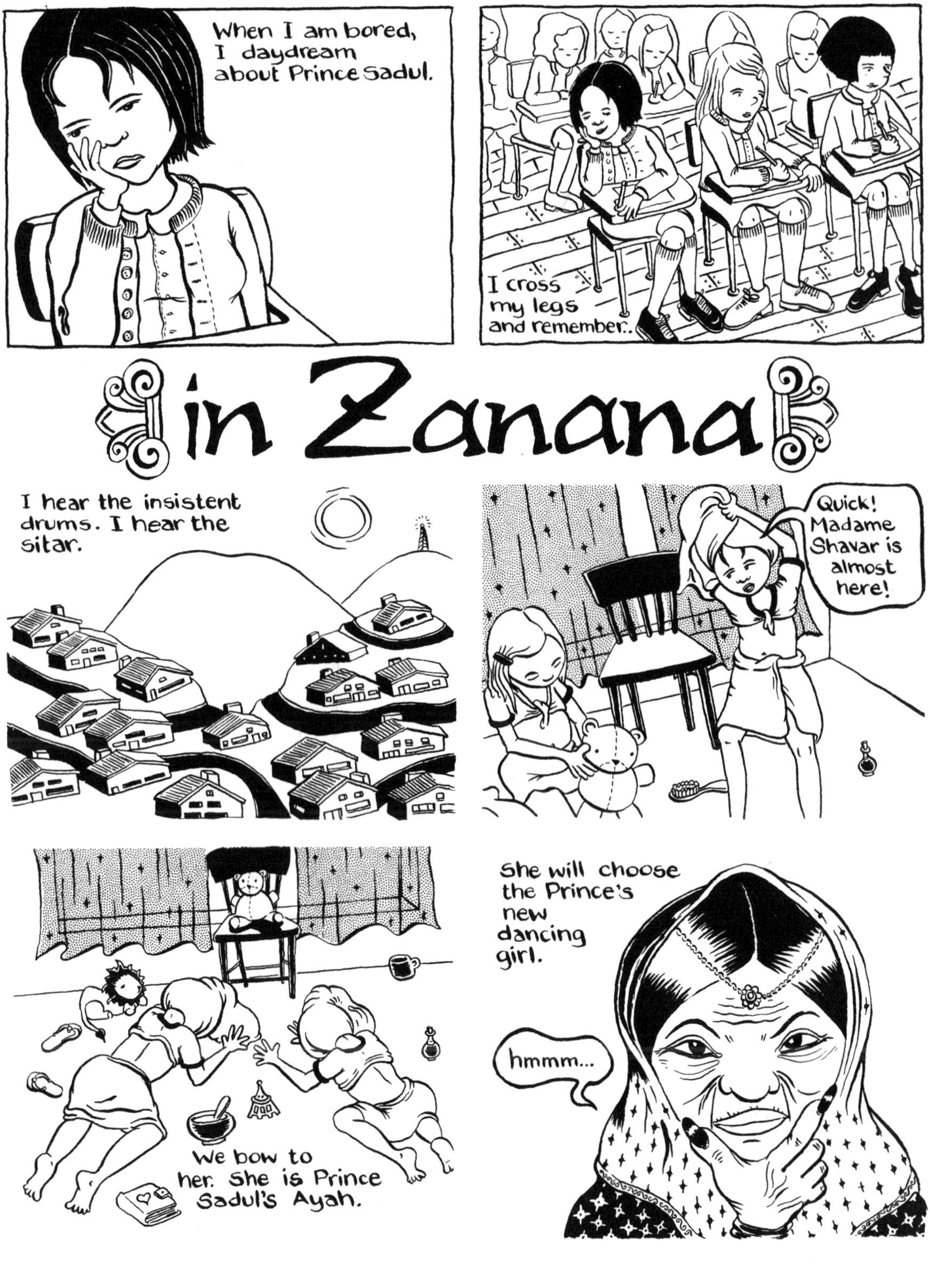
When I am bored, I daydream about Prince Sadul.
I cross my legs and remember...
in Zanana
I hear the insistent drums. I hear the sitar.
Quick! Madame Shavar is almost here!
We bow to her. She is Prince Sadul's Ayah.
She will choose the Prince's new dancing girl.
hmmm...

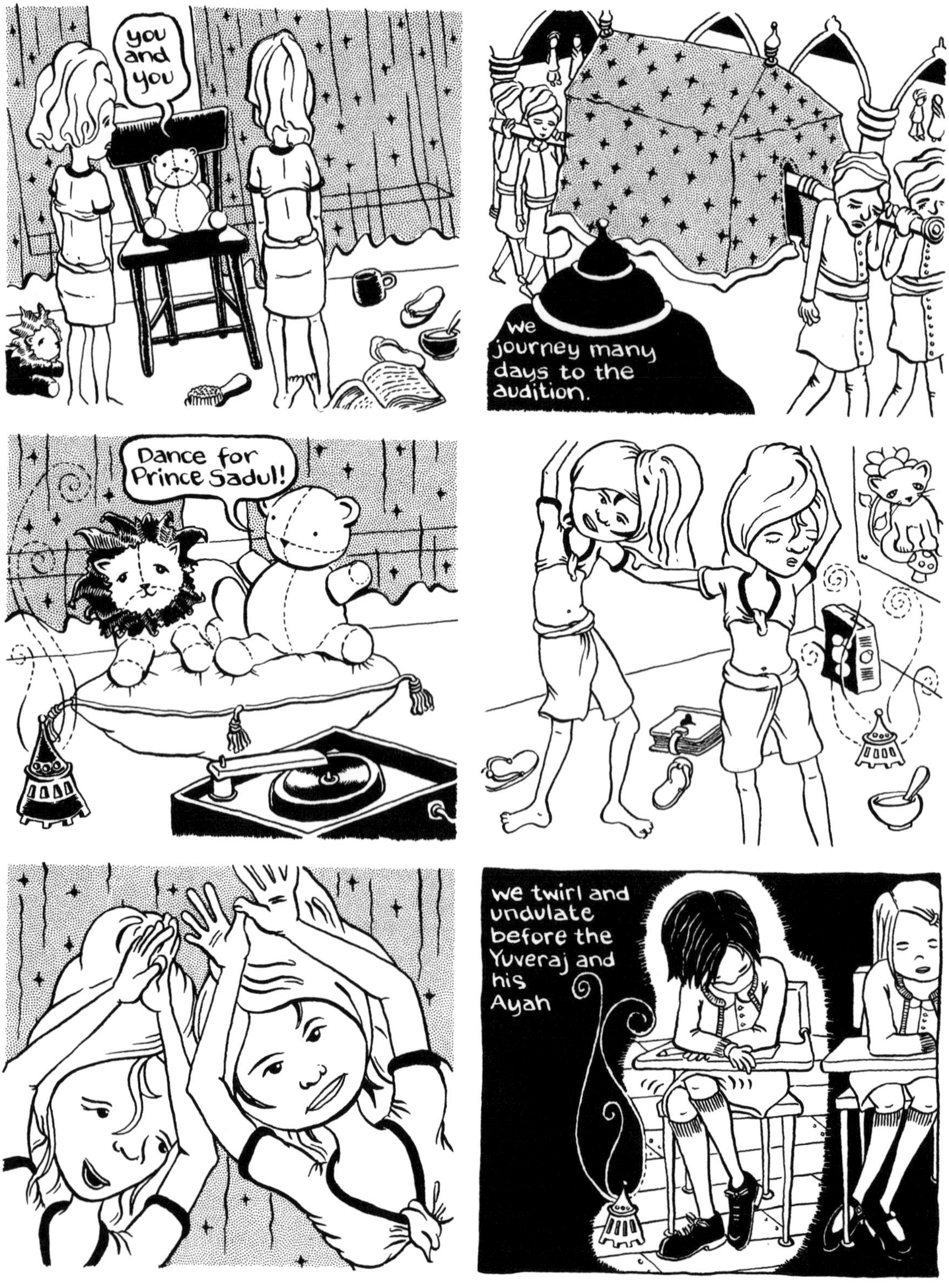
you and you
we journey many days to the audition.
Dance for Prince Sadul!
we twirl and undulate before the Yuveraj and his Ayah

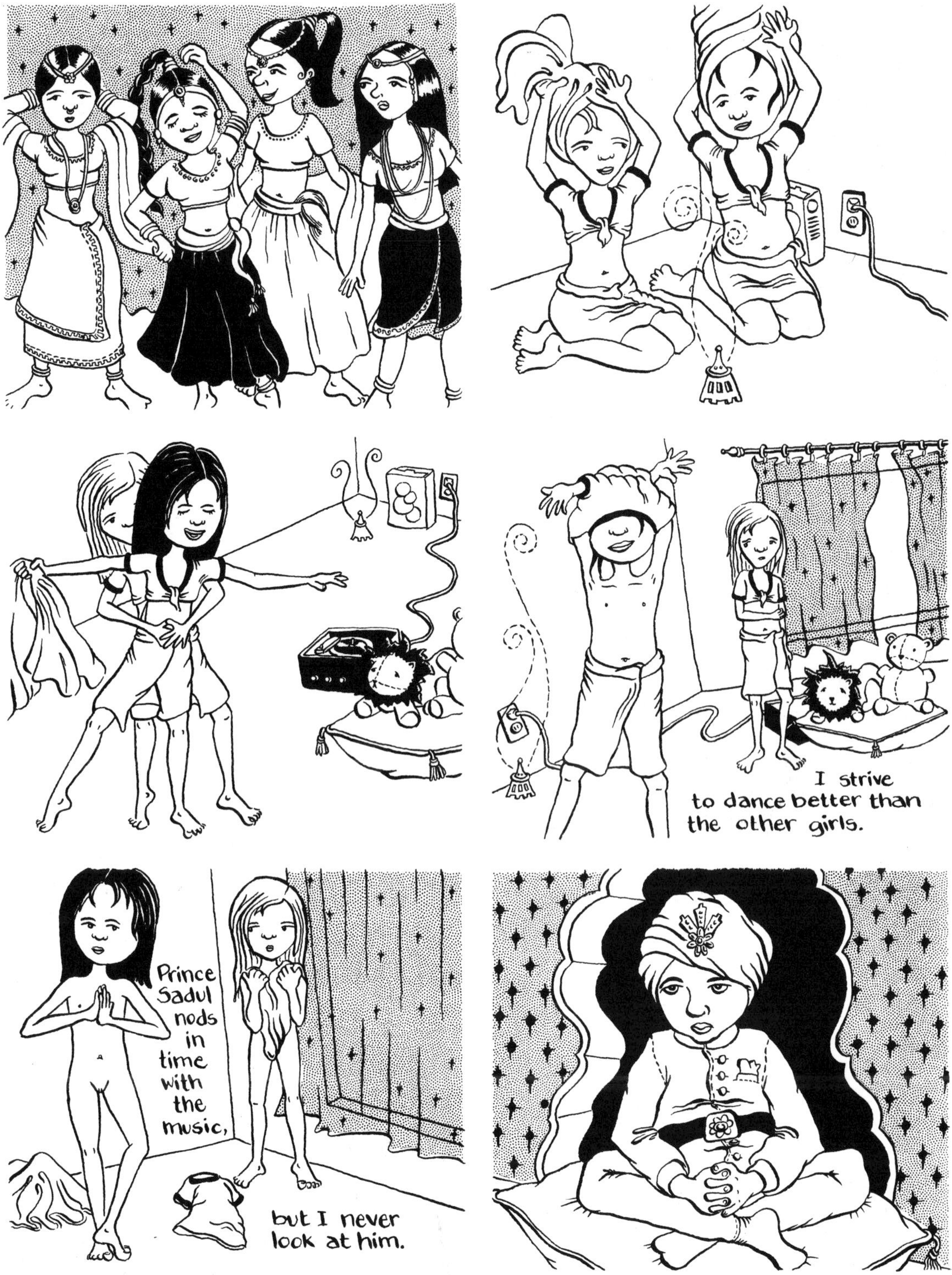
I strive to dance better than the other girls.
Prince Sadul nods in time with the music,
but I never look at him.

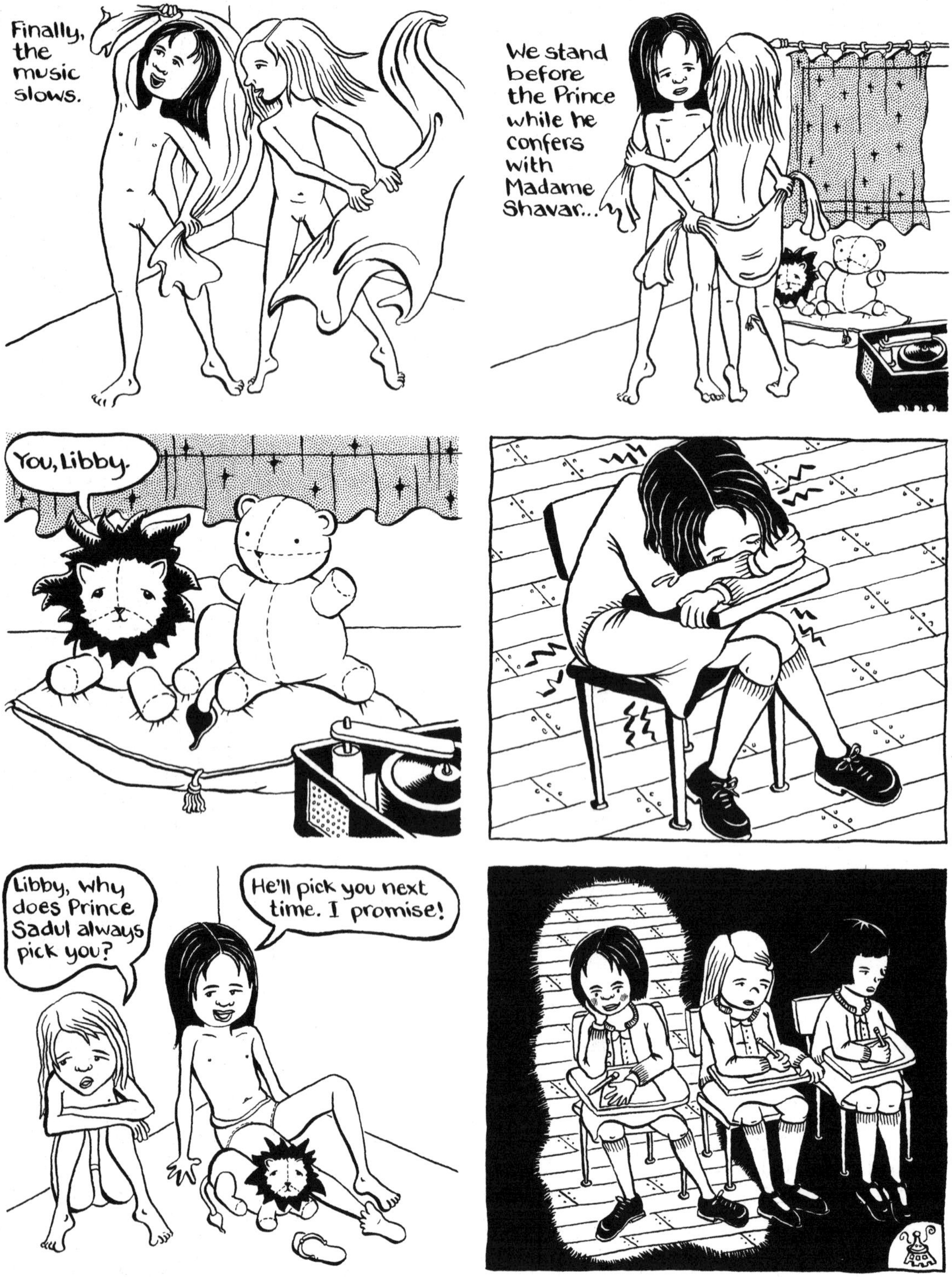
Finally, the music slows.
We stand before the Prince while he confers with Madame Shavar...
You, Libby.
Libby, why does Prince Sadul always pick you?
He'll pick you next time. I promise!

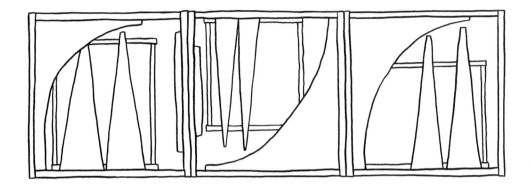

GLAMOUR

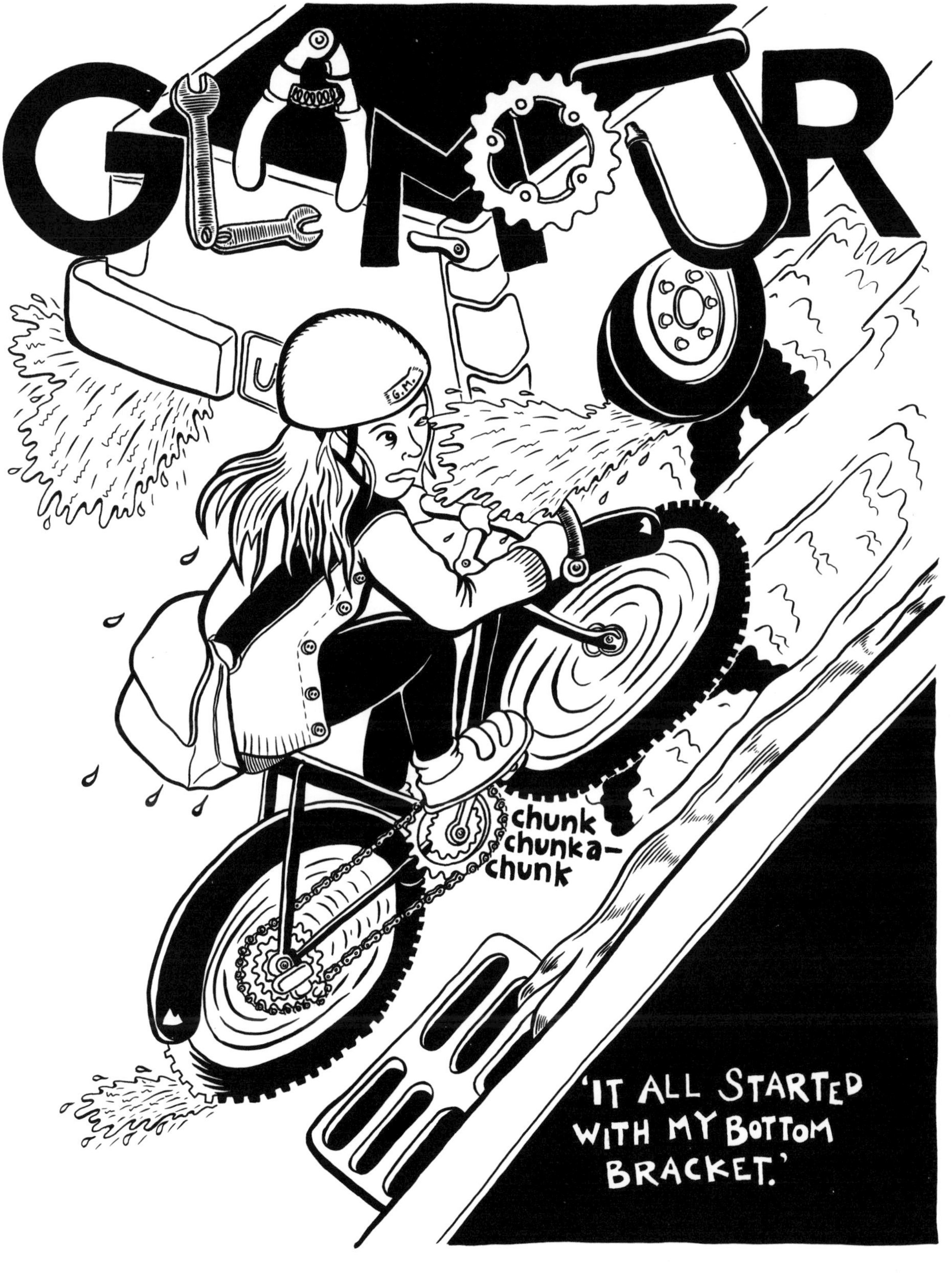
GLAMOUR
G.M.
chunk chunka-chunk
'IT ALL STARTED WITH MY BOTTOM BRACKET.'

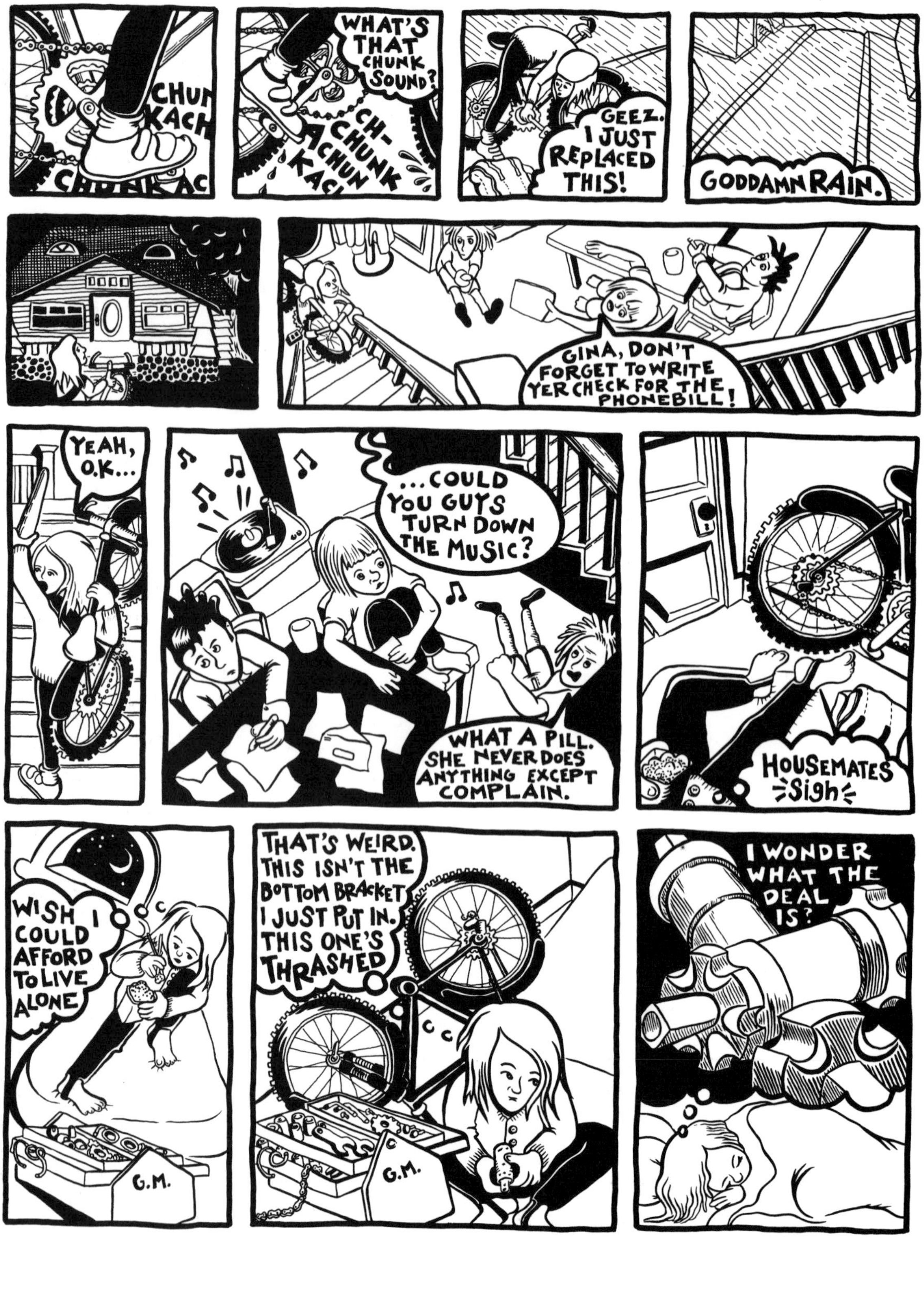
CHUN
KACH
CHUNK AC
WHAT'S THAT CHUNK SOUND?
CH-CHUNK
ACHUN
KACH
GEEZ. I JUST REPLACED THIS!
GODDAMN RAIN.
GINA, DON'T FORGET TO WRITE YER CHECK FOR THE PHONEBILL!
YEAH, O.K...
...COULD YOU GUYS TURN DOWN THE MUSIC?
WHAT A PILL. SHE NEVER DOES ANYTHING EXCEPT COMPLAIN.
HOUSEMATES
Sigh
WISH I COULD AFFORD TO LIVE ALONE
G.M.
THAT'S WEIRD. THIS ISN'T THE BOTTOM BRACKET I JUST PUT IN. THIS ONE'S THRASHED
G.M.
I WONDER WHAT THE DEAL IS?

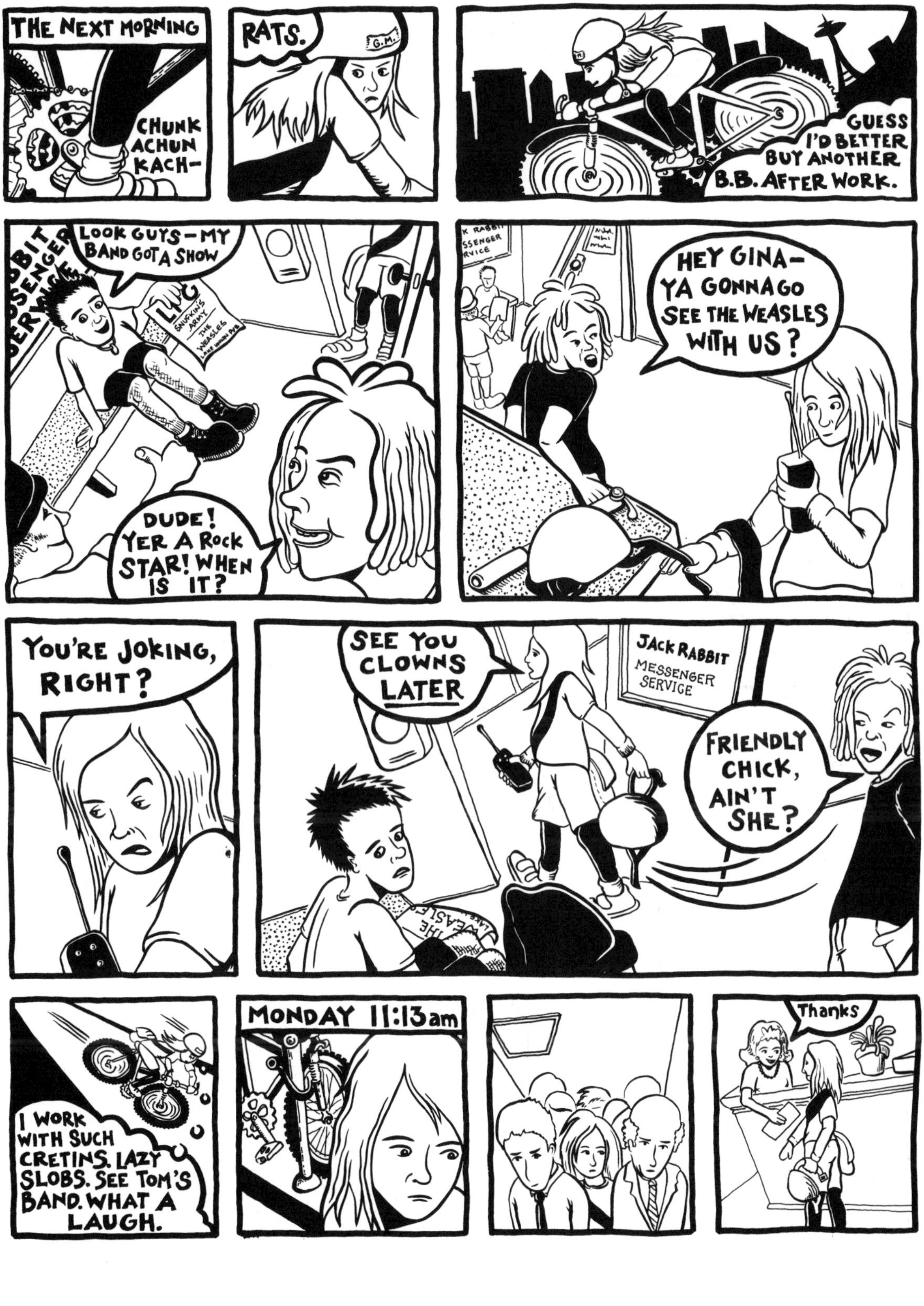
THE NEXT MORNING
CHUNK ACHUN KACH-
RATS.
GUESS I'D BETTER BUY ANOTHER B.B. AFTER WORK.
JACK RABBIT MESSENGER SERVICE
LOOK GUYS—MY BAND GOT A SHOW
DUDE! YER A ROCK STAR! WHEN IS IT?
HEY GINA— YA GONNA GO SEE THE WEASLES WITH US?
YOU'RE JOKING, RIGHT?
SEE YOU CLOWNS LATER
JACK RABBIT MESSENGER SERVICE
FRIENDLY CHICK, AIN'T SHE?
I WORK WITH SUCH CRETINS. LAZY SLOBS. SEE TOM'S BAND. WHAT A LAUGH.
MONDAY 11:13am
Thanks

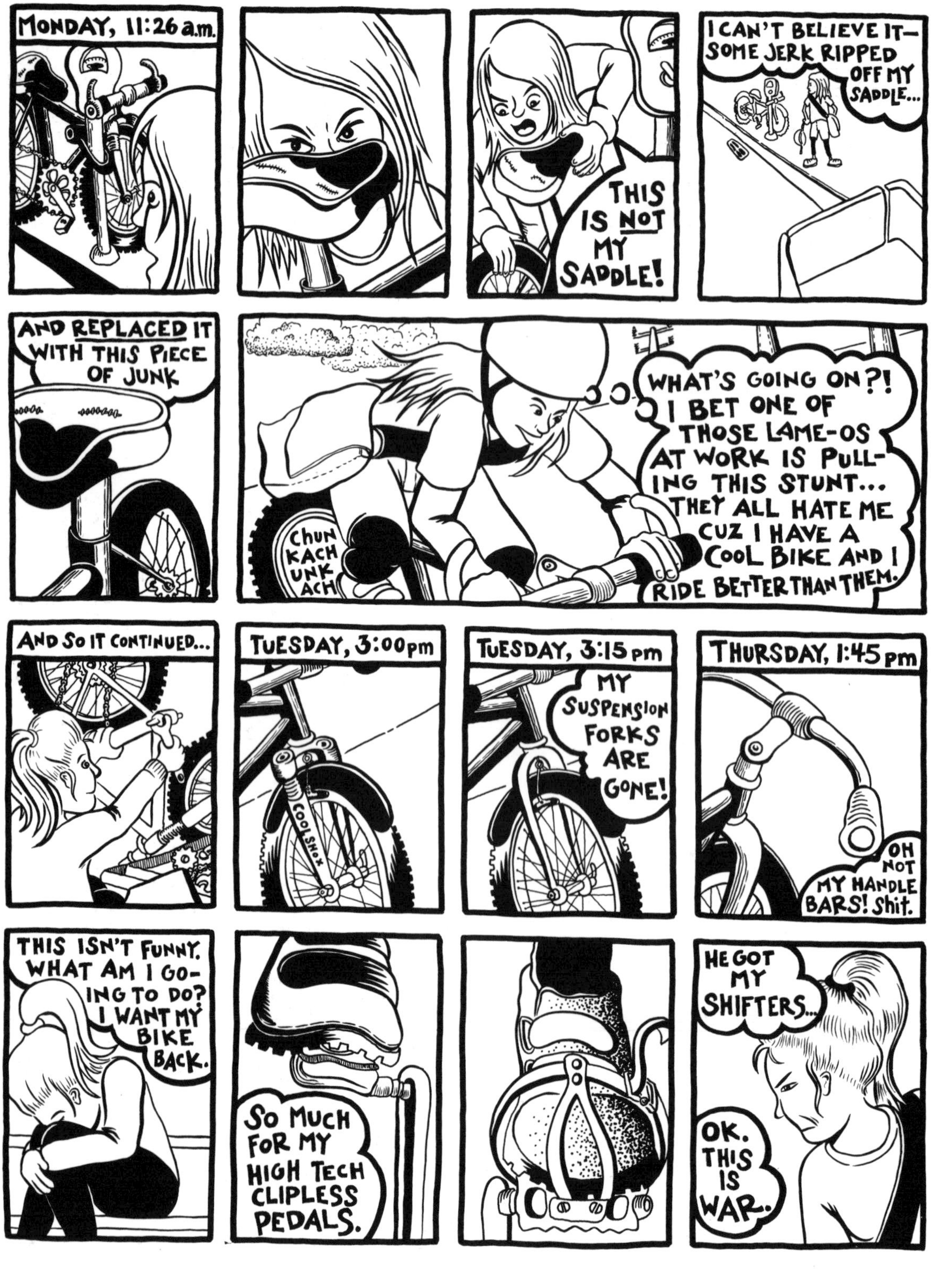
MONDAY, 11:26 a.m.
THIS IS NOT MY SADDLE!
I CAN'T BELIEVE IT— SOME JERK RIPPED OFF MY SADDLE...
AND REPLACED IT WITH THIS PIECE OF JUNK
WHAT'S GOING ON?! I BET ONE OF THOSE LAME-OS AT WORK IS PULLING THIS STUNT... THEY ALL HATE ME CUZ I HAVE A COOL BIKE AND I RIDE BETTER THAN THEM.
CHUN KACH UNK ACH
AND SO IT CONTINUED...
TUESDAY, 3:00pm
COOLSHOX
TUESDAY, 3:15 pm
MY SUSPENSION FORKS ARE GONE!
THURSDAY, 1:45 pm
OH NOT MY HANDLE BARS! Shit.
THIS ISN'T FUNNY. WHAT AM I GOING TO DO? I WANT MY BIKE BACK.
SO MUCH FOR MY HIGH TECH CLIPLESS PEDALS.
HE GOT MY SHIFTERS...
OK. THIS IS WAR.

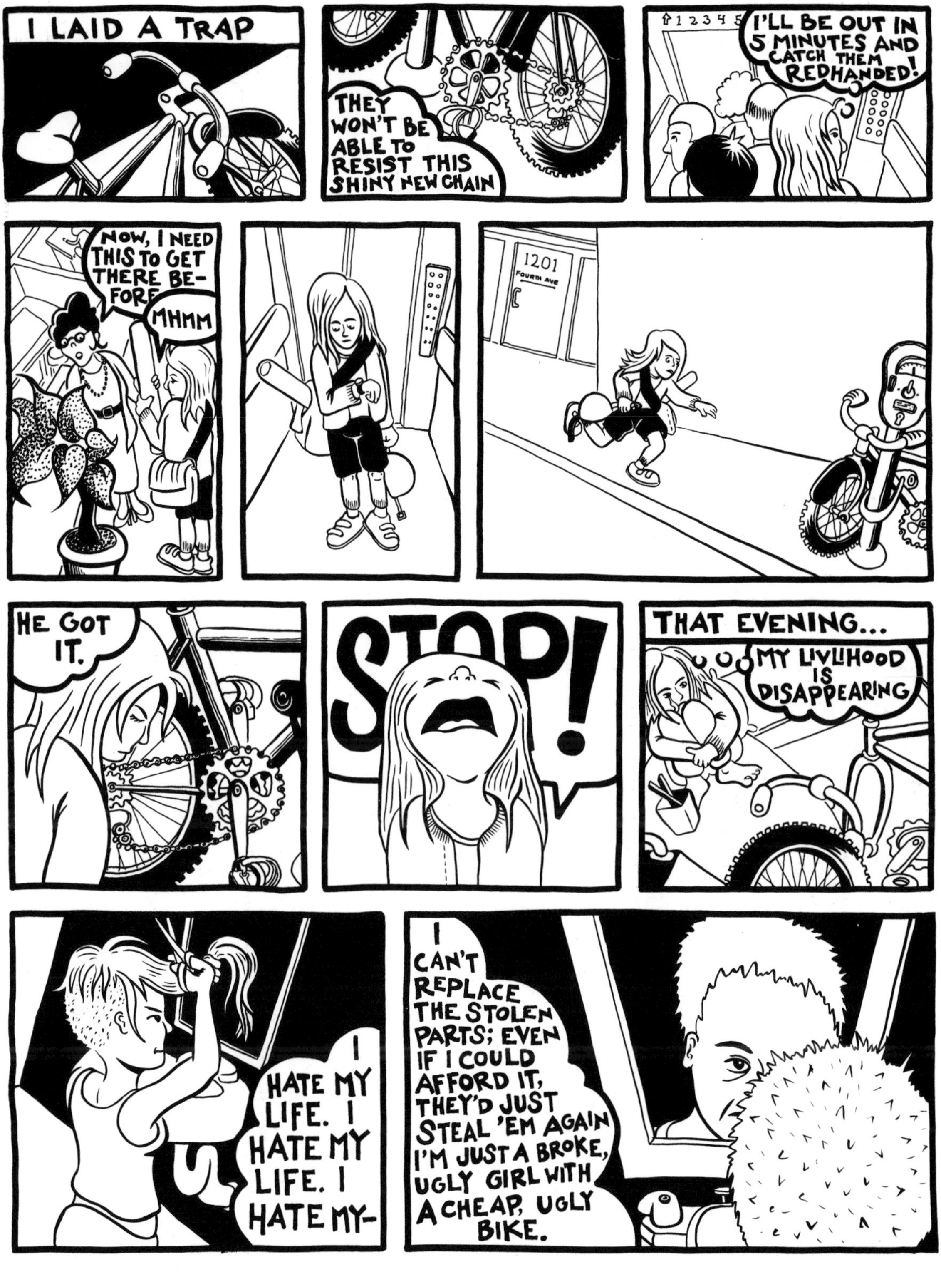

I LAID A TRAP
THEY WON'T BE ABLE TO RESIST THIS SHINY NEW CHAIN
I'LL BE OUT IN 5 MINUTES AND CATCH THEM REDHANDED!
NOW, I NEED THIS TO GET THERE BE-FORE
MHMM
1201 FOURTH AVE
HE GOT IT.
STOP!
THAT EVENING...
MY LIVLIHOOD IS DISAPPEARING
I HATE MY LIFE. I HATE MY LIFE. I HATE MY-
I CAN'T REPLACE THE STOLEN PARTS; EVEN IF I COULD AFFORD IT, THEY'D JUST STEAL 'EM AGAIN
I'M JUST A BROKE, UGLY GIRL WITH A CHEAP, UGLY BIKE.

A WEEK AND MANY BIKE PARTS LATER.

GOD GINA! YOU LOOK LIKE HELL! IS SOMETHING WRONG?

SPARE ME YER PITY. WE BOTH KNOW YER IN ON THIS HILARIOUS PRANK JOE

PRANK? I DON'T GET IT— WHAT PRANK

FINE, JOE. WHATEVER. BE CLUELESS. BUT I KNOW YOU AND YOUR PALS ARE BEHIND THIS SICK LITTLE—

BUT GINA, I'M NOT EVEN—

SAVE IT. I HAVETA GO DO SOME WORK.

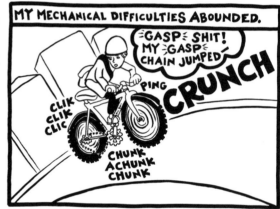
MY MECHANICAL DIFFICULTIES ABOUNDED.

GASP SHIT! MY GASP CHAIN JUMPED

CLIK CLIK CLIC

PING

CRUNCH

CHUNK ACHUNK CHUNK

SNAPPED BRAKE CABLE

HUFFY 2000

CRACKED FENDERS... BROKEN SPOKES, BENT AXLE... PITTED HEAD SET... WHERE WILL IT END?

GINA—WHAT'S GOIN' ON? YER ONE OF OUR BEST RIDERS, BUT YOU'VE BEEN MESSIN' UP LATELY. WHAT GIVES?

NOTHING, BOB

MY BIKE'S JUST A LITTLE OUT OF WHACK, NO BIG, I'M FIXING IT BACK UP.

IF HE FIRES ME, I'M SCREWED. I DON'T KNOW HOW TO DO ANYTHING ELSE!

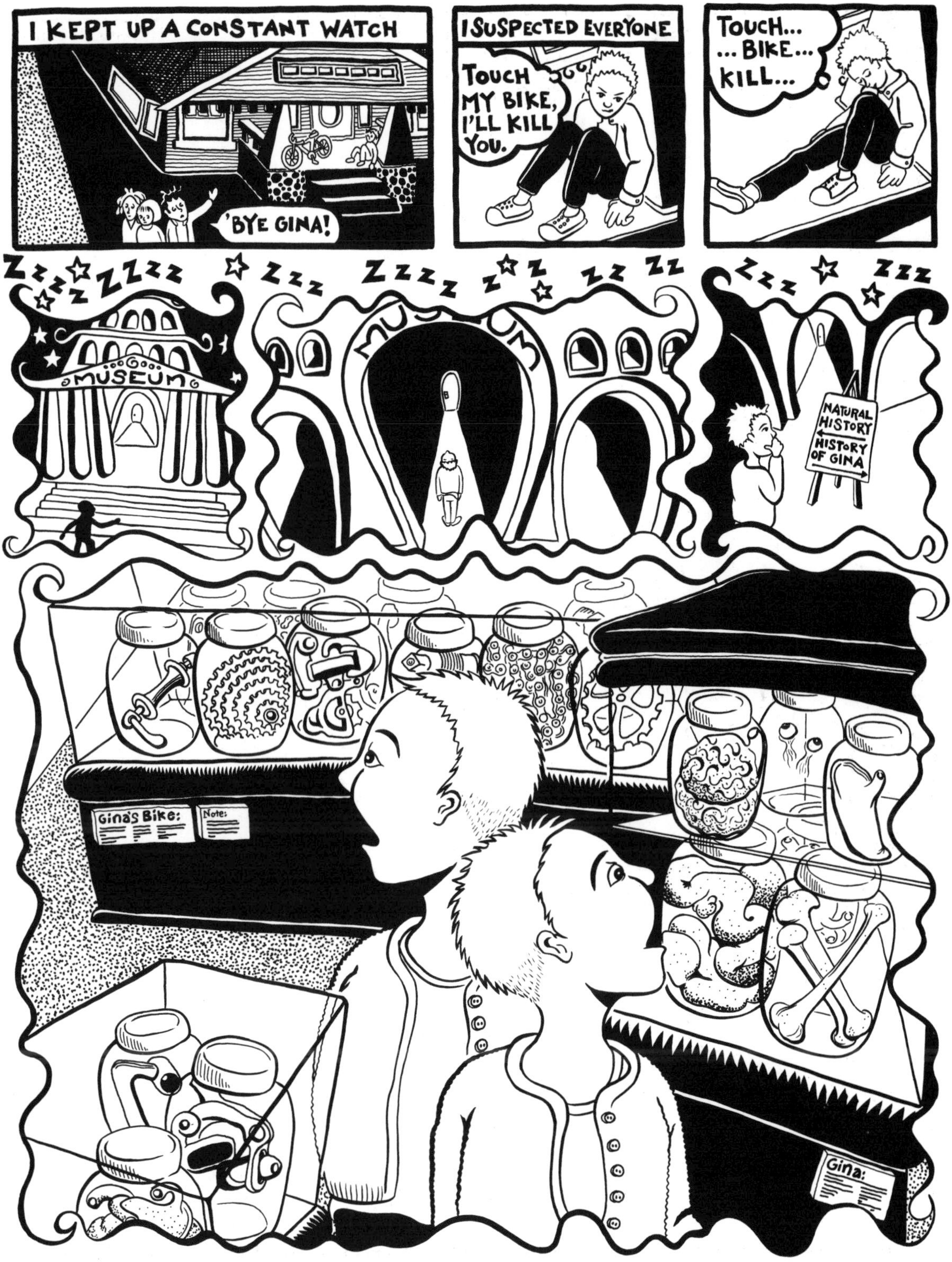
I KEPT UP A CONSTANT WATCH
'BYE GINA!
I SUSPECTED EVERYONE
TOUCH MY BIKE, I'LL KILL YOU.
TOUCH... ...BIKE... KILL...
MUSEUM
MUSEUM
NATURAL HISTORY
HISTORY OF GINA
Gina's Bike:
Note:
Gina:

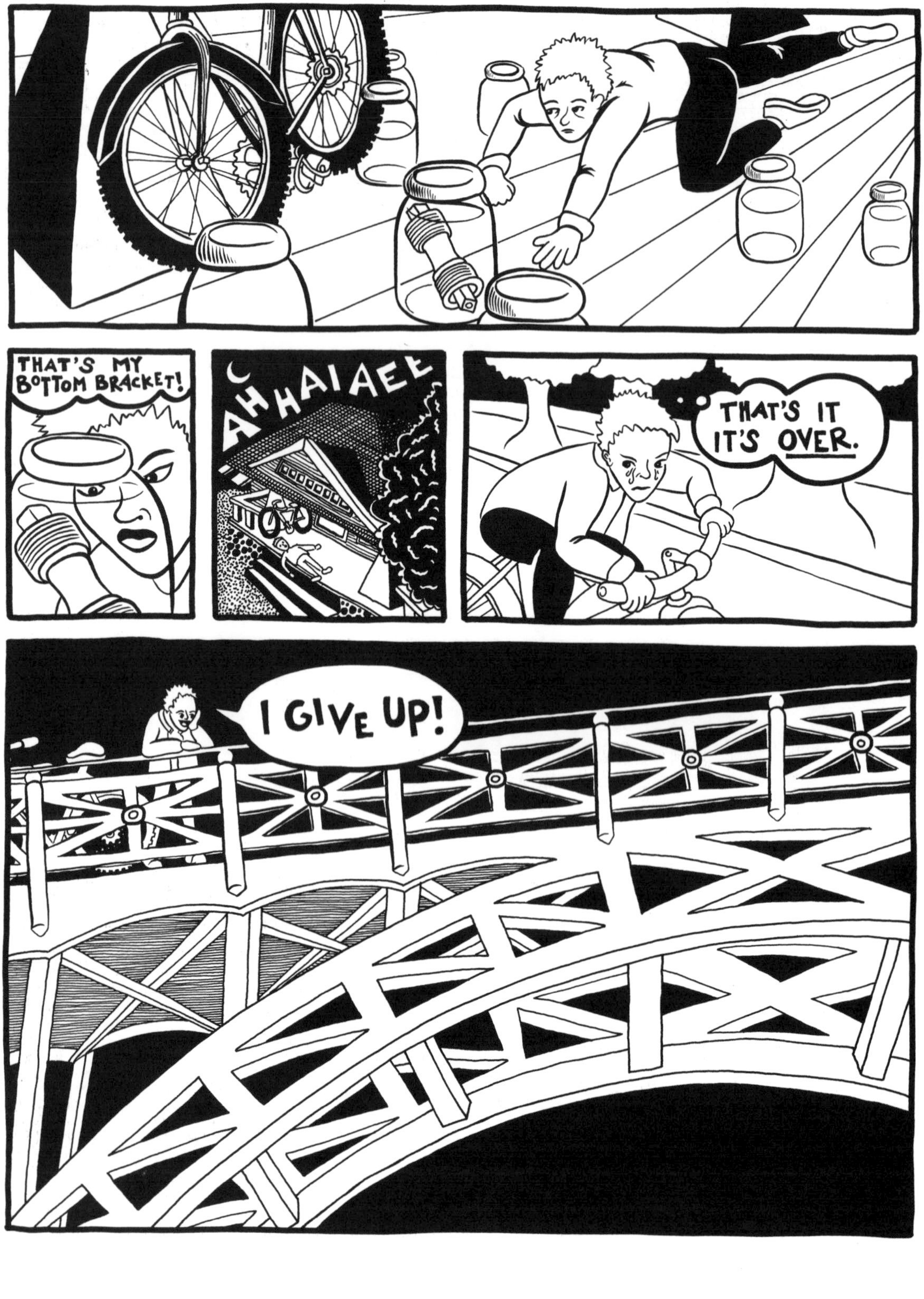
THAT'S MY BOTTOM BRACKET!
AHHAIAEE
THAT'S IT IT'S OVER.
I GIVE UP!

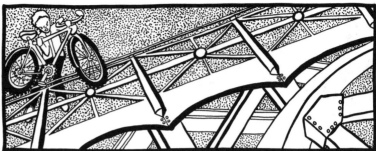

AFTERWARDS, FROZEN, I WALKED THROUGH THE DAWN.

I KILLED IT.

ALL I REMEMBER

IS FINDING THE KEYCHAIN

AND SO, I DECIDED TO COME HERE.

Pete's BODY SHOP
100 LAKE STREET
MINNEAPOLIS, MN

THE END

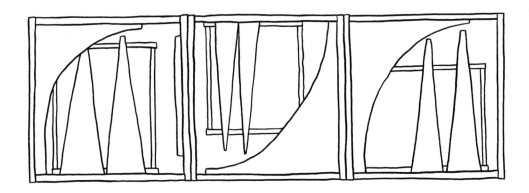

HER PEAS AND QUEUES

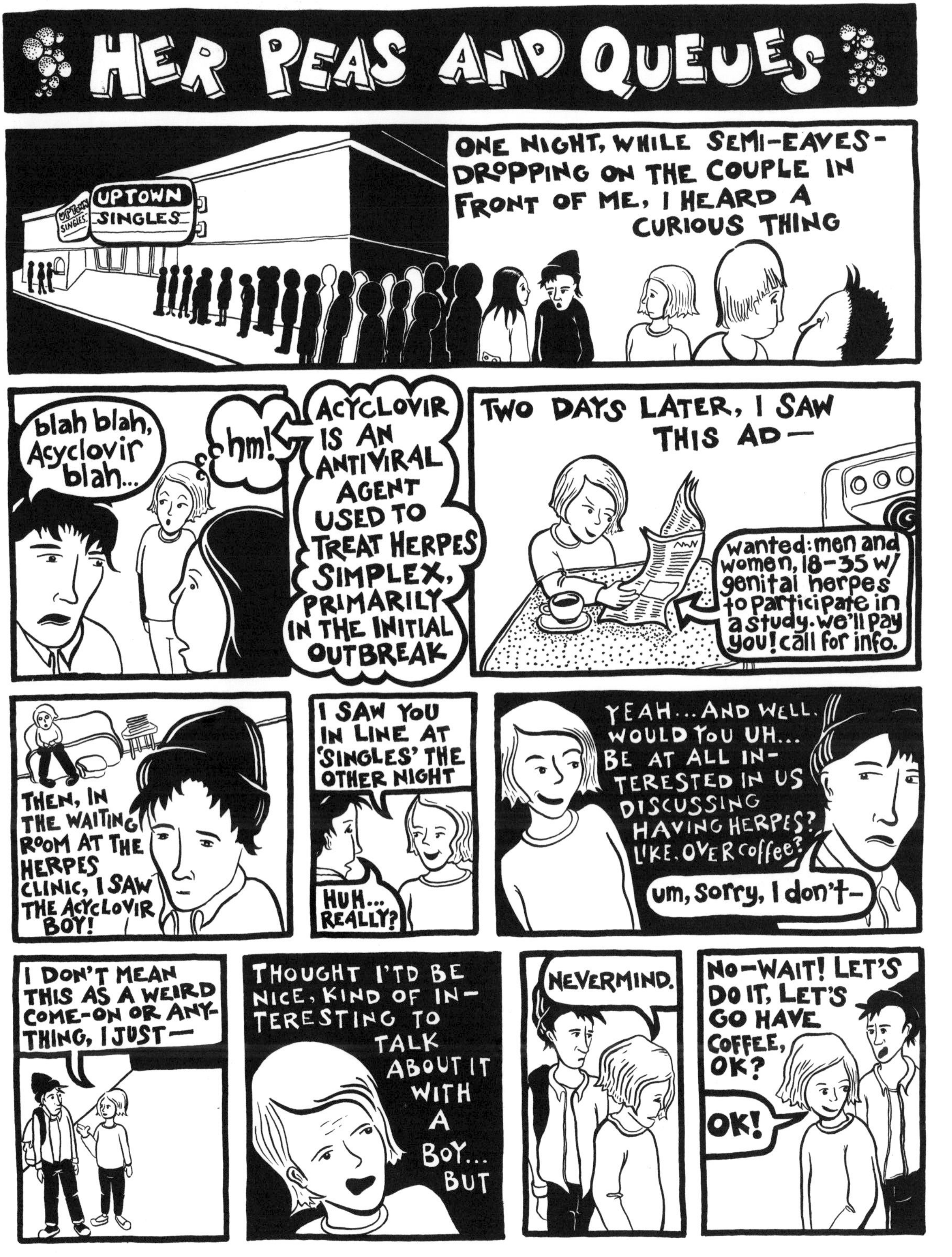
HER PEAS AND QUEUES
UPTOWN SINGLES
ONE NIGHT, WHILE SEMI-EAVES-DROPPING ON THE COUPLE IN FRONT OF ME, I HEARD A CURIOUS THING
blah blah, Acyclovir blah...
hm!
ACYCLOVIR IS AN ANTIVIRAL AGENT USED TO TREAT HERPES SIMPLEX, PRIMARILY IN THE INITIAL OUTBREAK
TWO DAYS LATER, I SAW THIS AD—
wanted: men and women, 18–35 w/ genital herpes to participate in a study. we'll pay you! call for info.
THEN, IN THE WAITING ROOM AT THE HERPES CLINIC, I SAW THE ACYCLOVIR BOY!
I SAW YOU IN LINE AT 'SINGLES' THE OTHER NIGHT
HUH... REALLY?
YEAH... AND WELL. WOULD YOU UH... BE AT ALL INTERESTED IN US DISCUSSING HAVING HERPES? LIKE, OVER coffee?
um, sorry, I don't—
I DON'T MEAN THIS AS A WEIRD COME-ON OR ANYTHING, I JUST—
THOUGHT I'TD BE NICE, KIND OF INTERESTING TO TALK ABOUT IT WITH A BOY... BUT
NEVERMIND.
NO—WAIT! LET'S DO IT, LET'S GO HAVE COFFEE, OK?
OK!

SO HOW'D YA GET IT?

YOU FIRST.

I WAS IN COLLEGE... MY BOYFRIEND TED AND I WERE IN THE PROCESS OF BREAKING UP. ONE NIGHT AT THE BROTHERHOOD TAVERN, I PICKED UP THIS COOL OLDER GUY, A CAR MECHANIC.

WANNA DANCE?

HOW OLD WAS HE?

WHY DO COLLEGE GIRLS THROW THEMSELVES AT OLDER BLUE COLLAR DUDES?

33, I THINK.

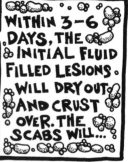

MMYUM.. DO YOU HAVE ANY DISEASES?

MMM...DON'T WORRY BABE, I'M CLEAN. OH BABE, I WANT YOU.

SO WE FUCKED UNPROTECTED AND A FEW WEEKS LATER...

AWW, C'MON, EVERYONE KNOWS THOSE OLDER GUYS SCREWED ANYTHING THAT MOVED BACK IN THE 60'S AND 70'S

I FELT THIS ITCHY PANG AND

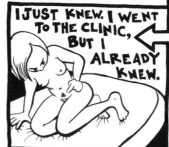

I JUST KNEW. I WENT TO THE CLINIC, BUT I ALREADY KNEW.

WITHIN 3-6 DAYS, THE INITIAL FLUID FILLED LESIONS WILL DRY OUT AND CRUST OVER. THE SCABS WILL...

BUMMER.

YEAH. THE WORST PART WAS, I'D HAD SEX WITH TED IN THE MEANTIME, SO I HAD TO TELL HIM ABOUT THE MECHANIC GUY AND HOW HE MIGHT BE INFECTED — LUCKILY HE WASN'T. BUT IT ALL JUST SUCKED.

YEAH, I'LL SAY — SUCKED FOR TED, THAT IS !!

GEEZ, SHE SOUNDS AS WIGGED OUT AS THE GIRL WHO GAVE ME HERPES.

THE GUY, THE MECHANIC, TOLD ME LATER HE HADN'T HAD AN OUT-BREAK IN 10 YEARS, SO HE THOUGHT IT WAS SAFE...NOT. BUT I'M PROUD THAT I HAVEN'T GIVEN IT TO ANYBODY.

YEAH, THAT'S GREAT NEVERMIND THAT YOU ALMOST INFECTED YOUR BOYFRIEND!

IT'S JUST — YA KNOW, YA LEARN TO DEAL.

HE DOESN'T SEEM VERY SYMPA-THETIC

MMM..

So, how about you? She was beautiful and crazy

My situation was different— I was in love. She was still in highschool. I'd just started college; she worked at 7-11. MHMM.. Had yourself a little townie girl. Typical

I knew she was more experienced than I, but she was only 15 — I didn't think she'd had TIME to catch anything.

Wow, herpes at 15? Yeah, I just never thought— God, that poor girl. Guess she got it from some other sleazy older guy...

Jenny— I've been to the doctor— hell, I've got sores all over my dick! You're the only one I could've gotten it from. Why didn't you tell me? SHUT UP! I don't have herpes ≷SNIFFLE≷ just get away from me!

She never would admit it— she was in complete denial, even when I threatened to tell her parents...finally I just gave up on her— THREATS! How effective. You're s'posed to be the mature one here BUB. —She was really messed up in other ways too.

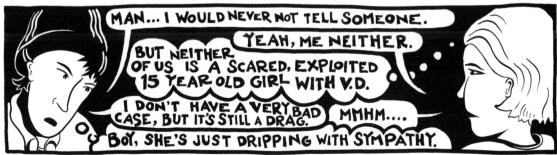

Man... I would never not tell someone. Yeah, me neither. But neither of us is a scared, exploited 15 year old girl with V.D. I don't have a very bad case, but it's still a drag. MMHM.... Boy, she's just dripping with sympathy.

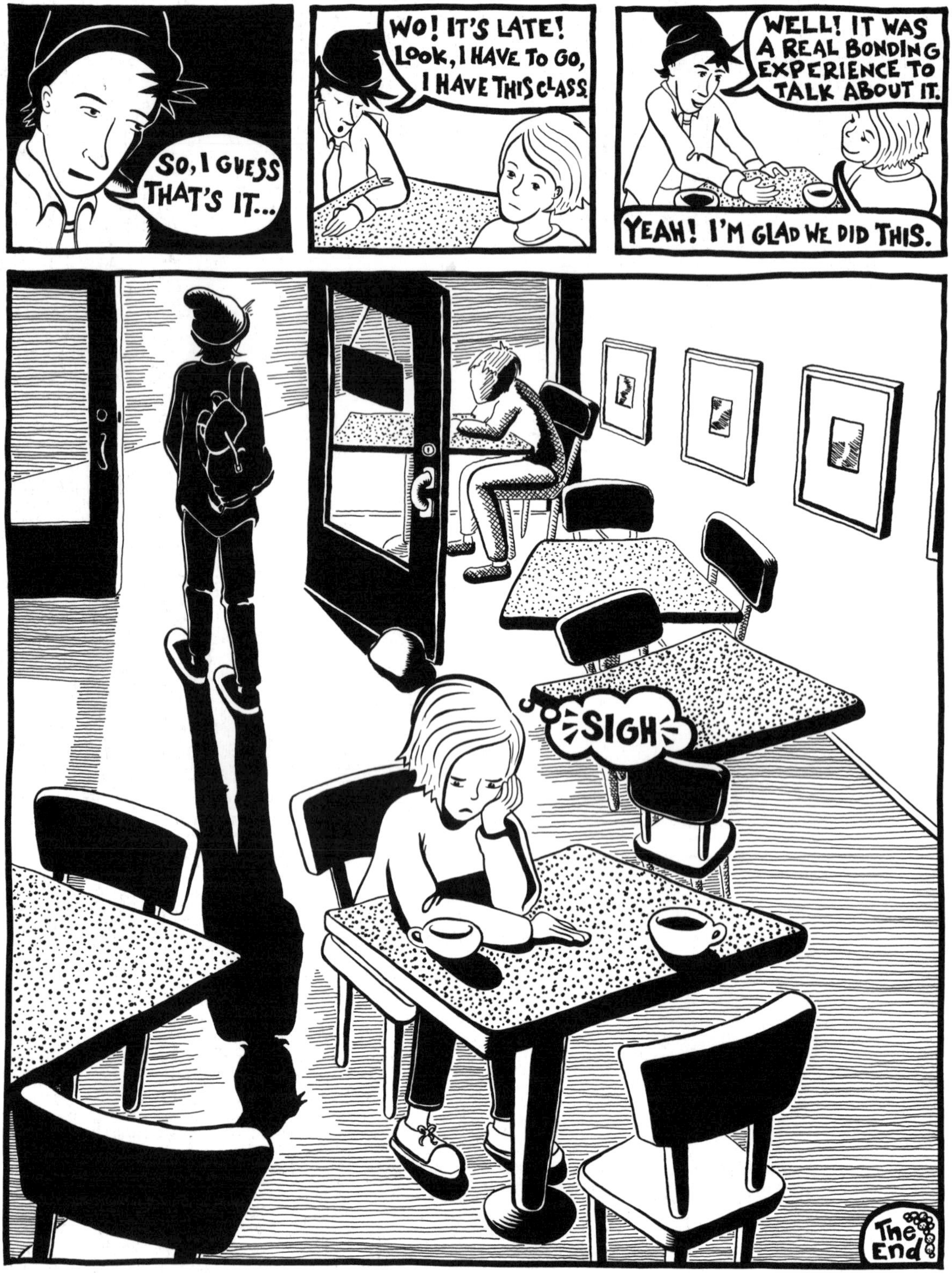
SO, I GUESS THAT'S IT...
WO! IT'S LATE! LOOK, I HAVE TO GO, I HAVE THIS CLASS.
WELL! IT WAS A REAL BONDING EXPERIENCE TO TALK ABOUT IT.
YEAH! I'M GLAD WE DID THIS.
SIGH
The End

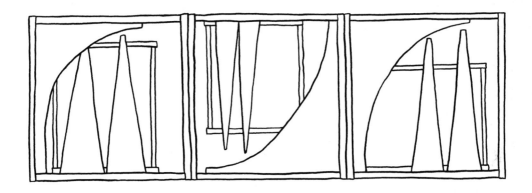

COMPOSITION

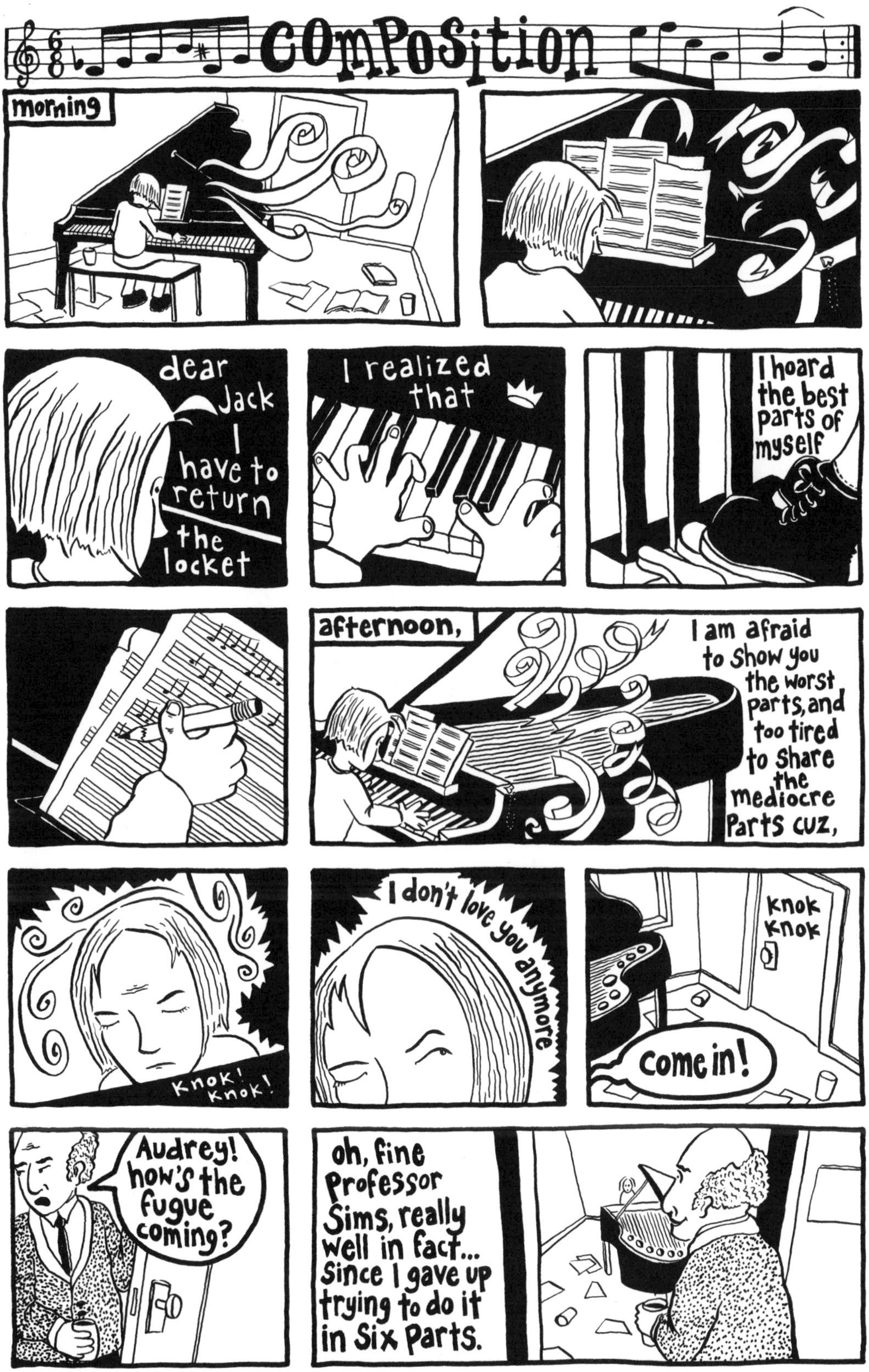
composition
morning
dear Jack I have to return the locket
I realized that
I hoard the best parts of myself
afternoon,
I am afraid to show you the worst parts, and too tired to share the mediocre parts cuz,
knok! knok!
I don't love you anymore
knok knok
come in!
Audrey! how's the fugue coming?
oh, fine Professor Sims, really well in fact... since I gave up trying to do it in six parts.

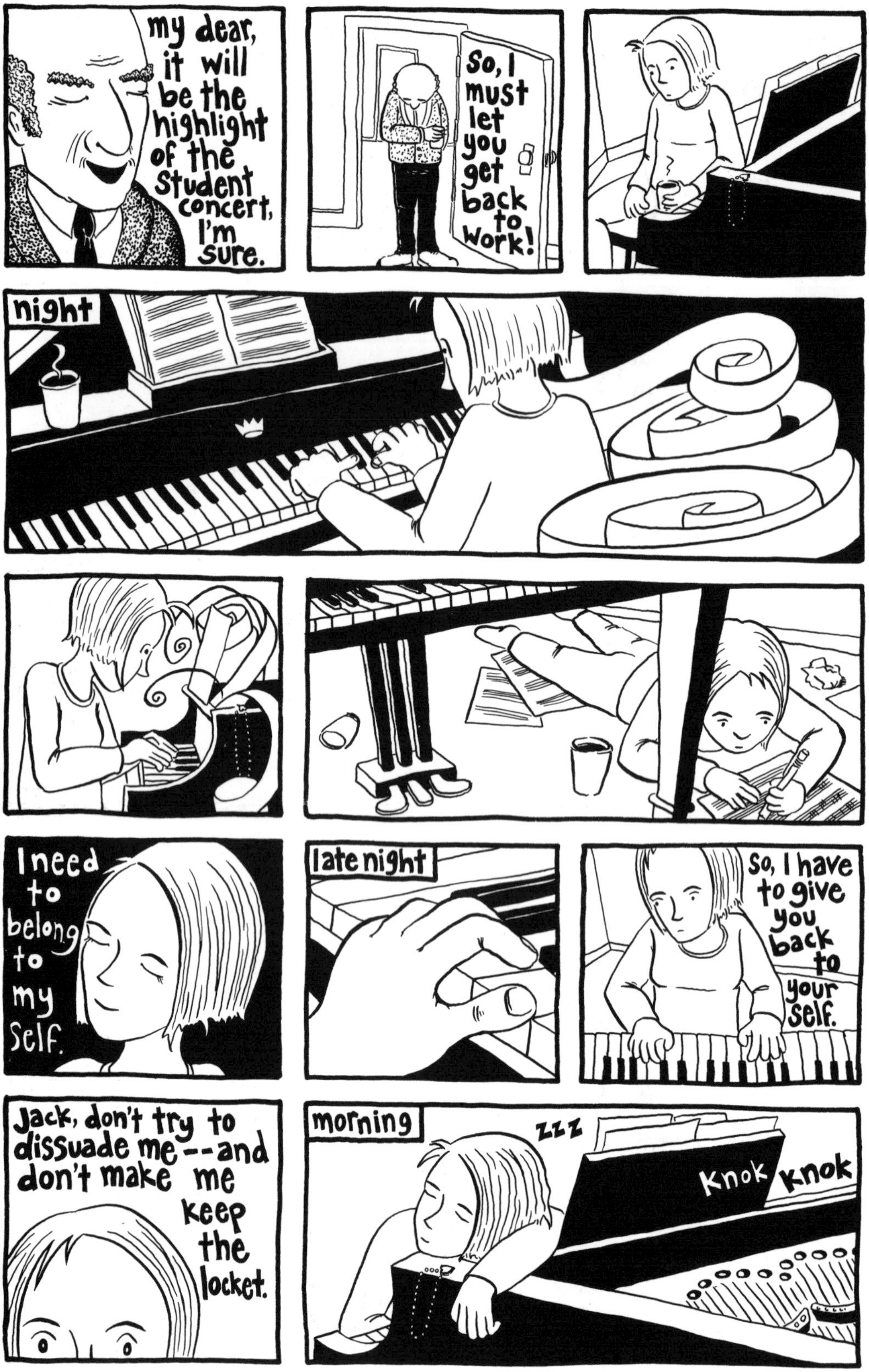
my dear, it will be the highlight of the student concert, I'm sure.
So, I must let you get back to work!
night
I need to belong to my self.
late night
So, I have to give you back to your self.
Jack, don't try to dissuade me--and don't make me keep the locket.
morning
zzz
knok knok

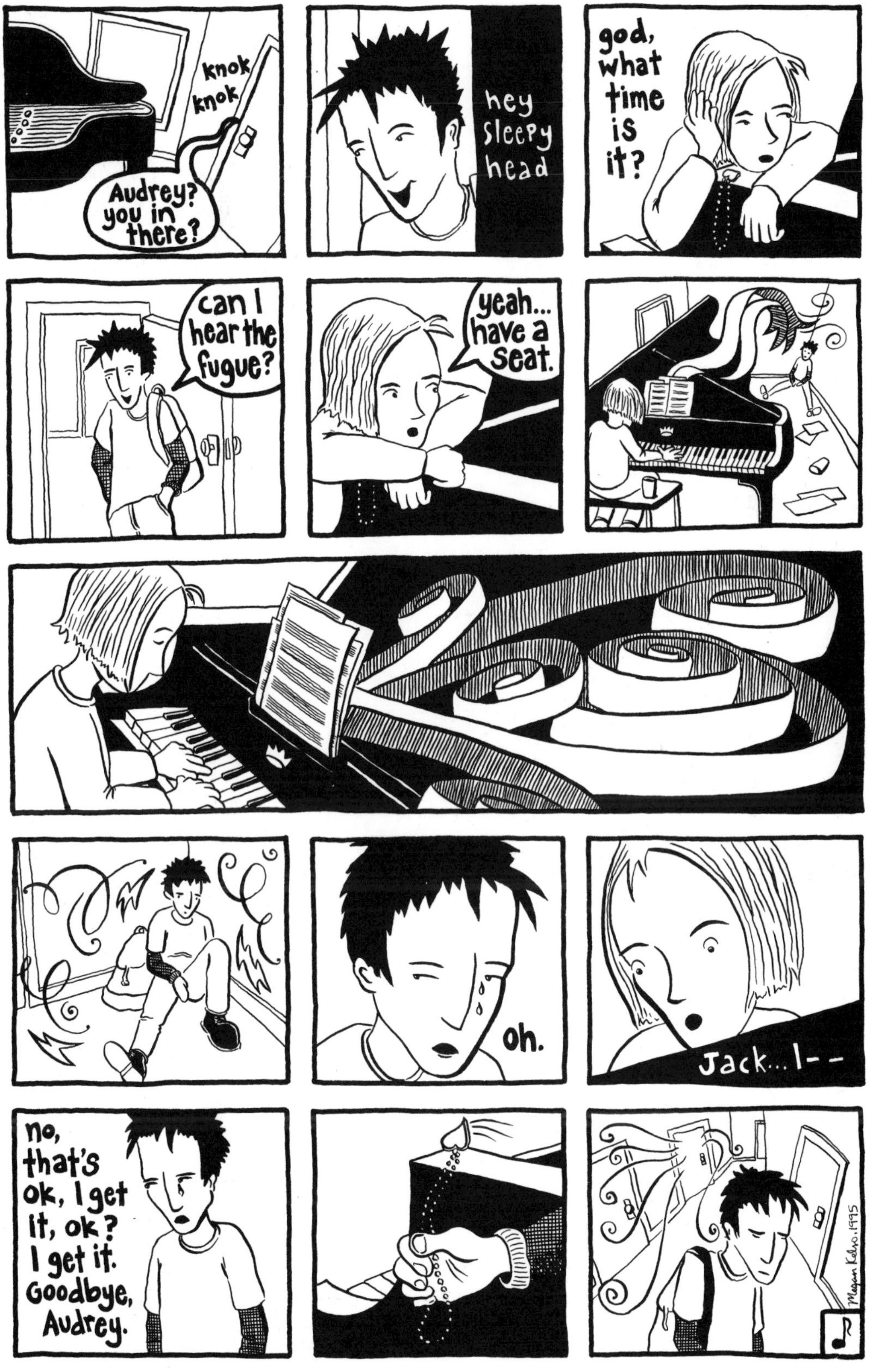
knok knok
Audrey? you in there?
hey sleepy head
god, what time is it?
can I hear the fugue?
yeah... have a seat.
oh.
Jack... I- -
no, that's ok, I get it, ok? I get it. Goodbye, Audrey.
Megan Kelso, 1995

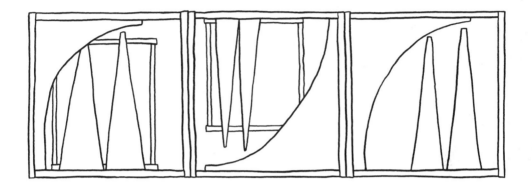

QUEEN OF THE BLACK BLACK

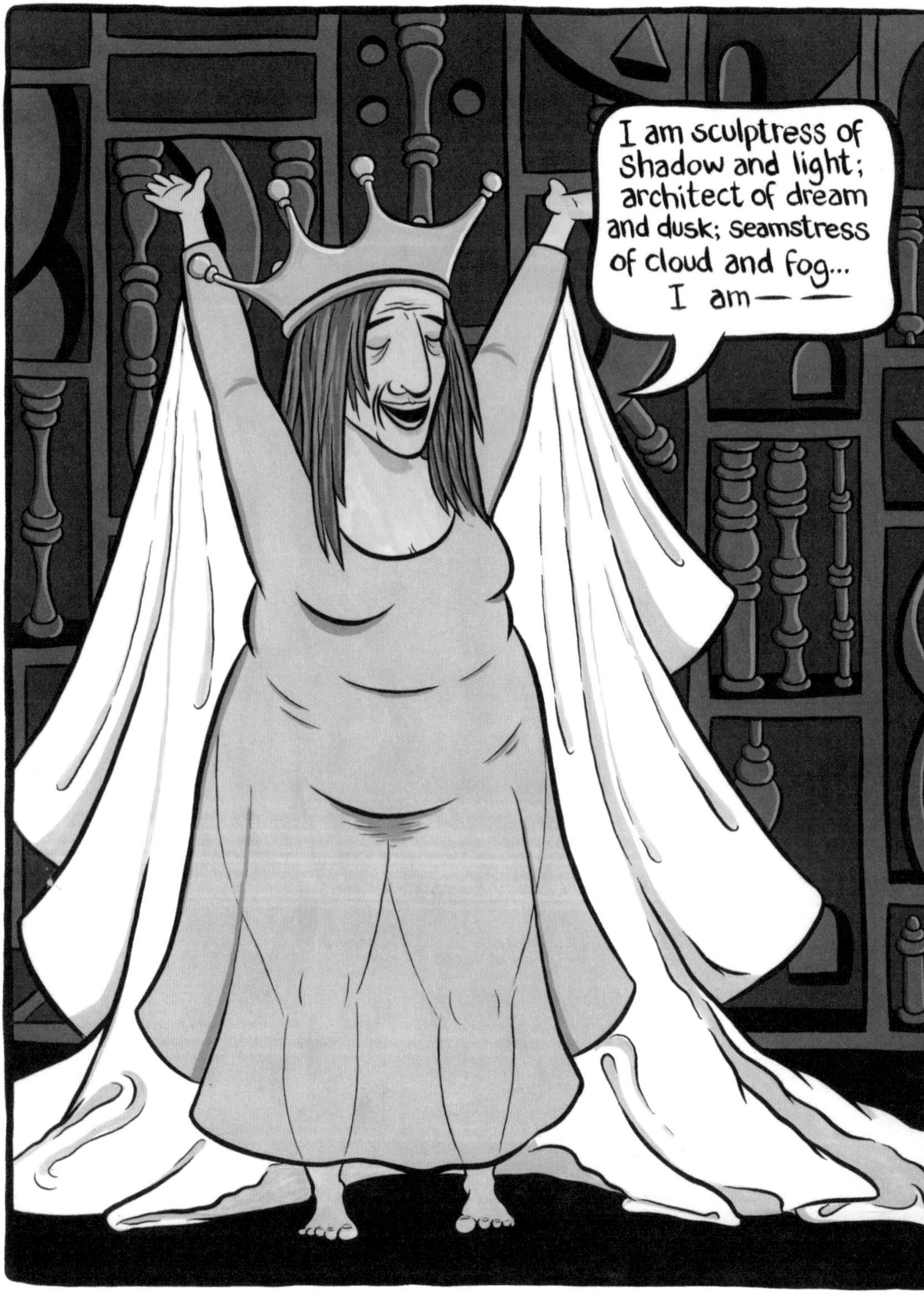
I am sculptress of shadow and light; architect of dream and dusk; seamstress of cloud and fog... I am——

QUEEN
of the BLACK
BLACK

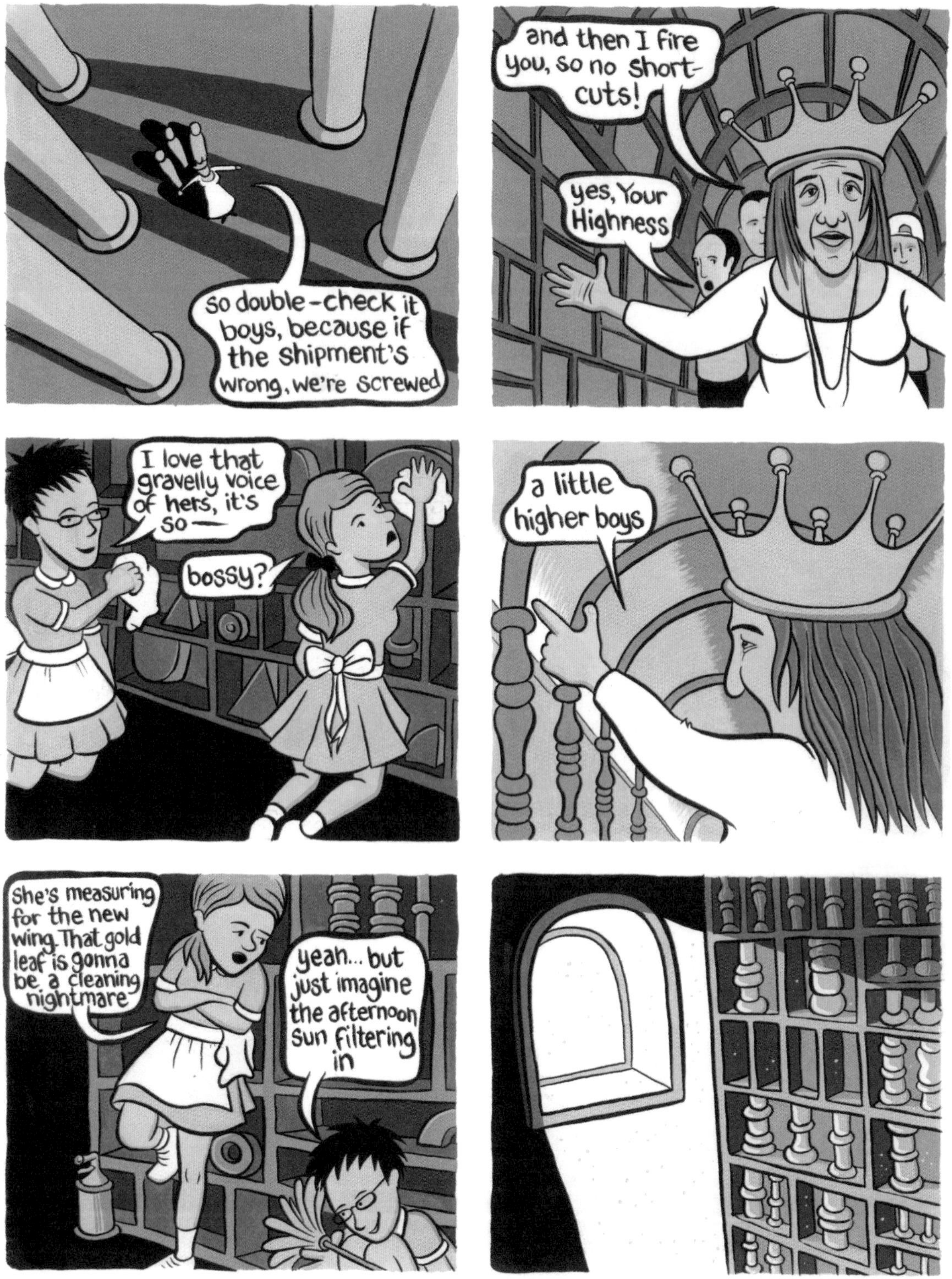
so double-check it boys, because if the shipment's wrong, we're screwed
and then I fire you, so no short-cuts!
yes, Your Highness
I love that gravelly voice of hers, it's so—
bossy?
a little higher boys
She's measuring for the new wing. That gold leaf is gonna be a cleaning nightmare
yeah... but just imagine the afternoon sun filtering in

SO.

You're the nocturnal horn blower I've been hearing, eh? What's your name?

Billie, your playing is DIVINE. No need to bow and scrape, You, my dear, are an ARTIST

But I still have so much to--

False modesty!

FALSE MODESTY. Be done with it! if you know you're good, you must PROCLAIM it. PROCLAIM! First to yourself, then to the world.

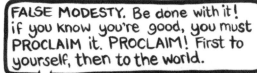

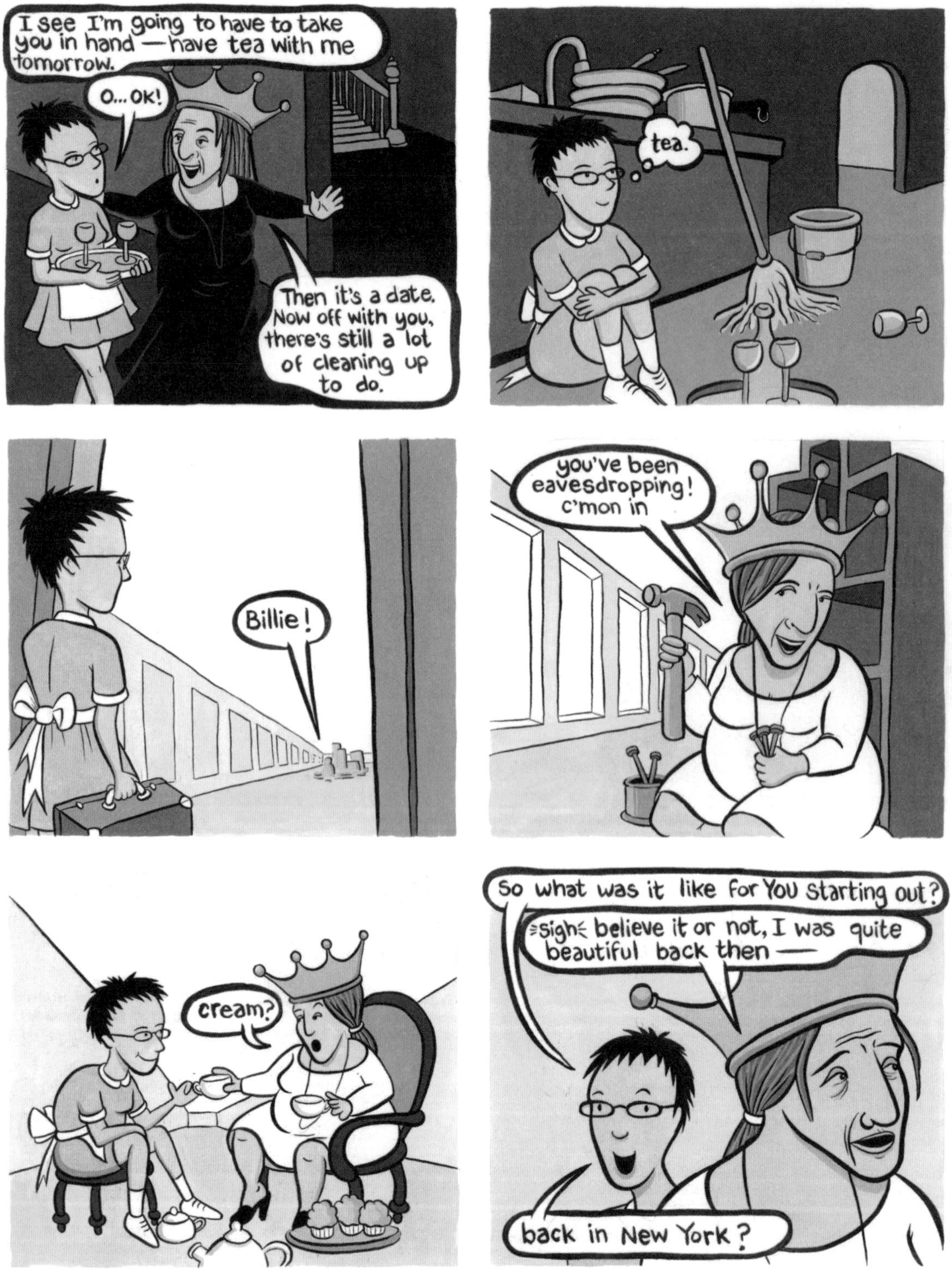
I see I'm going to have to take you in hand —have tea with me tomorrow.
O...OK!
Then it's a date. Now off with you, there's still a lot of cleaning up to do.
tea.
Billie!
you've been eavesdropping! c'mon in
cream?
So what was it like for YOU starting out?
back in New York?
≋sigh≋ believe it or not, I was quite beautiful back then —

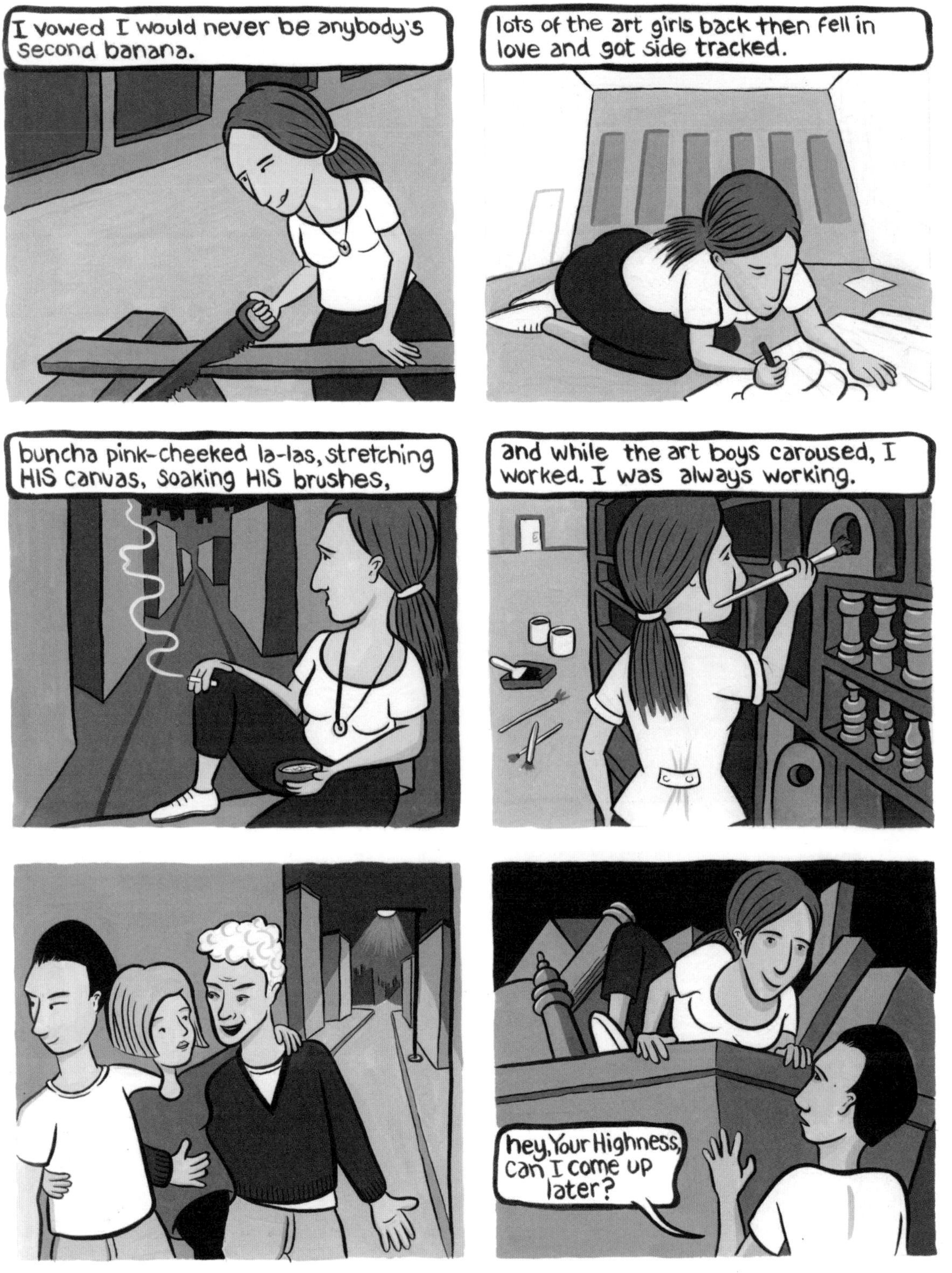
I vowed I would never be anybody's second banana.
lots of the art girls back then fell in love and got side tracked.
buncha pink-cheeked la-las, stretching HIS canvas, soaking HIS brushes,
and while the art boys caroused, I worked. I was always working.
hey, Your Highness, can I come up later?

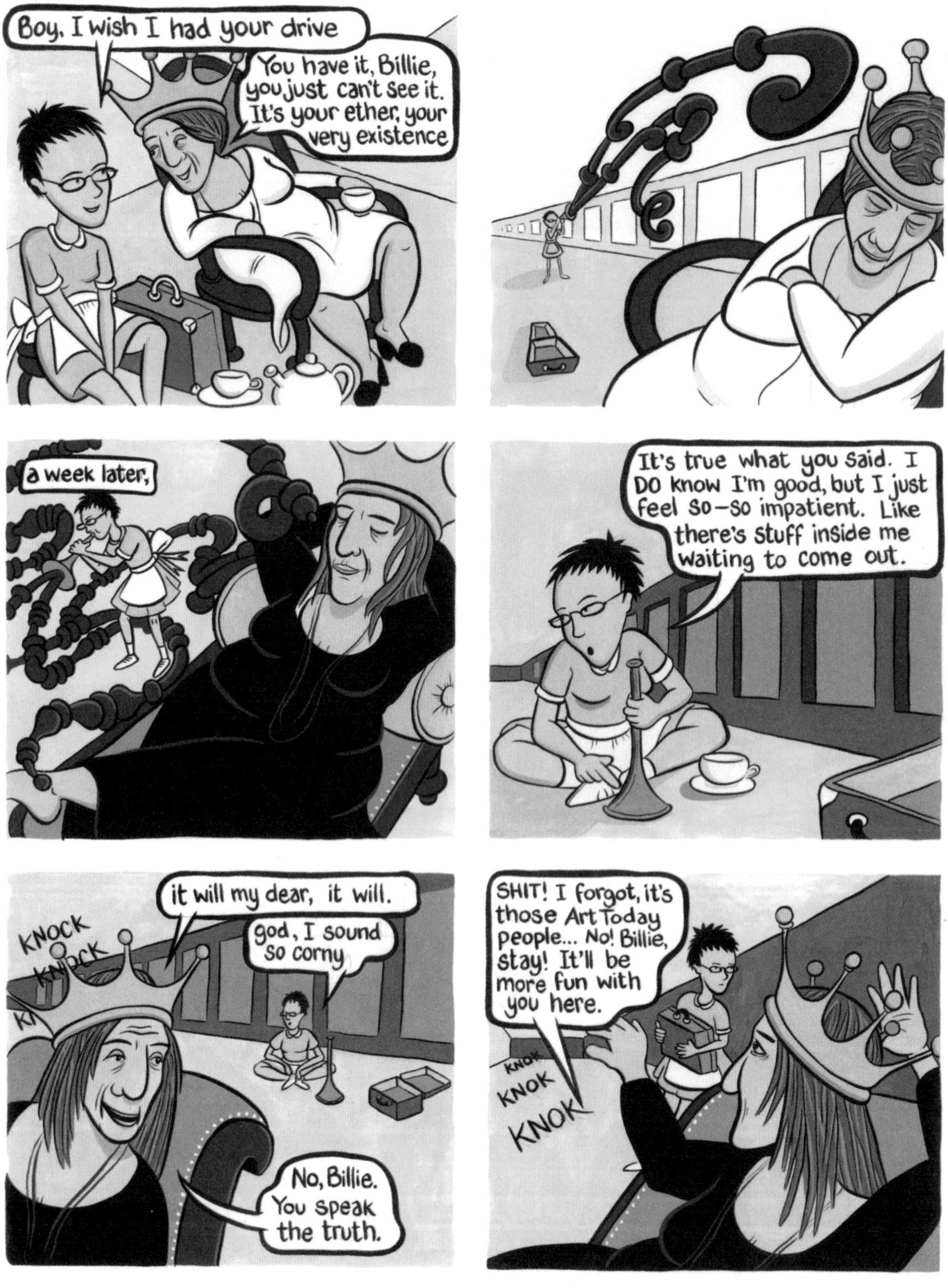

Boy, I wish I had your drive
You have it, Billie, you just can't see it. It's your ether, your very existence
a week later,
It's true what you said. I DO know I'm good, but I just feel so—so impatient. Like there's stuff inside me waiting to come out.
KNOCK
KNOCK
it will my dear, it will.
god, I sound so corny
No, Billie. You speak the truth.
SHIT! I forgot, it's those Art Today people... No! Billie, stay! It'll be more fun with you here.
KNOK
KNOK
KNOK

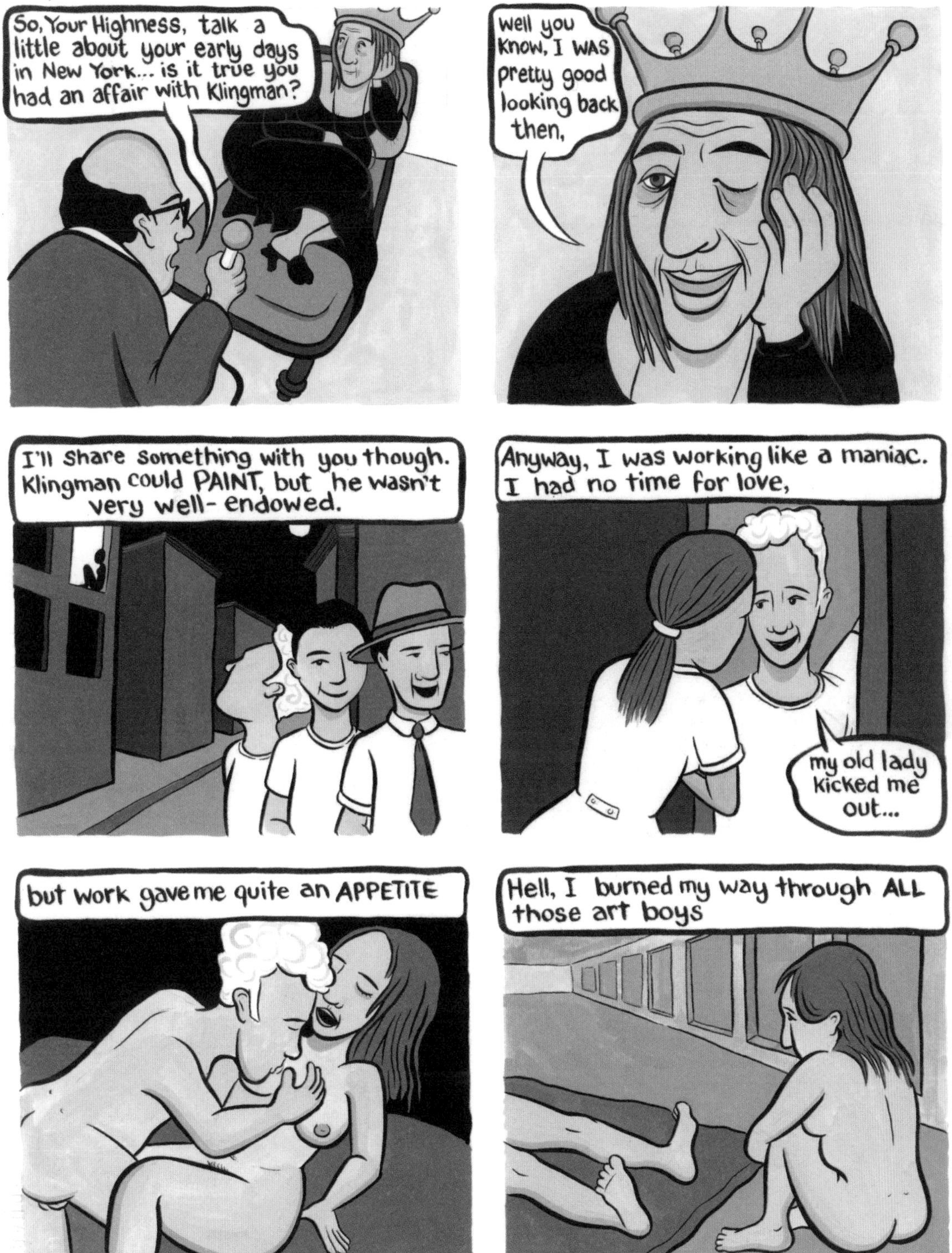
So, Your Highness, talk a little about your early days in New York... is it true you had an affair with Klingman?
Well you know, I WAS pretty good looking back then,
I'll share something with you though. Klingman could PAINT, but he wasn't very well-endowed.
Anyway, I was working like a maniac. I had no time for love,
my old lady kicked me out...
but work gave me quite an APPETITE
Hell, I burned my way through ALL those art boys

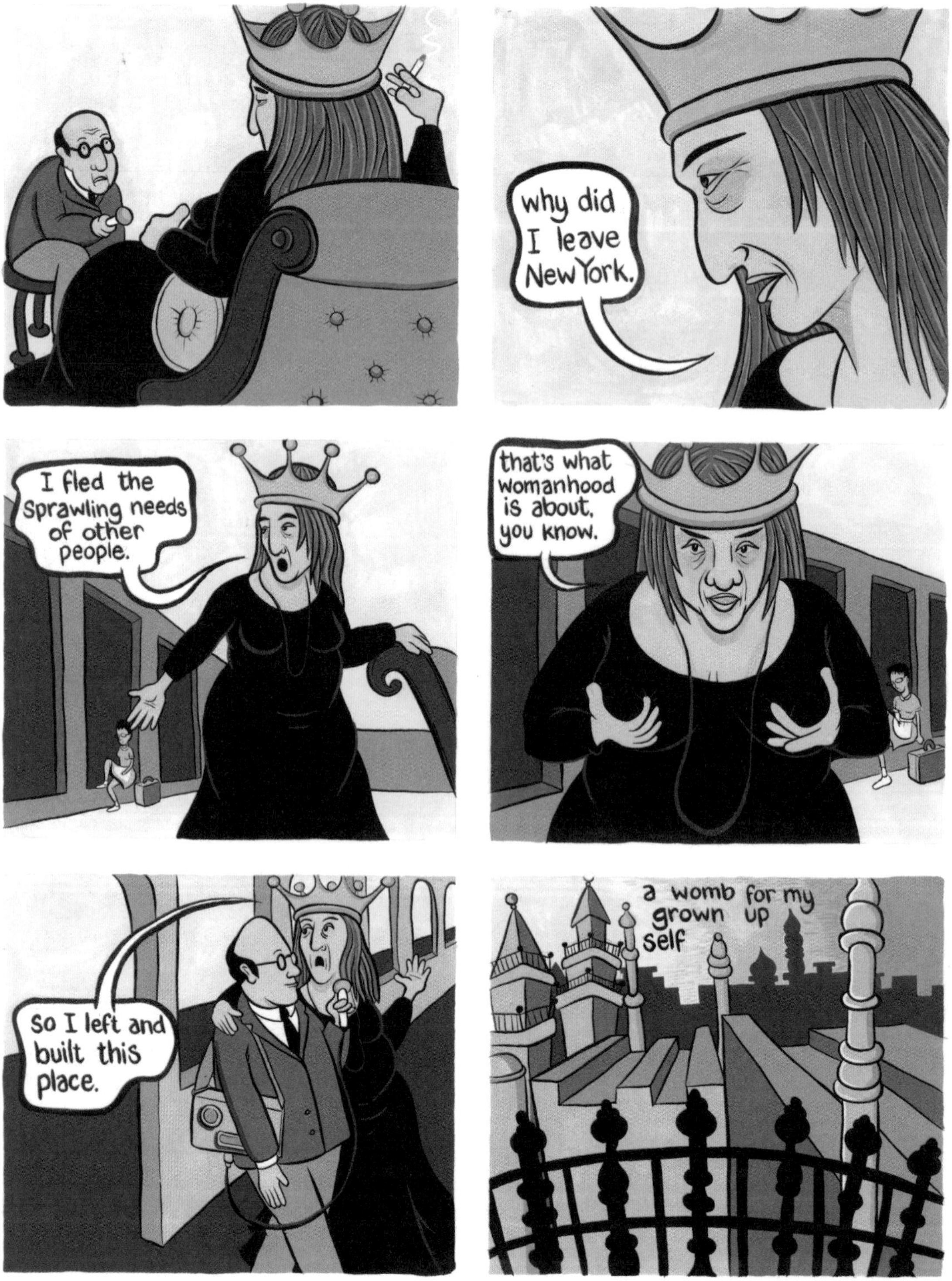
why did I leave New York.
I fled the sprawling needs of other people.
that's what womanhood is about, you know.
So I left and built this place.
a womb for my grown up self

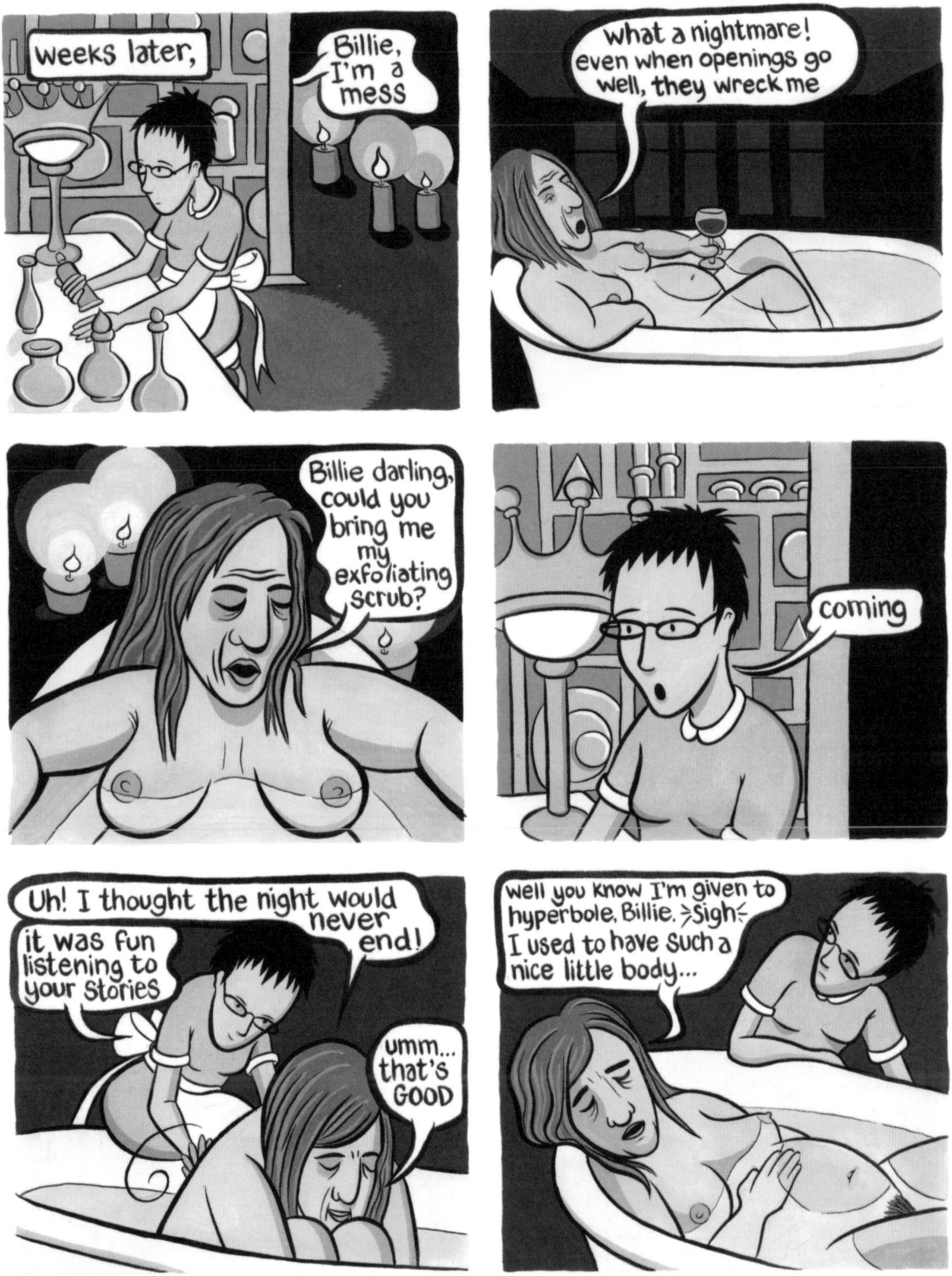
weeks later,
Billie, I'm a mess
what a nightmare! even when openings go well, they wreck me
Billie darling, could you bring me my exfoliating scrub?
coming
Uh! I thought the night would never end!
it was fun listening to your stories
umm... that's GOOD
well you know I'm given to hyperbole, Billie. Sigh I used to have such a nice little body...

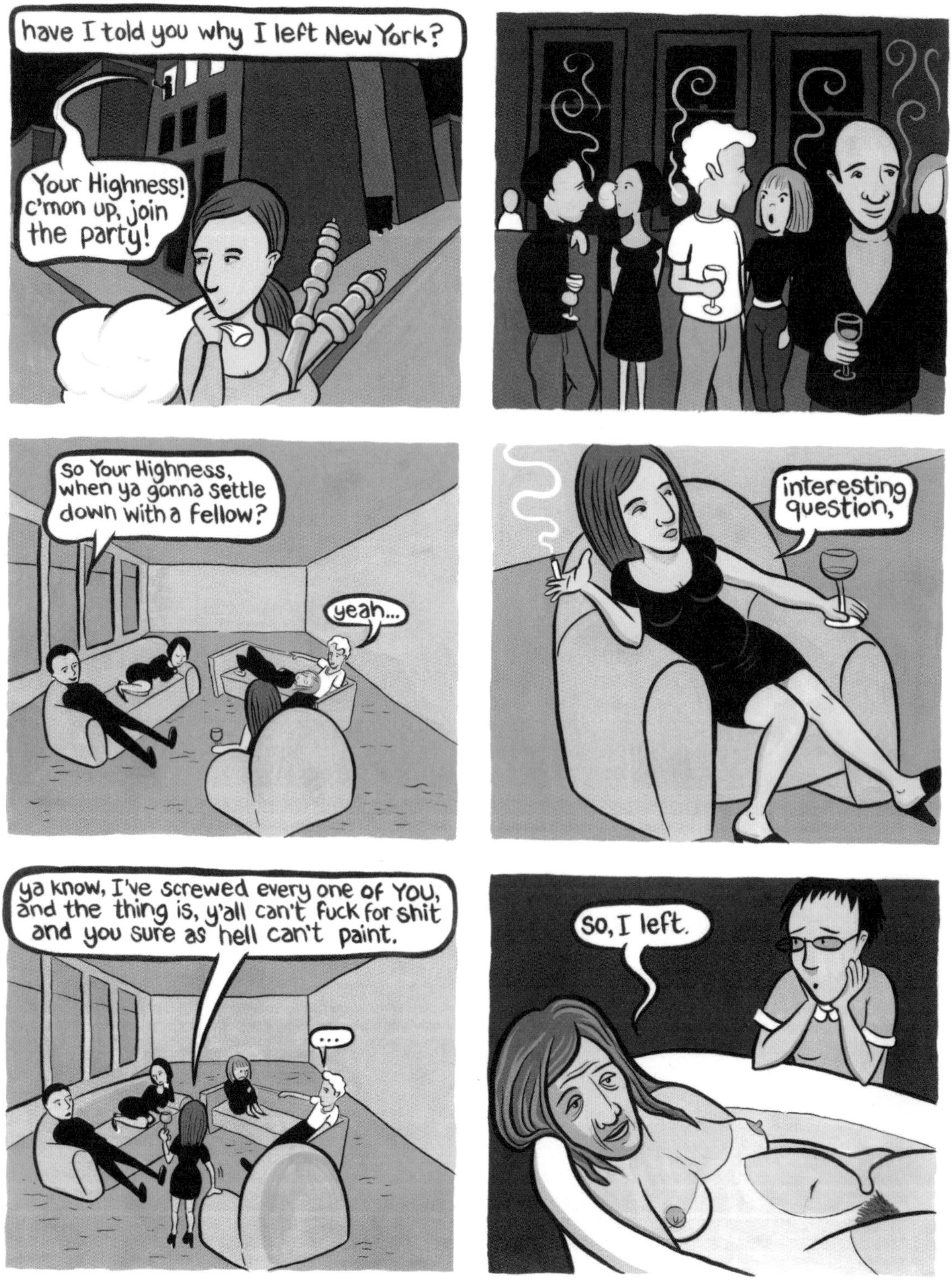
have I told you why I left New York?
Your Highness! c'mon up, join the party!
So Your Highness, when ya gonna settle down with a fellow?
yeah...
interesting question,
ya know, I've screwed every one of YOU, and the thing is, y'all can't fuck for shit and you sure as hell can't paint.
...
So, I left.

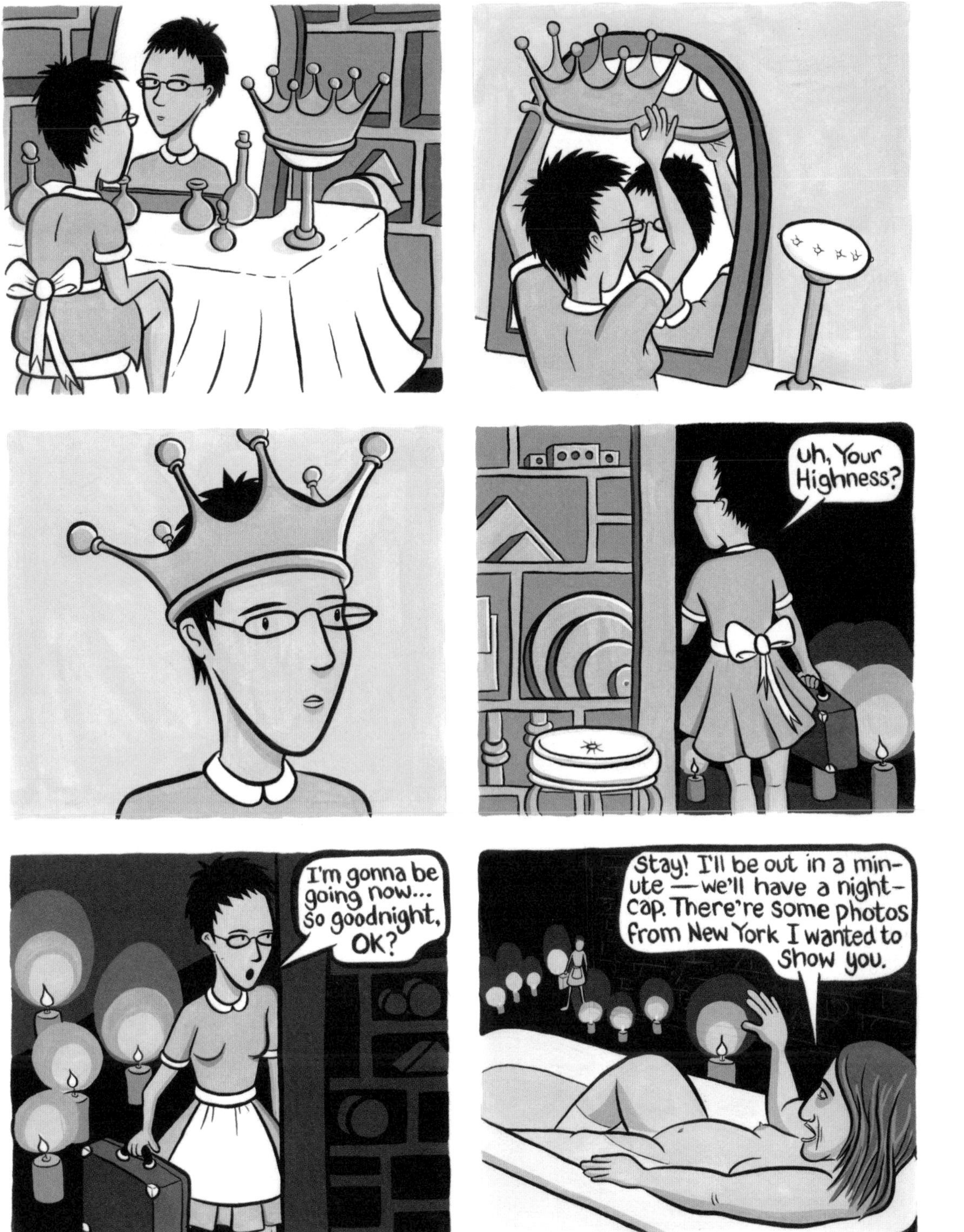
Uh, Your Highness?
I'm gonna be going now... so goodnight, OK?
Stay! I'll be out in a minute — we'll have a nightcap. There're some photos from New York I wanted to show you.

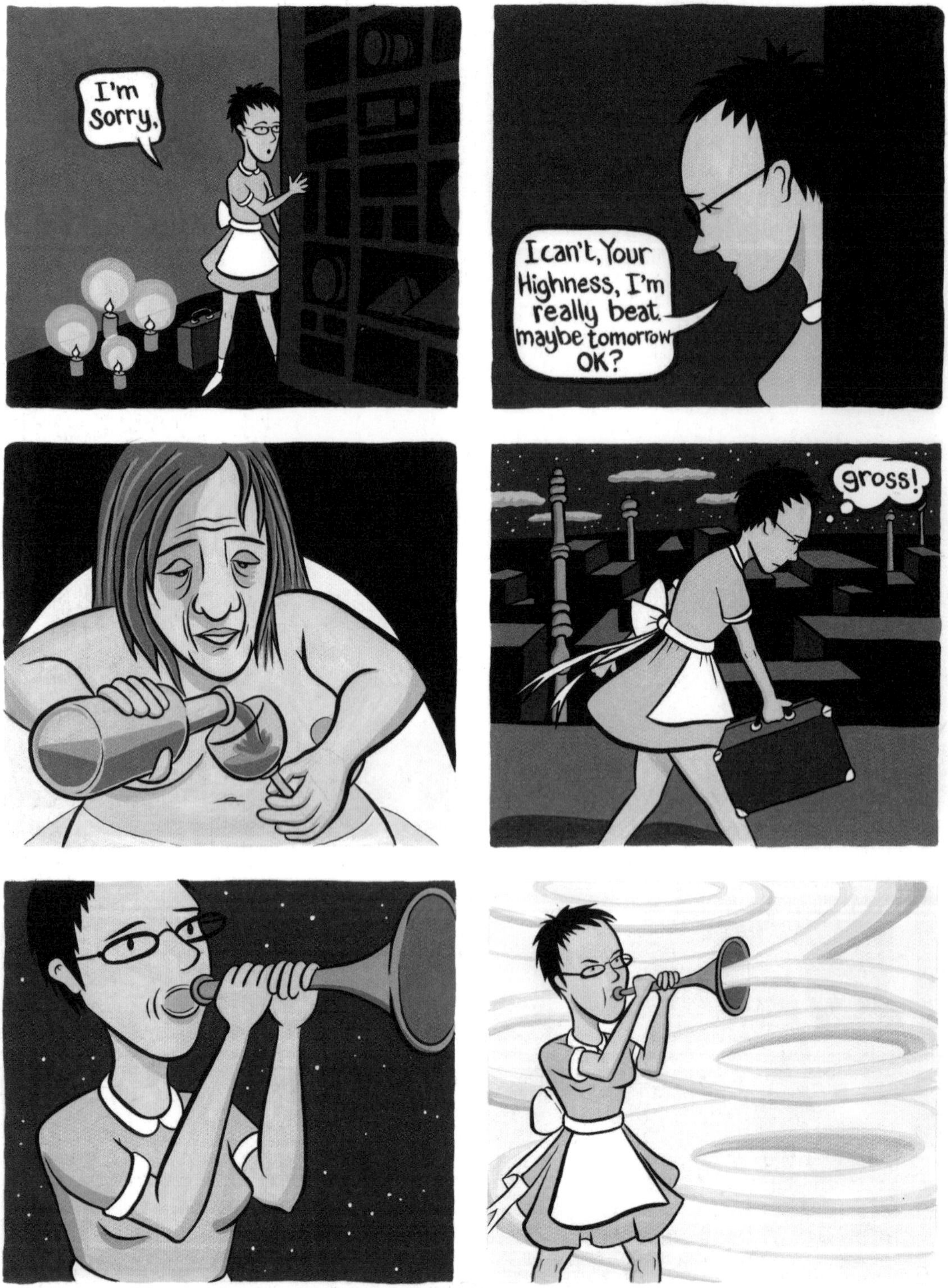
I'm sorry,
I can't, Your Highness, I'm really beat. maybe tomorrow OK?
gross!

THE MARRIED MAN

the MARRIED man
KL
KWIK
break time!
WILLIAMS
-KATT-
SCIENCE
BUILDING

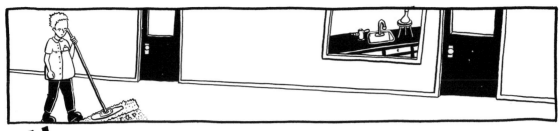

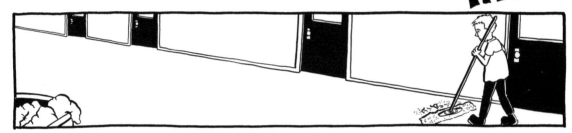

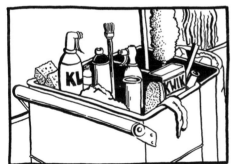

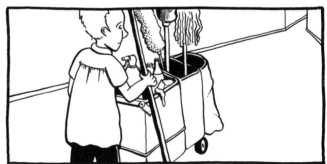

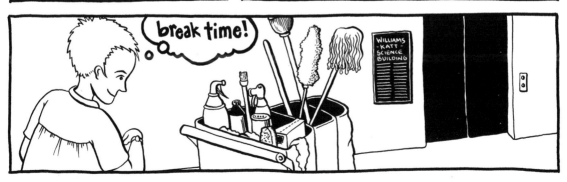

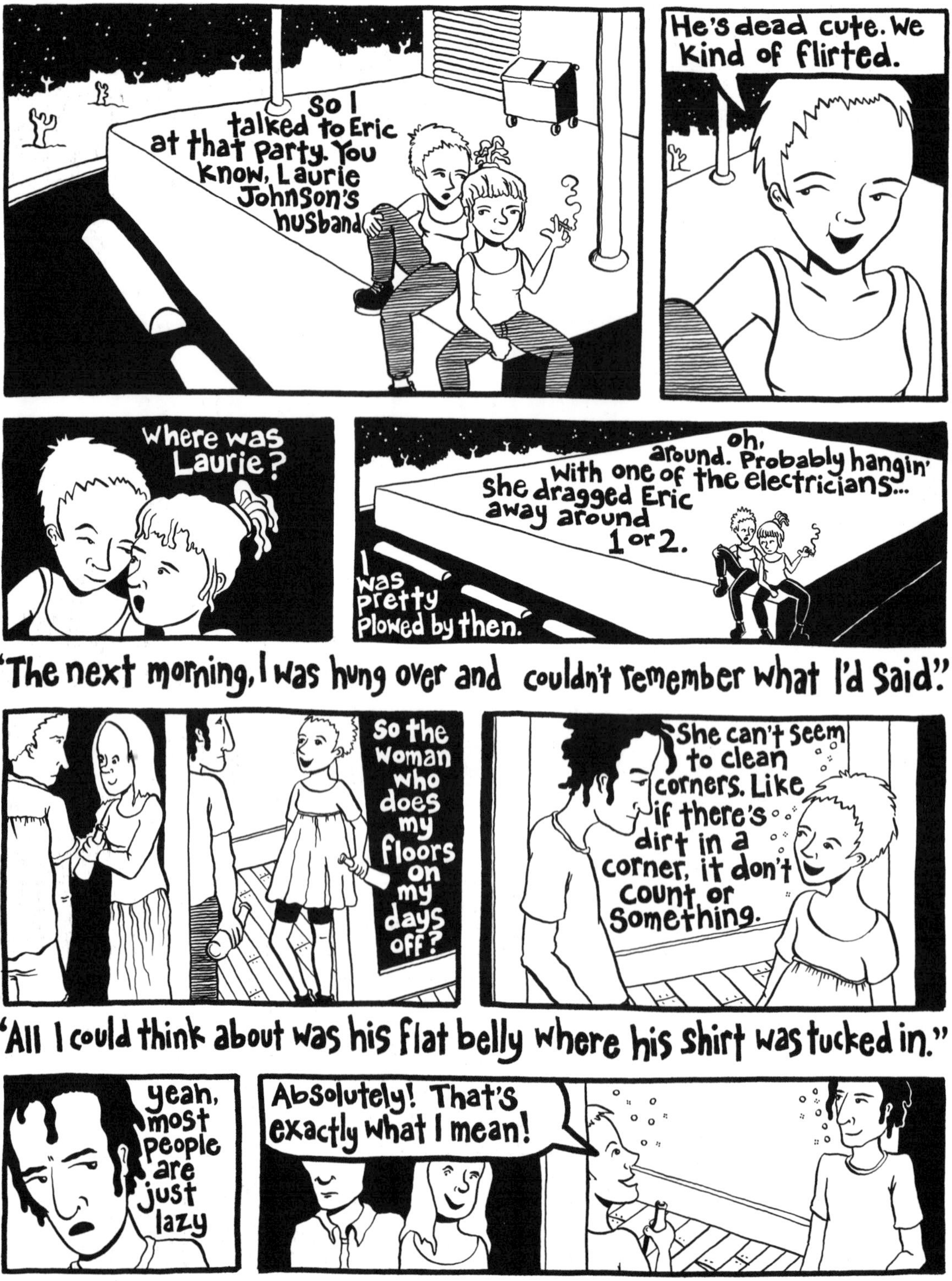
So I talked to Eric at that party. You know, Laurie Johnson's husband
He's dead cute. We kind of flirted.
Where was Laurie?
oh, around. Probably hangin' with one of the electricians... She dragged Eric away around 1 or 2.
I was pretty plowed by then.
"The next morning, I was hung over and couldn't remember what I'd said."
So the woman who does my floors on my days off?
She can't seem to clean corners. Like if there's dirt in a corner, it don't count or something.
"All I could think about was his flat belly where his shirt was tucked in."
yeah, most people are just lazy
Absolutely! That's exactly what I mean!

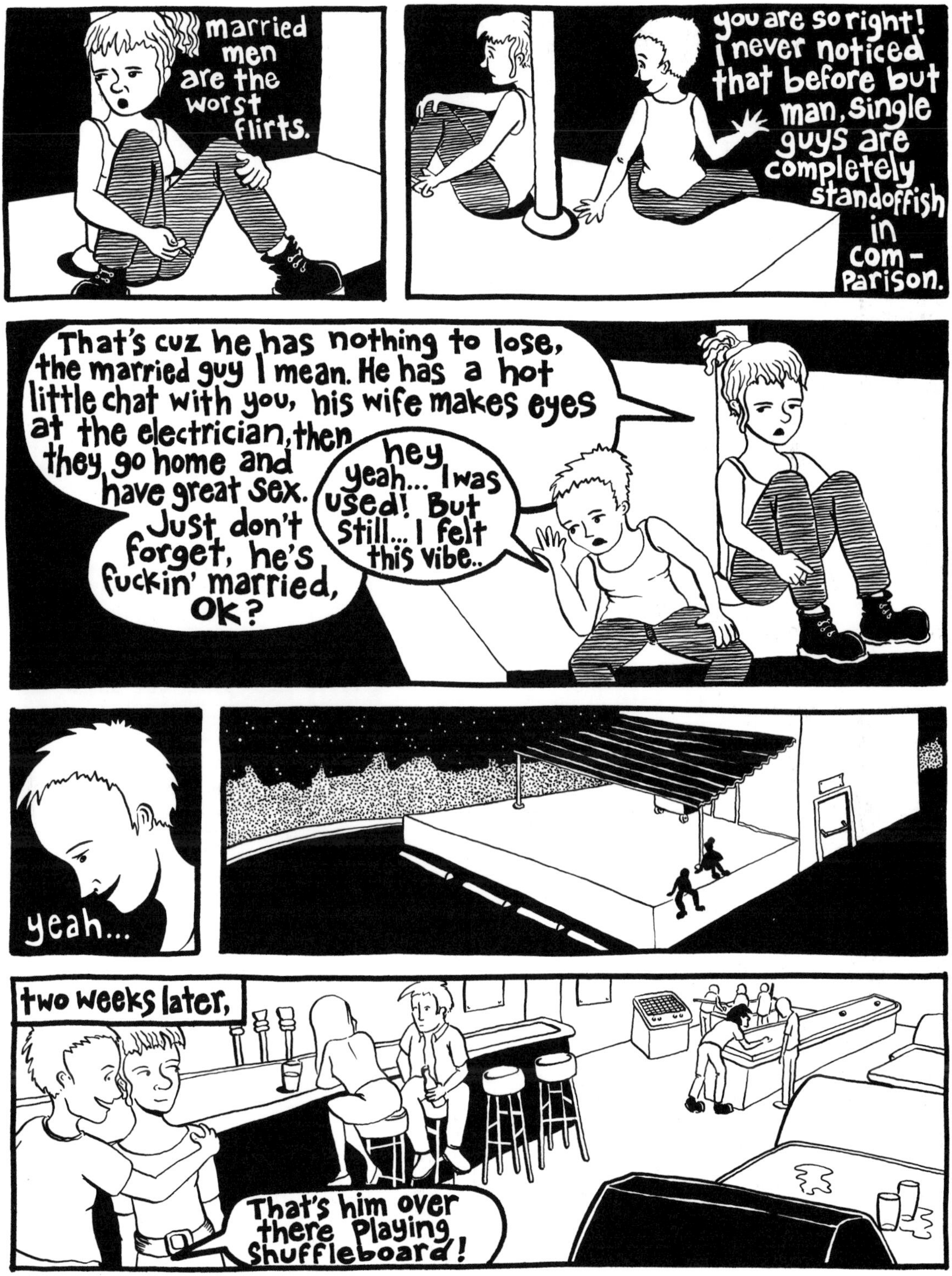
married men are the worst flirts.
you are so right! I never noticed that before but man, single guys are completely standoffish in com-parison.
That's cuz he has nothing to lose, the married guy I mean. He has a hot little chat with you, his wife makes eyes at the electrician, then they go home and have great sex. Just don't forget, he's fuckin' married, OK?
hey yeah... I was used! But still... I felt this vibe..
yeah...
two weeks later,
That's him over there Playing Shuffleboard!

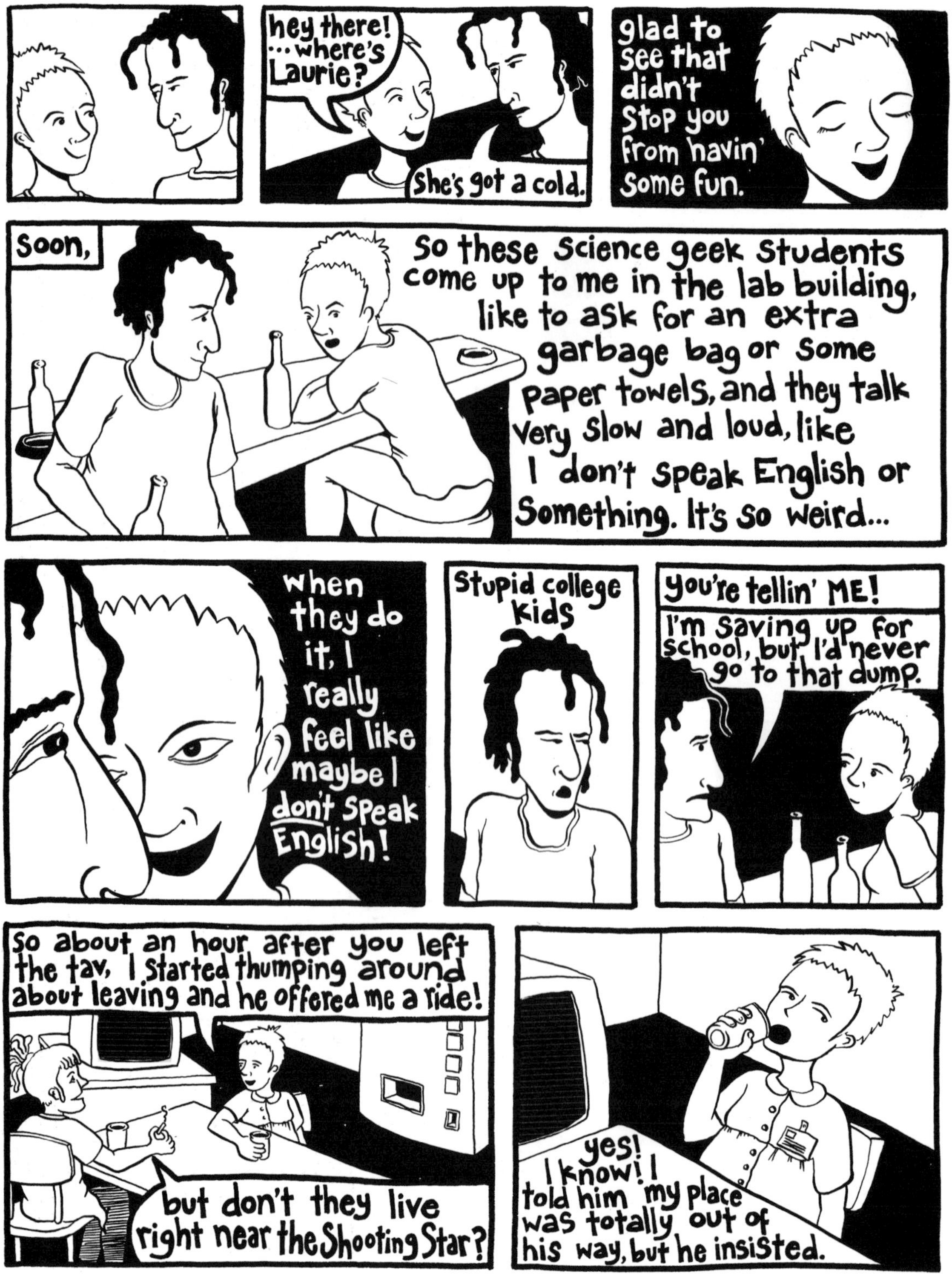
hey there! ...where's Laurie?
She's got a cold.
glad to see that didn't stop you from havin' some fun.
Soon,
So these science geek students come up to me in the lab building, like to ask for an extra garbage bag or some paper towels, and they talk very slow and loud, like I don't speak English or something. It's so weird...
when they do it, I really feel like maybe I don't speak English!
Stupid college kids
You're tellin' ME!
I'm saving up for school, but I'd never go to that dump.
So about an hour after you left the tav, I started thumping around about leaving and he offered me a ride!
but don't they live right near the Shooting Star?
yes! I know! I told him my place was totally out of his way, but he insisted.

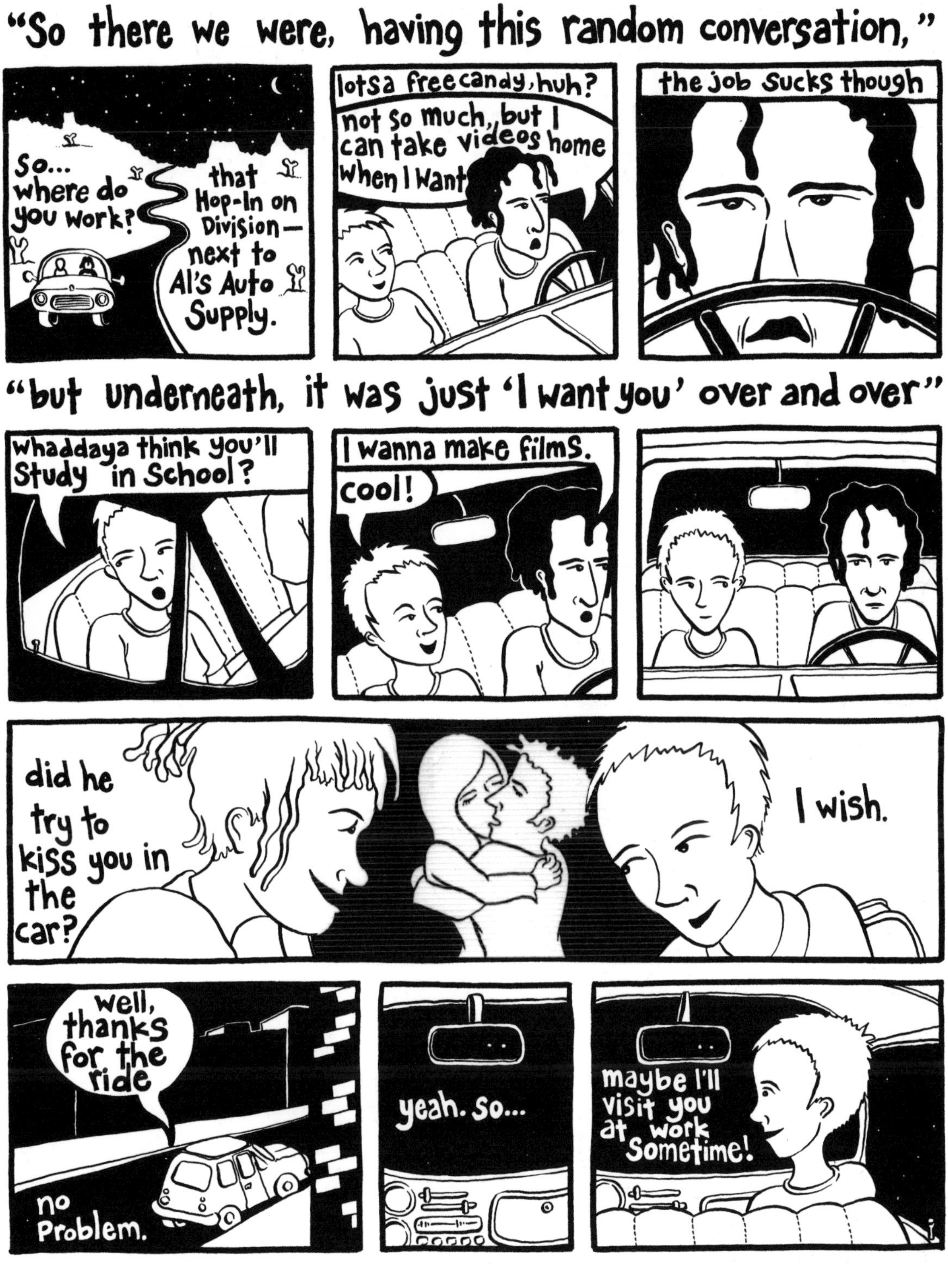
"So there we were, having this random conversation,"
So... where do you work?
that Hop-In on Division— next to Al's Auto Supply.
lotsa free candy, huh?
not so much, but I can take videos home when I want
the job sucks though
"but underneath, it was just 'I want you' over and over"
whaddaya think you'll study in school?
I wanna make films.
cool!
did he try to kiss you in the car?
I wish.
well, thanks for the ride
no Problem.
yeah. so...
maybe I'll visit you at work sometime!

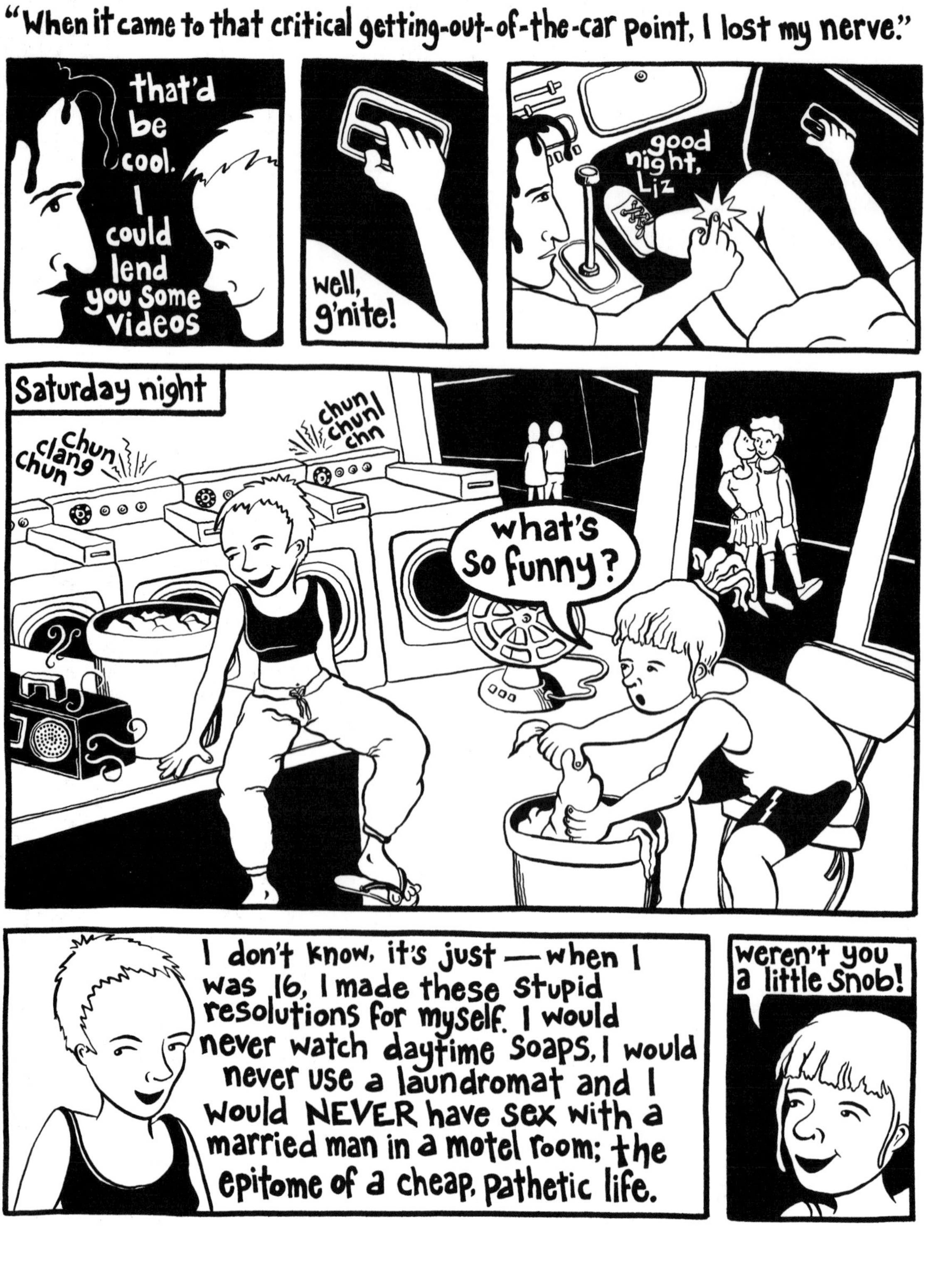
"When it came to that critical getting-out-of-the-car point, I lost my nerve."
that'd be cool. I could lend you some videos
well, g'nite!
good night, Liz
Saturday night
chun clang chun
chun chun! chn
what's so funny?
I don't know, it's just — when I was 16, I made these stupid resolutions for myself. I would never watch daytime soaps, I would never use a laundromat and I would NEVER have sex with a married man in a motel room; the epitome of a cheap, pathetic life.
weren't you a little snob!

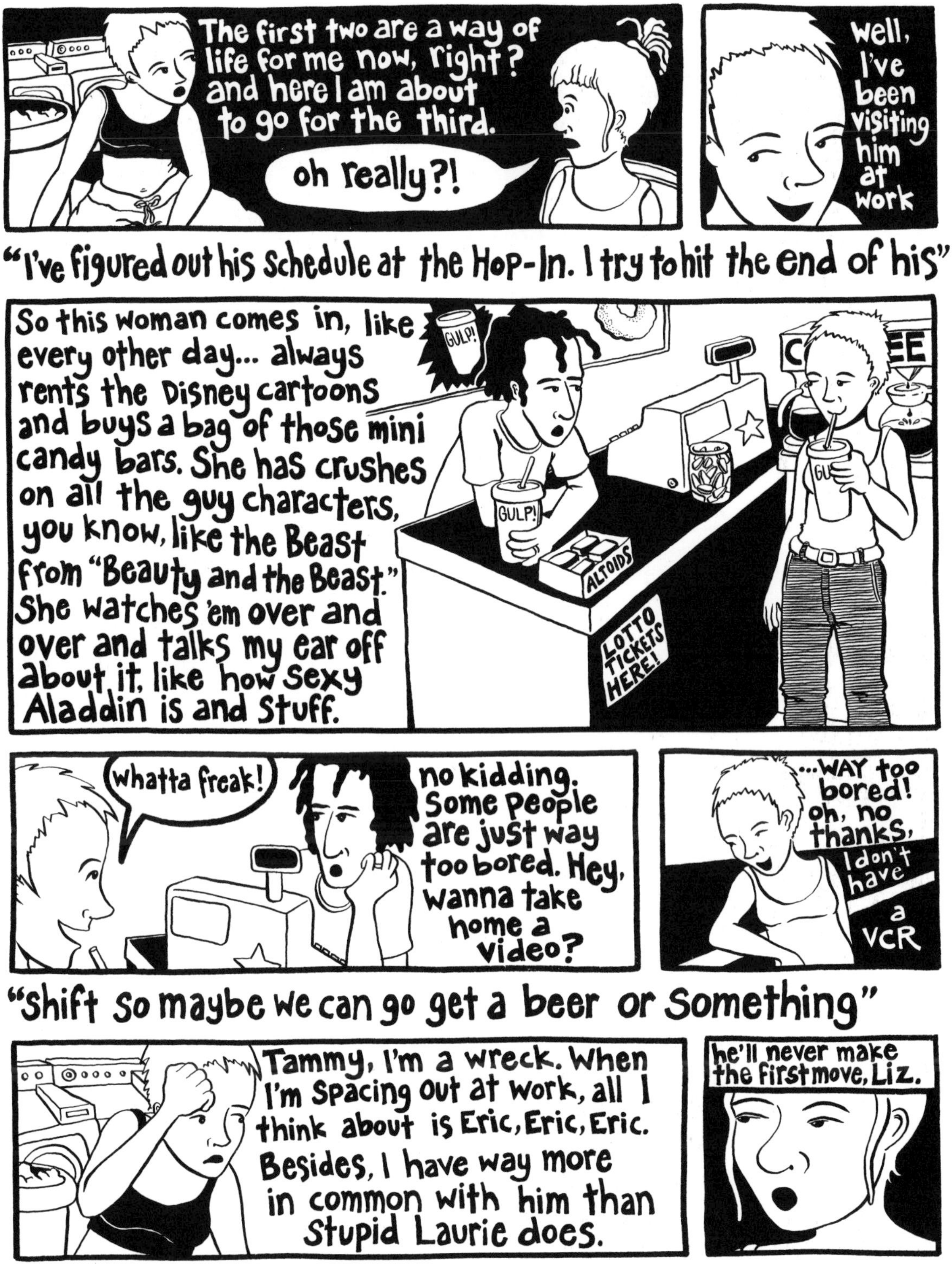

The first two are a way of life for me now, right? and here I am about to go for the third.
oh really?!
Well, I've been visiting him at work
"I've figured out his schedule at the Hop-In. I try to hit the end of his"
So this woman comes in, like every other day... always rents the Disney cartoons and buys a bag of those mini candy bars. She has crushes on all the guy characters, you know, like the Beast from "Beauty and the Beast." She watches 'em over and over and talks my ear off about it, like how sexy Aladdin is and stuff.
GULP!
GULP!
ALTOIDS
LOTTO TICKETS HERE!
whatta freak!
no kidding. Some people are just way too bored. Hey, wanna take home a video?
...WAY too bored! oh, no thanks, I don't have a VCR
"shift so maybe we can go get a beer or something"
Tammy, I'm a wreck. When I'm spacing out at work, all I think about is Eric, Eric, Eric. Besides, I have way more in common with him than stupid Laurie does.
he'll never make the first move, Liz.

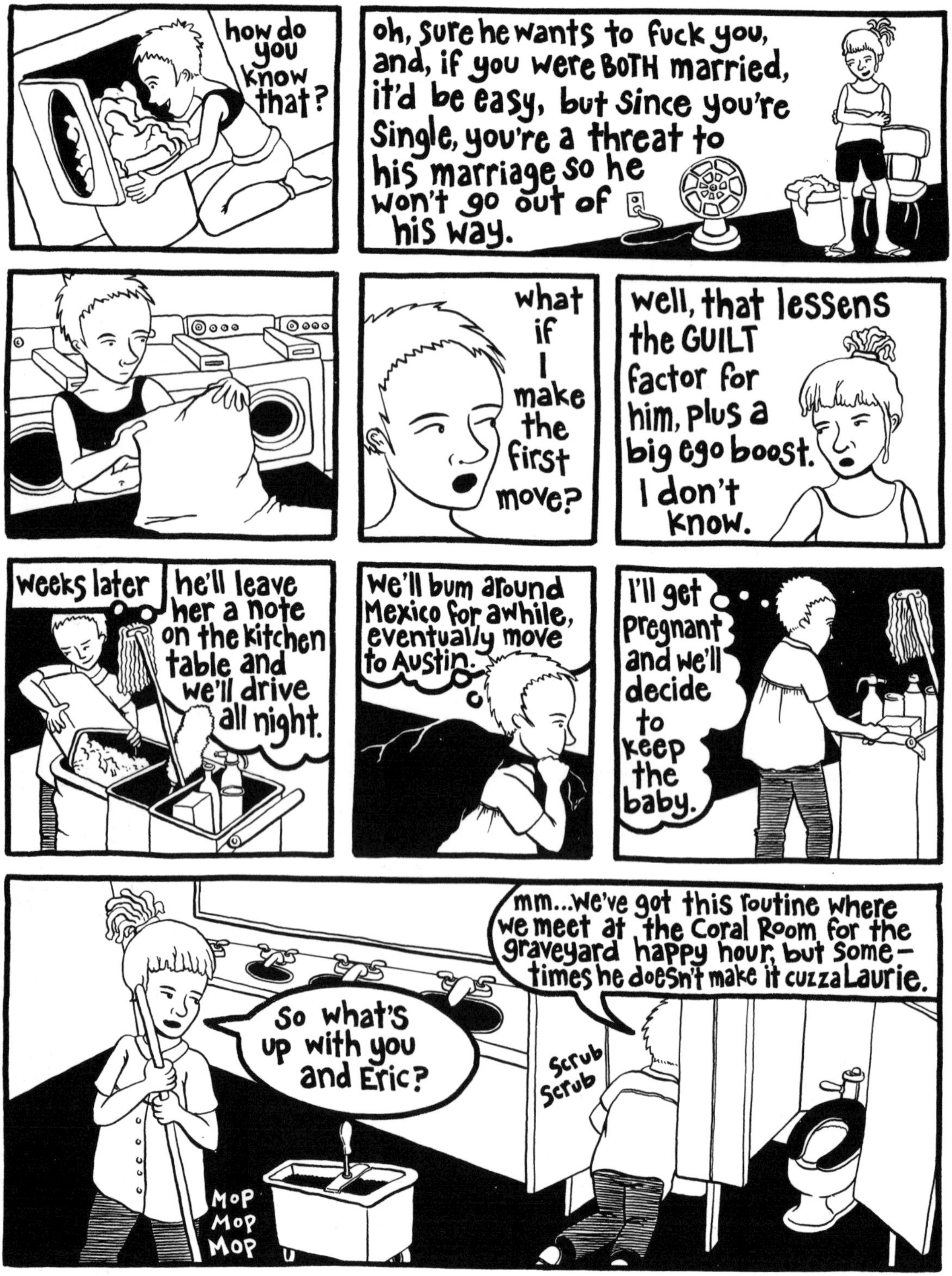
how do you know that?
oh, sure he wants to fuck you, and, if you were BOTH married, it'd be easy, but since you're single, you're a threat to his marriage so he won't go out of his way.
what if I make the first move?
well, that lessens the GUILT factor for him, plus a big ego boost.
I don't know.
weeks later
he'll leave her a note on the kitchen table and we'll drive all night.
We'll bum around Mexico for awhile, eventually move to Austin.
I'll get pregnant and we'll decide to keep the baby.
So what's up with you and Eric?
mm...we've got this routine where we meet at the Coral Room for the graveyard happy hour, but some-times he doesn't make it cuzza Laurie.
Scrub Scrub
Mop Mop Mop

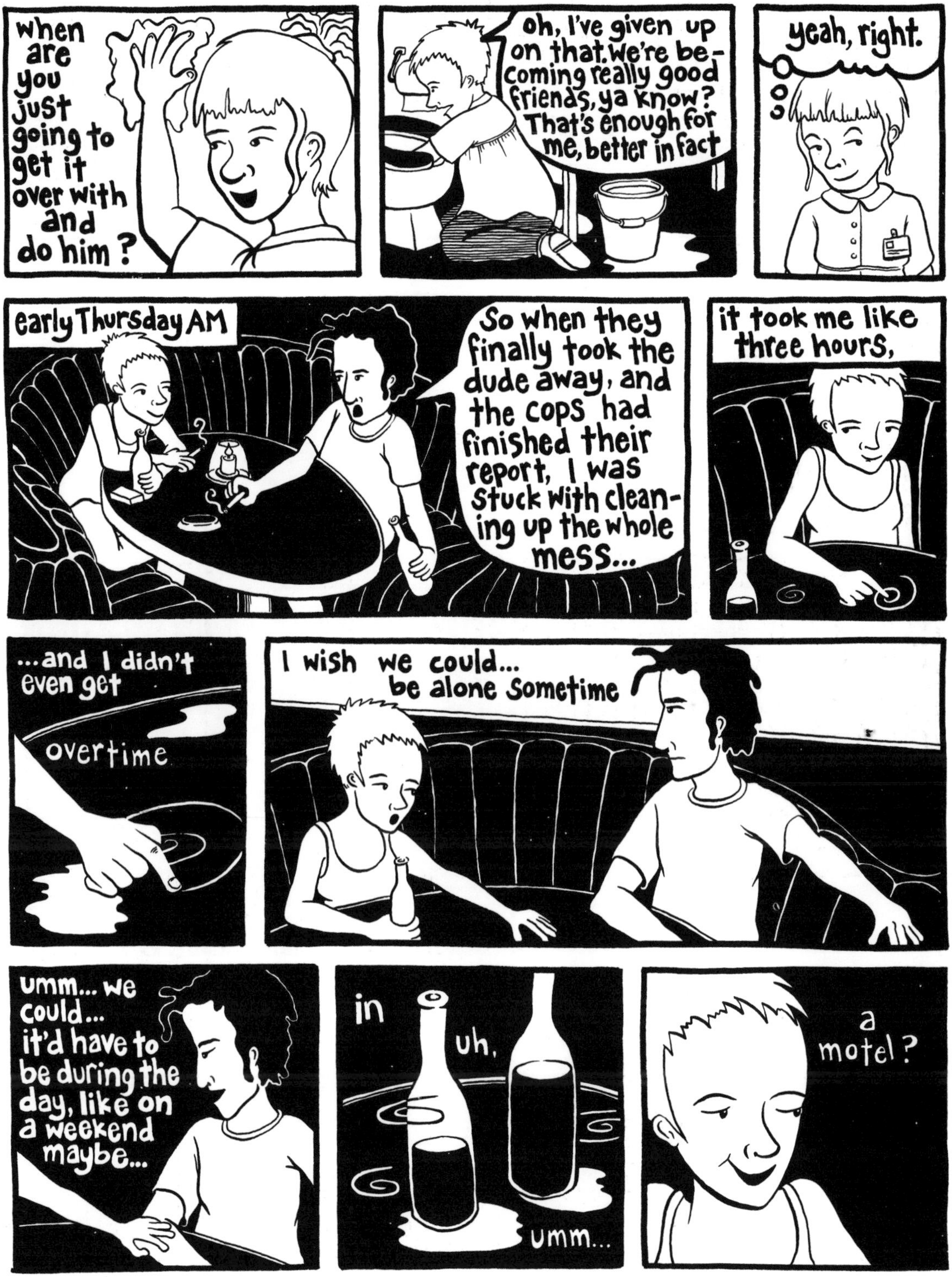
when are you just going to get it over with and do him?
oh, I've given up on that. We're be-coming really good friends, ya know? That's enough for me, better in fact
yeah, right.
early Thursday AM
So when they finally took the dude away, and the cops had finished their report, I was stuck with clean-ing up the whole mess...
it took me like three hours,
...and I didn't even get
overtime
I wish we could...
be alone sometime
umm... we could... it'd have to be during the day, like on a weekend maybe...
in
uh,
umm...
a motel?

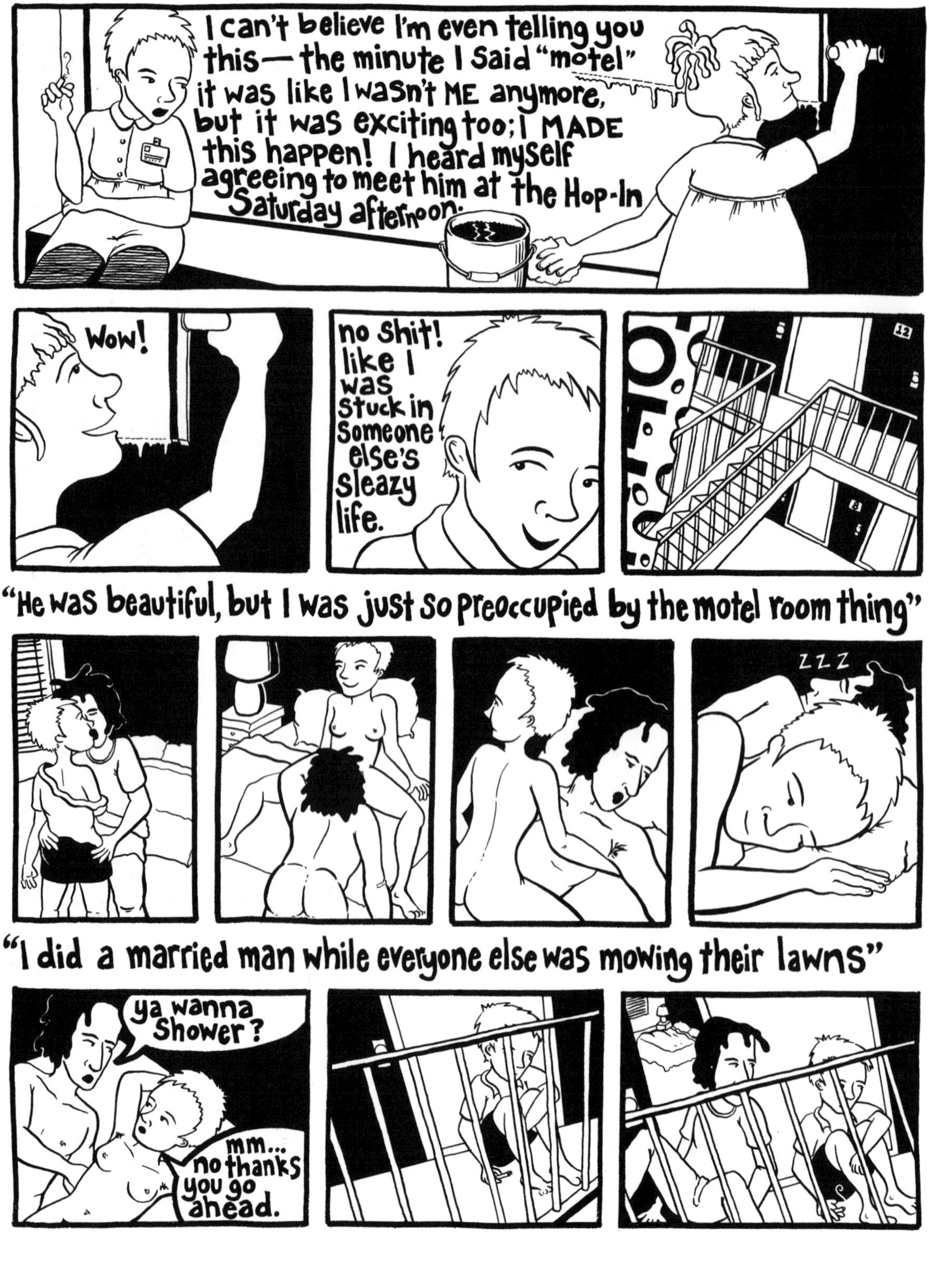
I can't believe I'm even telling you this— the minute I said "motel" it was like I wasn't ME anymore, but it was exciting too; I MADE this happen! I heard myself agreeing to meet him at the Hop-In Saturday afternoon.
Wow!
no shit! like I was stuck in someone else's sleazy life.
"He was beautiful, but I was just so preoccupied by the motel room thing"
ZZZ
"I did a married man while everyone else was mowing their lawns"
ya wanna shower?
mm... no thanks you go ahead.

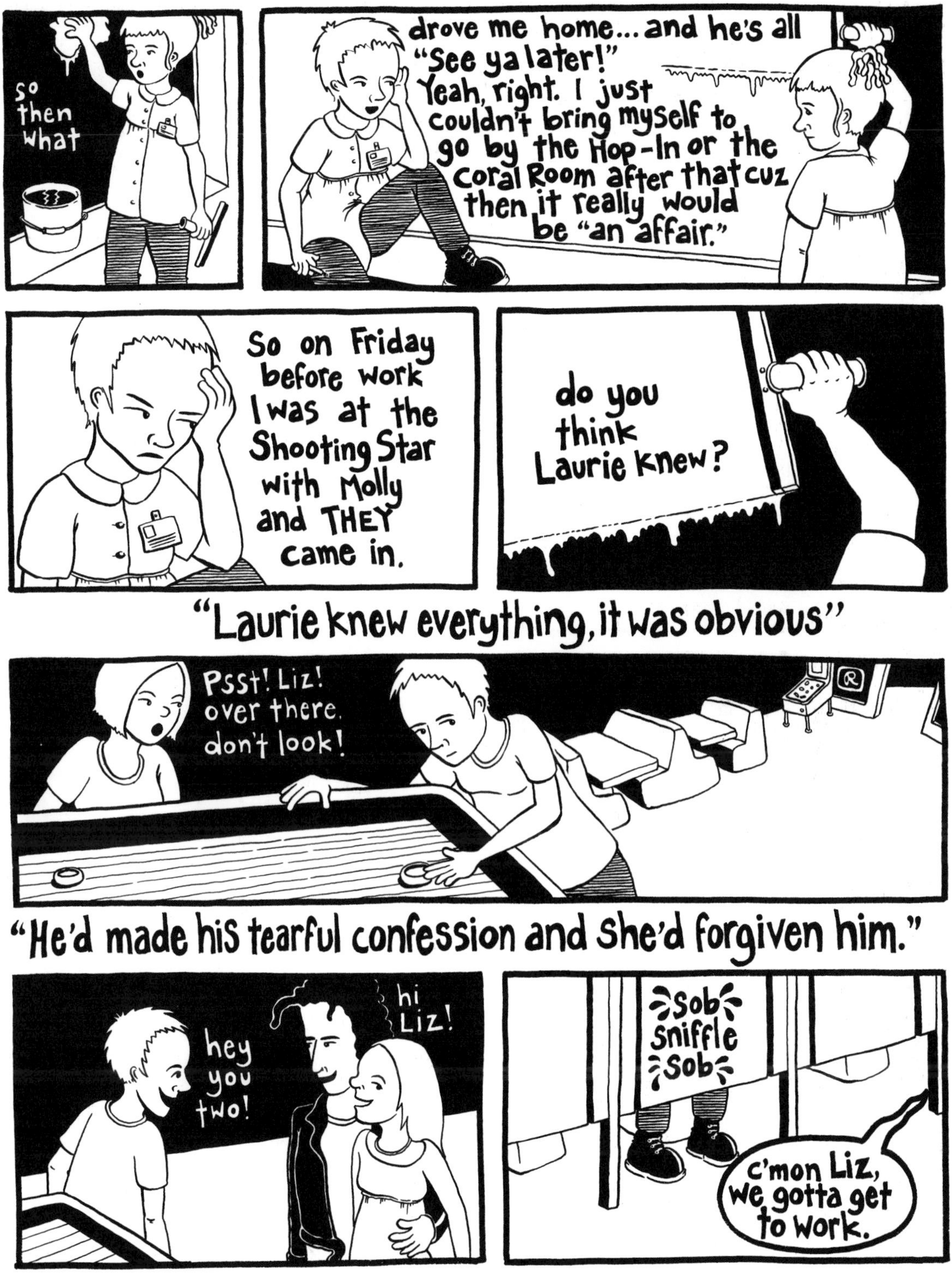
so then what
drove me home... and he's all "See ya later!" Yeah, right. I just couldn't bring myself to go by the Hop-In or the Coral Room after that cuz then it really would be "an affair."
So on Friday before work I was at the Shooting Star with Molly and THEY came in.
do you think Laurie knew?
"Laurie knew everything, it was obvious"
Psst! Liz! over there. don't look!
"He'd made his tearful confession and she'd forgiven him."
hey you two!
hi Liz!
Sob
Sniffle
Sob
c'mon Liz, we gotta get to work.

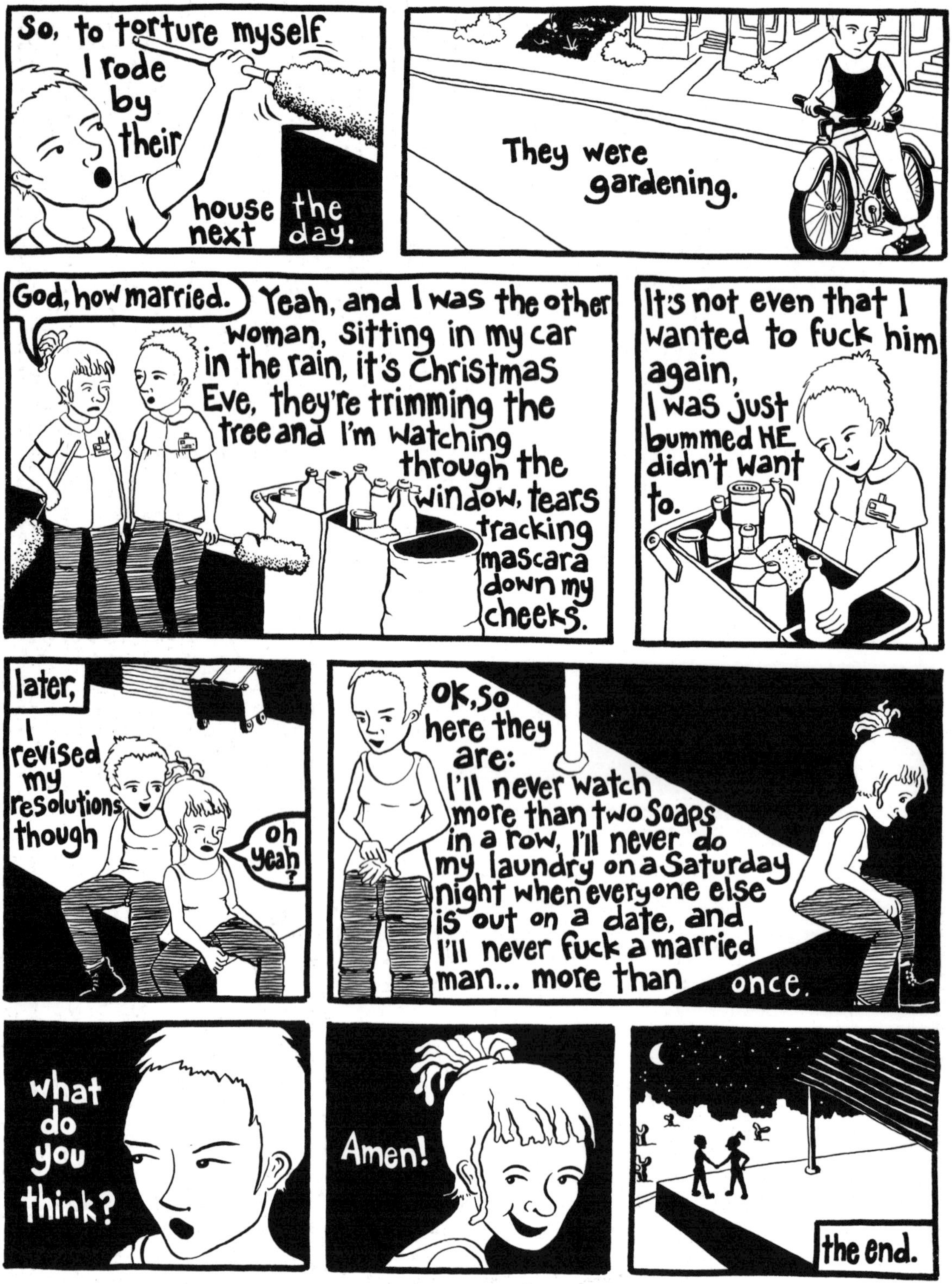
So, to torture myself I rode by their house the next day.
They were gardening.
God, how married.
Yeah, and I was the other woman, sitting in my car in the rain, it's Christmas Eve, they're trimming the tree and I'm watching through the window, tears tracking mascara down my cheeks.
It's not even that I wanted to fuck him again, I was just bummed HE didn't want to.
later,
I revised my resolutions though
oh yeah?
OK, so here they are: I'll never watch more than two soaps in a row, I'll never do my laundry on a Saturday night when everyone else is out on a date, and I'll never fuck a married man... more than once.
what do you think?
Amen!
the end.

THE ART OF BEING
A SUCCESSFUL BUSINESS GIRL

THE ART OF BEING A SUCCESSFUL BUSINESS GIRL

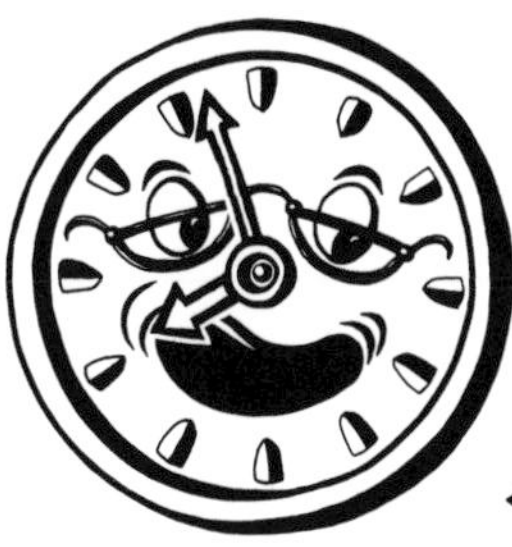

THIS IS A CAUTIONARY TALE OF TWO YOUNG BUSINESS GIRLS WHO MAY NOT ADVANCE IN THEIR CAREERS AS QUICKLY AS THEY EXPECT BECAUSE OF THEIR FAILURE TO ABIDE BY SOME IMPORTANT OFFICE RULES. NO MATTER WHAT OTHERS DO ABOUT RULES, YOU STICK BY 'EM! SOME DAY YOU'LL BE GLAD YOU DID...

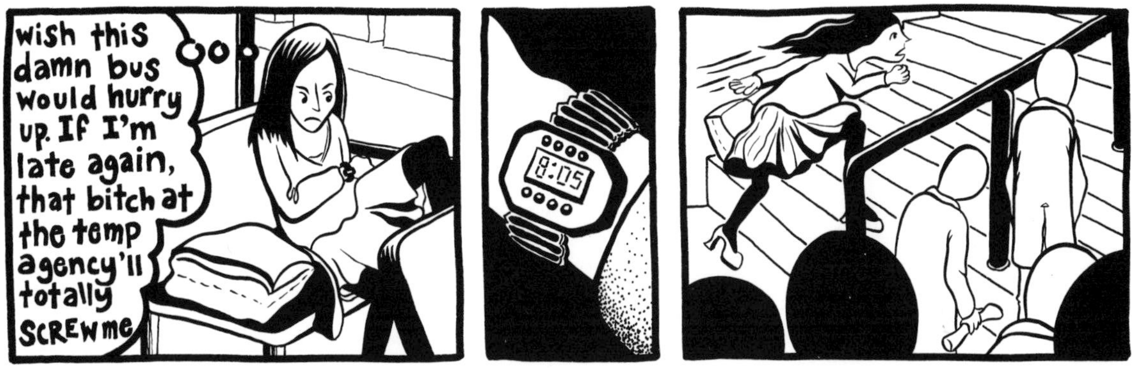
wish this damn bus would hurry up. If I'm late again, that bitch at the temp agency'll totally SCREW me
8:05

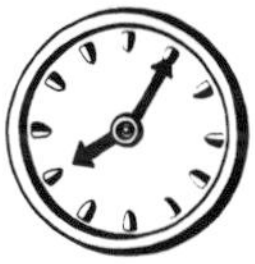

ALWAYS ARRIVE AT THE OFFICE IN THE MORNING AT LEAST FIFTEEN MINUTES BEFORE YOU ARE DUE!

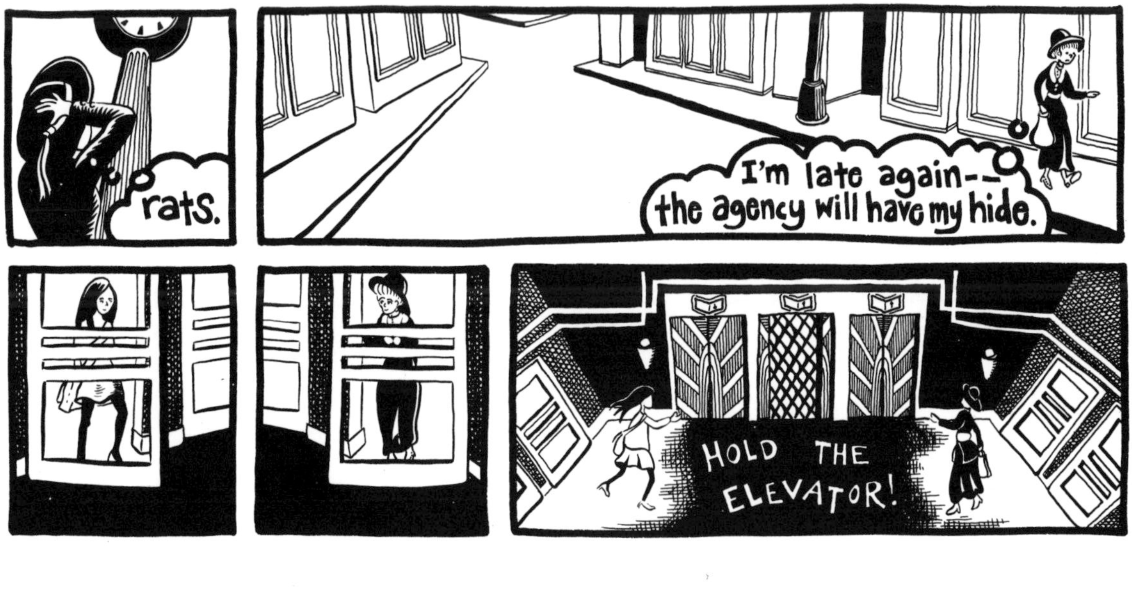
rats.
I'm late again-- the agency will have my hide.
HOLD THE ELEVATOR!

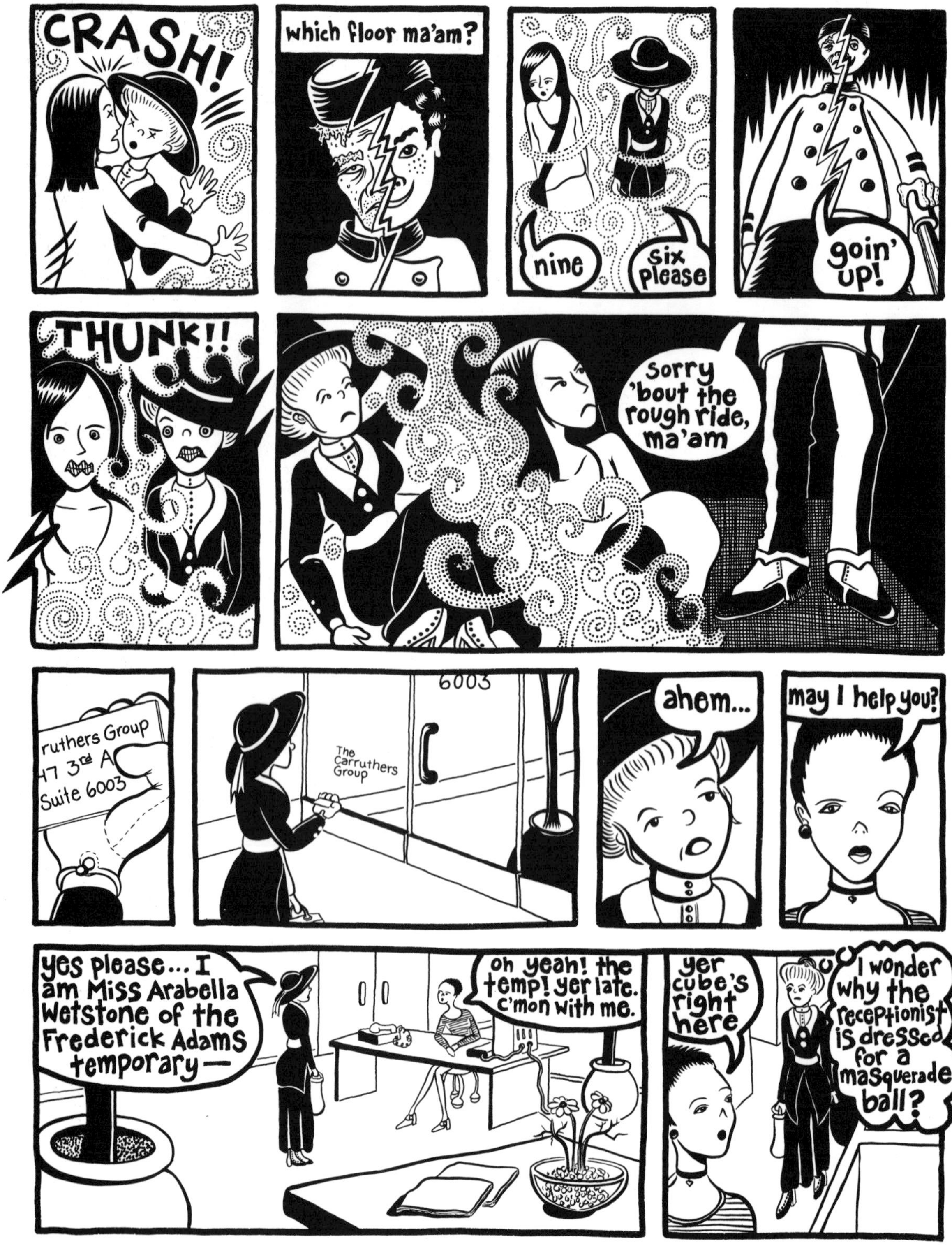
CRASH!
which floor ma'am?
nine
six please
goin' up!
THUNK!!
sorry 'bout the rough ride, ma'am
ruthers Group
47 3rd A
Suite 6003
6003
The Carruthers Group
ahem...
may I help you?
yes please... I am Miss Arabella Wetstone of the Frederick Adams temporary—
oh yeah! the temp! yer late. c'mon with me.
yer cube's right here
I wonder why the receptionist is dressed for a masquerade ball?

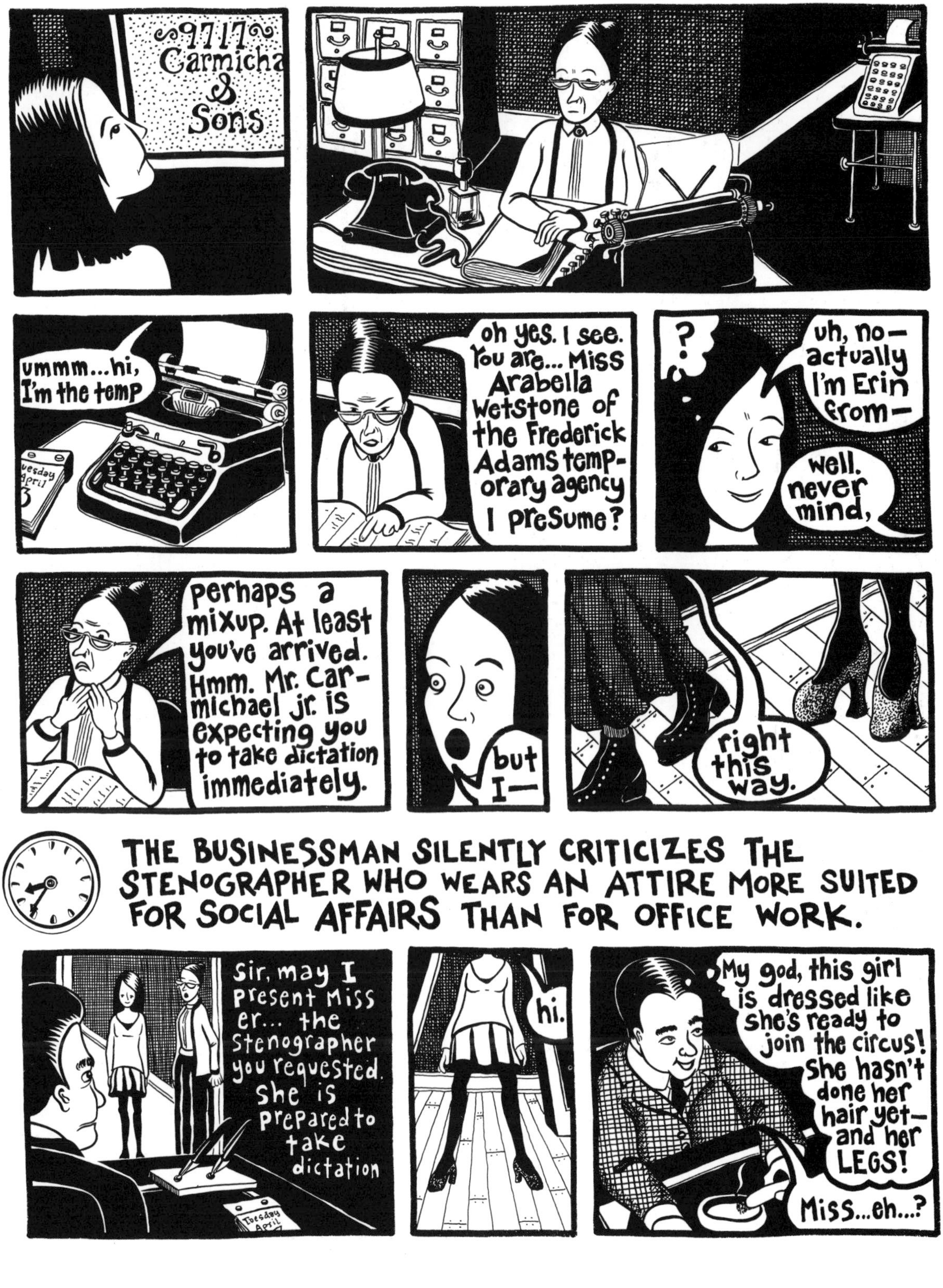
9717 Carmicha
& Sons
ummm...hi, I'm the temp
Tuesday April 3
oh yes. I see. You are... Miss Arabella Wetstone of the Frederick Adams temporary agency I presume?
?
uh, no— actually I'm Erin from—
well. never mind,
perhaps a mixup. At least you've arrived. Hmm. Mr. Carmichael jr. is expecting you to take dictation immediately.
but I—
right this way.
THE BUSINESSMAN SILENTLY CRITICIZES THE STENOGRAPHER WHO WEARS AN ATTIRE MORE SUITED FOR SOCIAL AFFAIRS THAN FOR OFFICE WORK.
Sir, may I present Miss er... the stenographer you requested. She is prepared to take dictation
Tuesday April
hi.
My god, this girl is dressed like she's ready to join the circus! She hasn't done her hair yet— and her LEGS!
Miss...eh...?

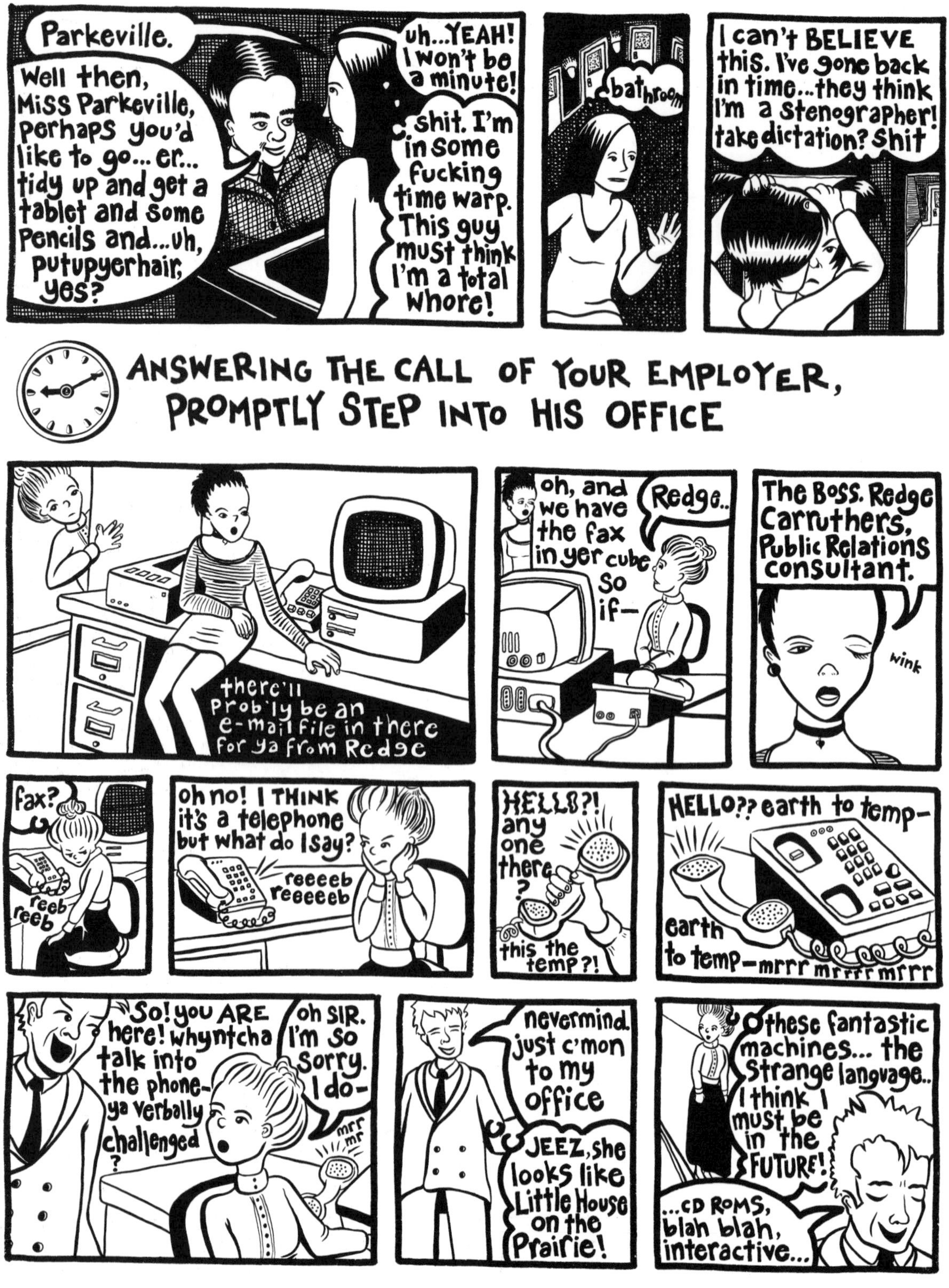

Parkeville.
Well then, Miss Parkeville, perhaps you'd like to go... er... tidy up and get a tablet and some pencils and...uh, putupyerhair, yes?
uh...YEAH! I won't be a minute!
shit. I'm in some fucking time warp. This guy must think I'm a total whore!
bathroom
I can't BELIEVE this. I've gone back in time...they think I'm a stenographer! take dictation? shit
ANSWERING THE CALL OF YOUR EMPLOYER, PROMPTLY STEP INTO HIS OFFICE
there'll prob'ly be an e-mail file in there for ya from Redge
oh, and we have the fax in yer cube so if—
Redge..
The Boss. Redge Carruthers, Public Relations consultant.
wink
fax?
reeb reeb
oh no! I THINK it's a telephone but what do I say?
reeeeb reeeeeb
HELLO?! any one there? this the temp?!
HELLO?? earth to temp—
earth to temp—mrrr mrrrr mrrr
So! you ARE here! whyntcha talk into the phone-ya verbally challenged?
oh SIR. I'm so sorry. I do-
mrr mr
nevermind. just c'mon to my office
JEEZ, she looks like Little House on the Prairie!
these fantastic machines... the strange language.. I think I must be in the FUTURE!
...CD ROMS, blah blah, interactive...

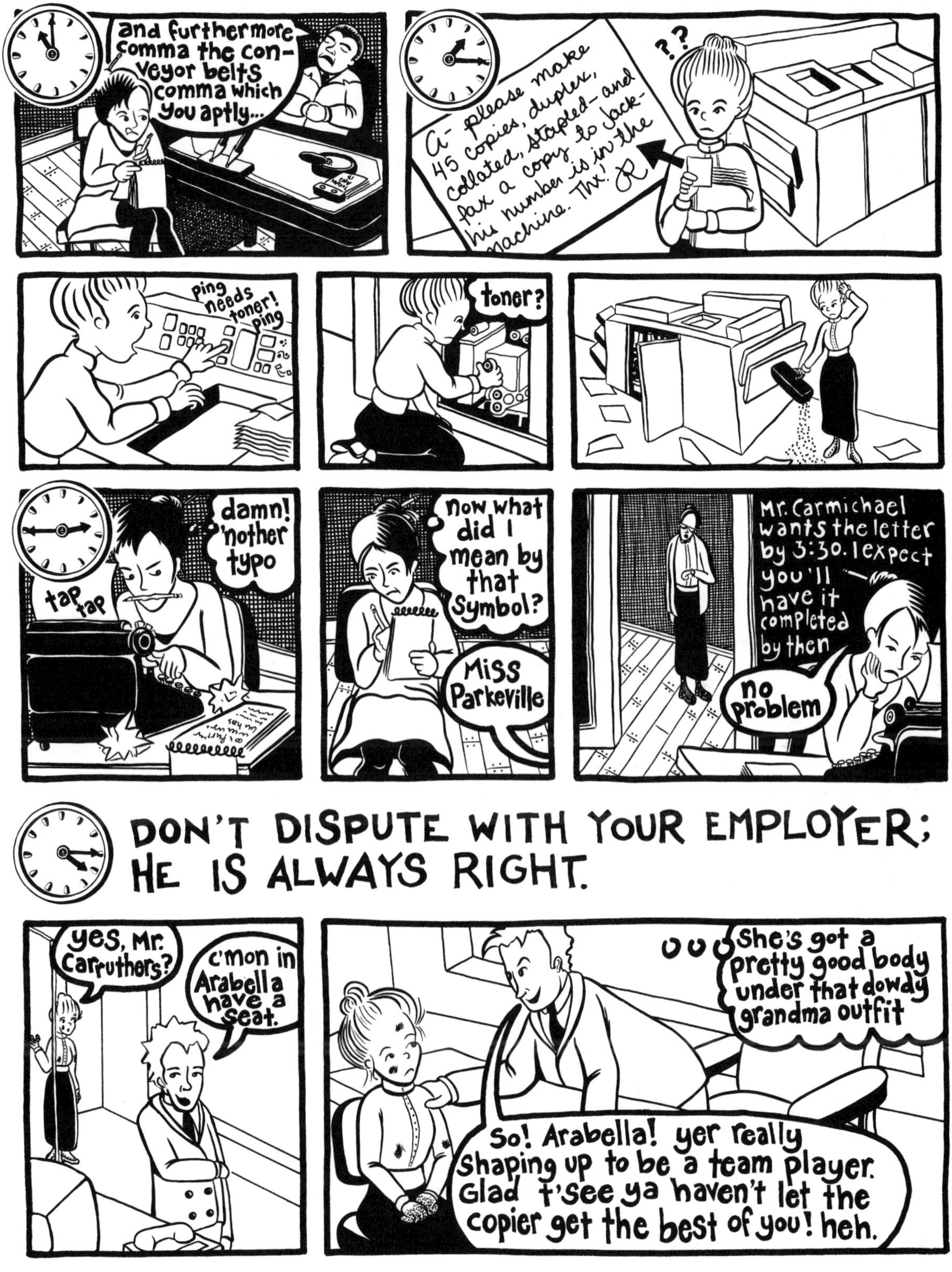
and furthermore comma the conveyor belts comma which you aptly...
A- please make 45 copies, duplex, collated, stapled - and fax a copy to Jack - his number is in the machine. Thx! JR
??
ping needs toner! ping
toner?
damn! 'nother typo
tap tap
now what did I mean by that symbol?
Miss Parkeville
Mr. Carmichael wants the letter by 3:30. I expect you'll have it completed by then
no problem
DON'T DISPUTE WITH YOUR EMPLOYER; HE IS ALWAYS RIGHT.
yes, Mr. Carruthers?
c'mon in Arabella have a seat.
She's got a pretty good body under that dowdy grandma outfit
So! Arabella! yer really shaping up to be a team player. Glad t'see ya haven't let the copier get the best of you! heh.

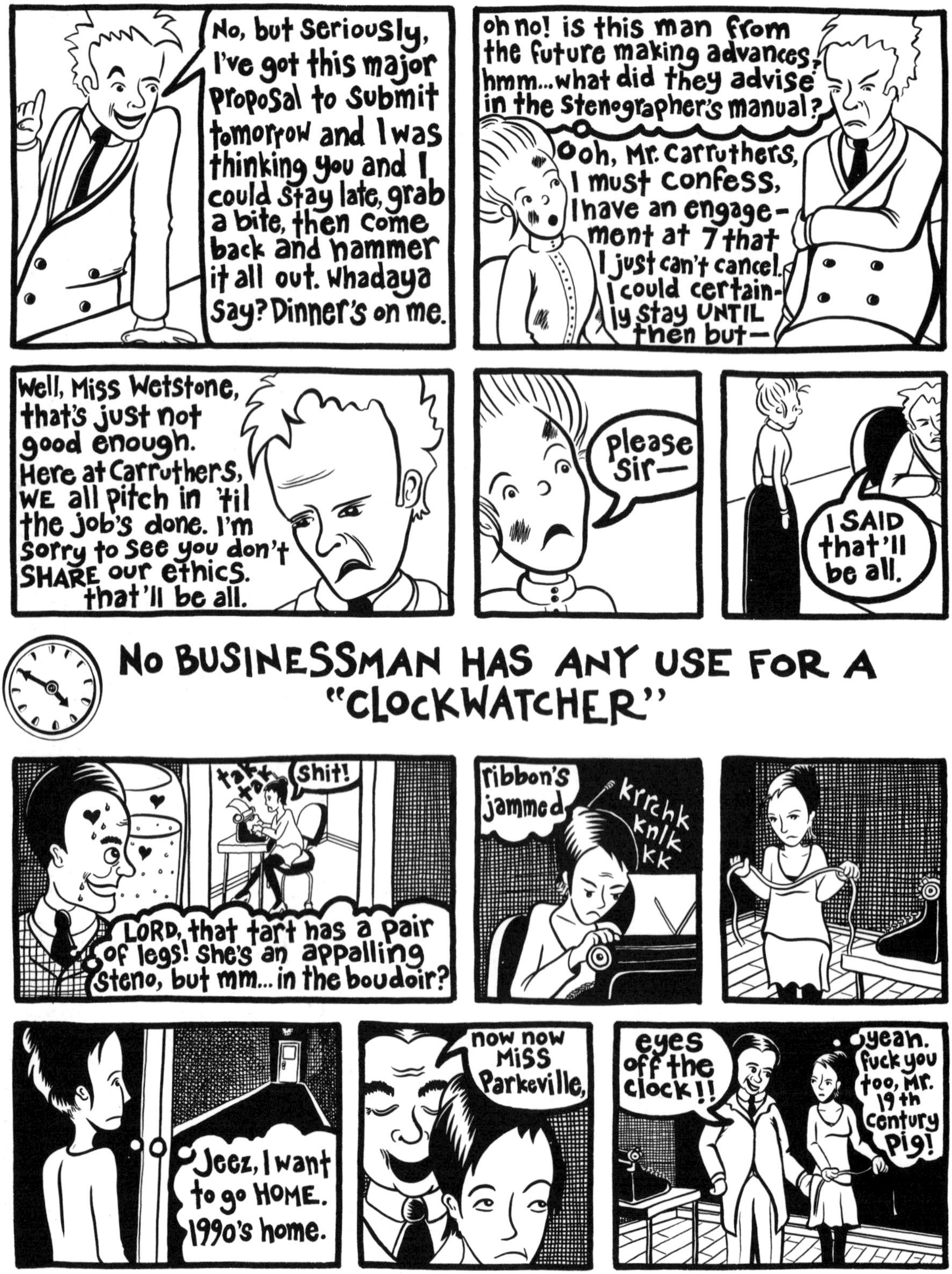

No, but seriously, I've got this major proposal to submit tomorrow and I was thinking you and I could stay late, grab a bite, then come back and hammer it all out. Whadaya say? Dinner's on me.
oh no! is this man from the future making advances? hmm...what did they advise in the stenographer's manual?
Ooh, Mr. Carruthers, I must confess, I have an engage-ment at 7 that I just can't cancel. I could certain-ly stay UNTIL then but—
Well, Miss Wetstone, that's just not good enough. Here at Carruthers, WE all pitch in 'til the job's done. I'm sorry to see you don't SHARE our ethics. that'll be all.
Please sir—
I SAID that'll be all.
NO BUSINESSMAN HAS ANY USE FOR A "CLOCKWATCHER"
tak tak
Shit!
LORD, that tart has a pair of legs! She's an appalling steno, but mm... in the boudoir?
ribbon's jammed
krrchk knlk kk
Jeez, I want to go HOME. 1990's home.
now now MISS Parkeville,
eyes off the clock!!
yeah. fuck you too, Mr. 19th century Pig!

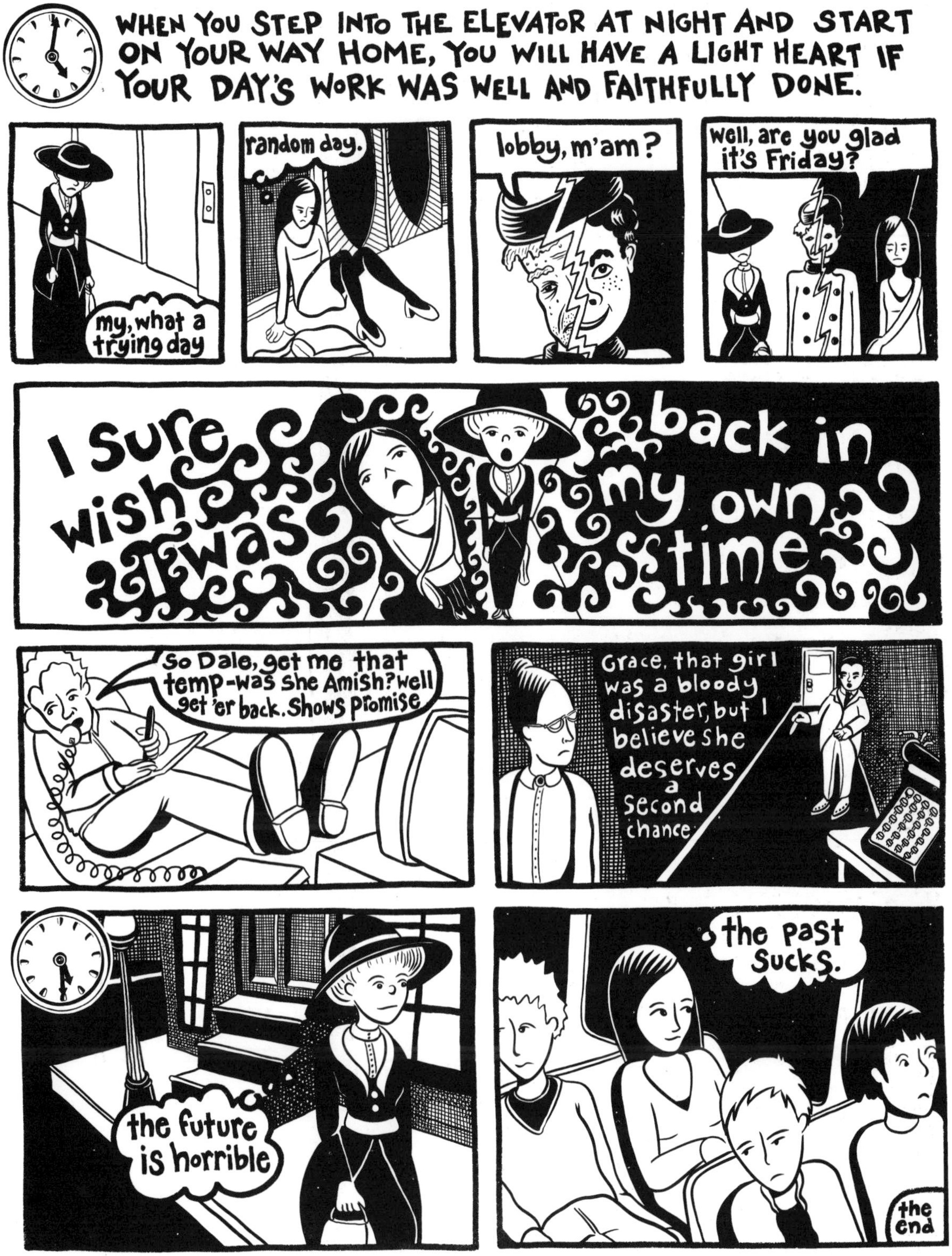
WHEN YOU STEP INTO THE ELEVATOR AT NIGHT AND START ON YOUR WAY HOME, YOU WILL HAVE A LIGHT HEART IF YOUR DAY'S WORK WAS WELL AND FAITHFULLY DONE.
my, what a trying day
random day.
lobby, m'am?
well, are you glad it's Friday?
I sure wish I was back in my own time
So Dale, get me that temp-was she Amish? well get 'er back. Shows promise
Grace, that girl was a bloody disaster, but I believe she deserves a second chance.
the future is horrible
the past sucks.
the end

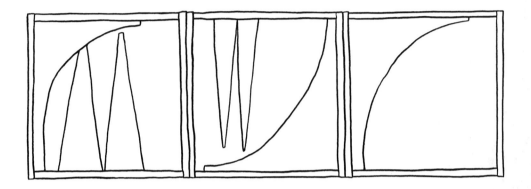

PENNYROYAL TEA

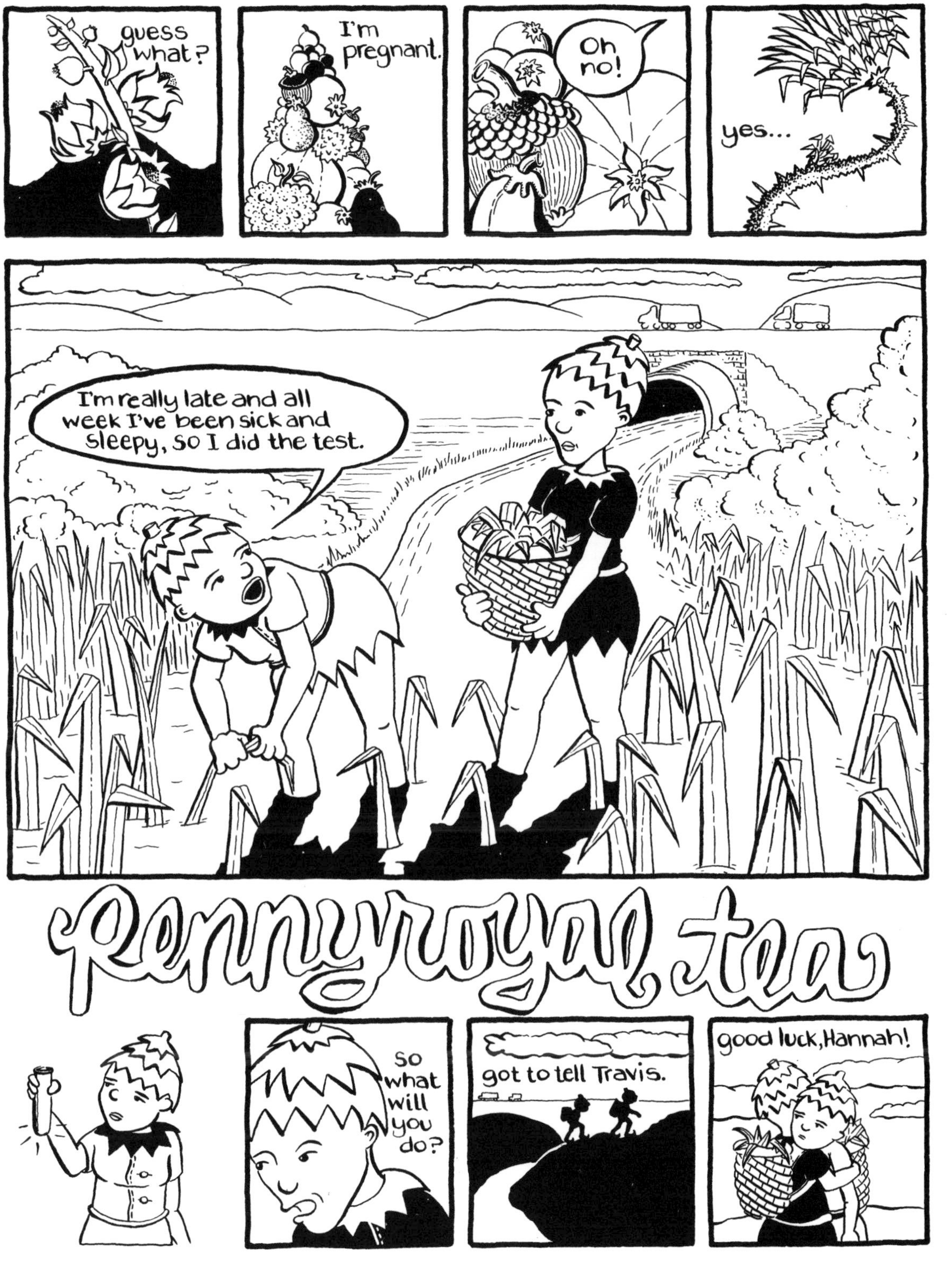
guess what?
I'm pregnant.
Oh no!
yes...
I'm really late and all week I've been sick and sleepy, so I did the test.
Pennyroyal tea
So what will you do?
got to tell Travis.
good luck, Hannah!

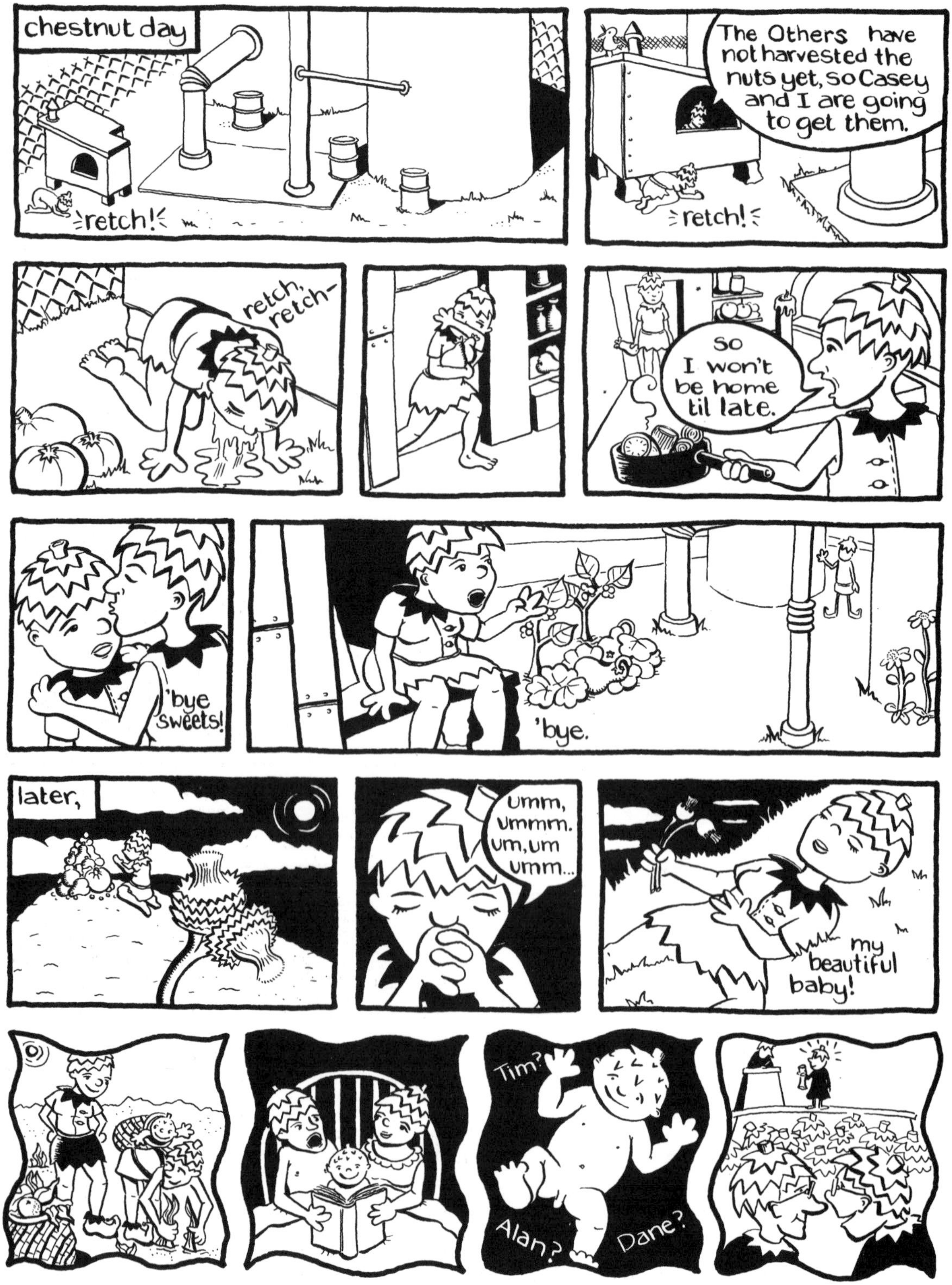

chestnut day
retch!
retch!
The Others have not harvested the nuts yet, so Casey and I are going to get them.
retch, retch-
So I won't be home til late.
'bye sweets!
'bye.
later,
umm, ummm. um, um umm...
my beautiful baby!
Tim?
Alan?
Dane?

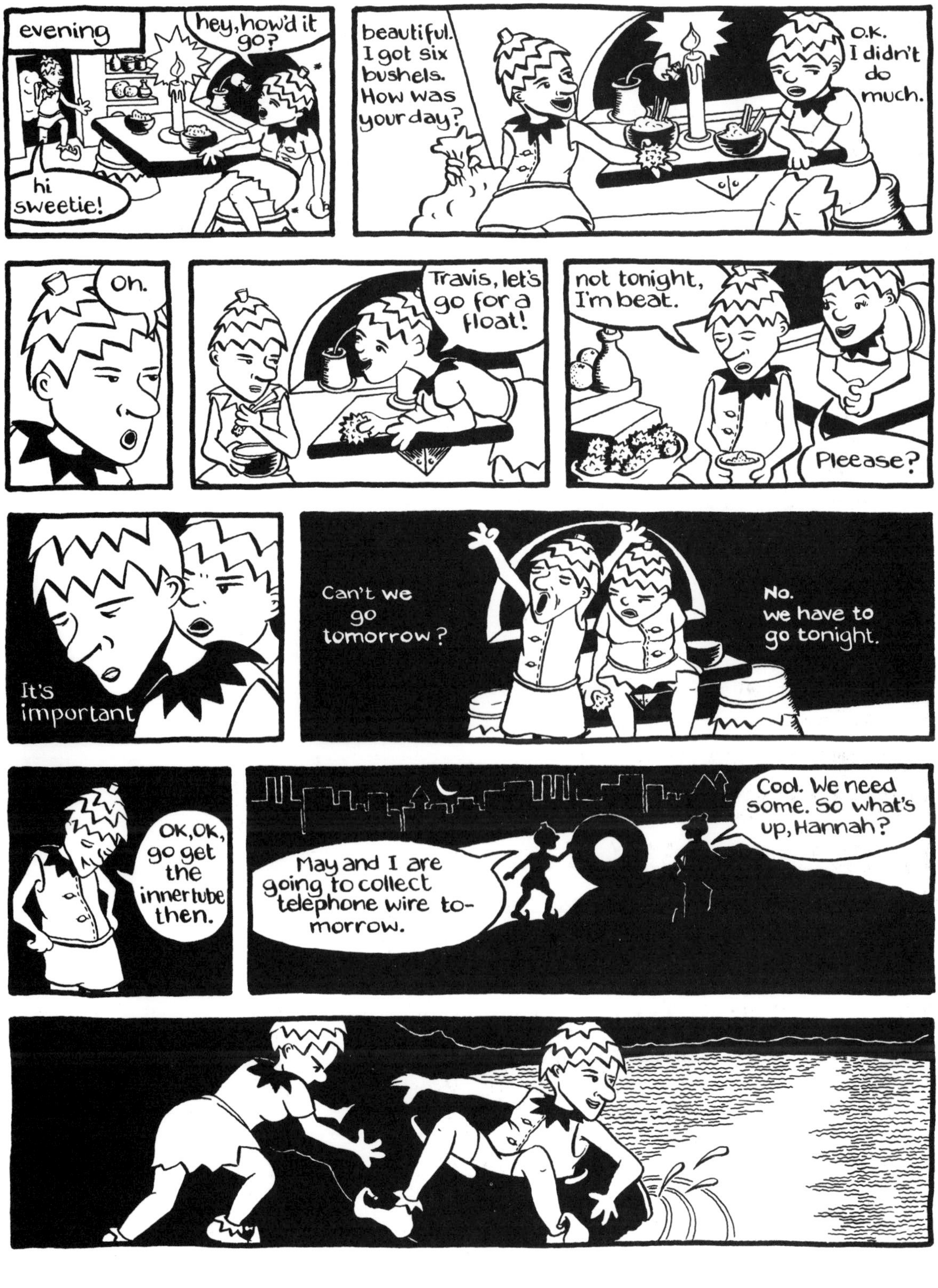

evening
hey, how'd it go?
hi sweetie!
beautiful. I got six bushels. How was your day?
O.K. I didn't do much.
Oh.
Travis, let's go for a float!
not tonight, I'm beat.
Pleease?
It's important
Can't we go tomorrow?
No. we have to go tonight.
OK, OK, go get the innertube then.
May and I are going to collect telephone wire to-morrow.
Cool. We need some. So what's up, Hannah?

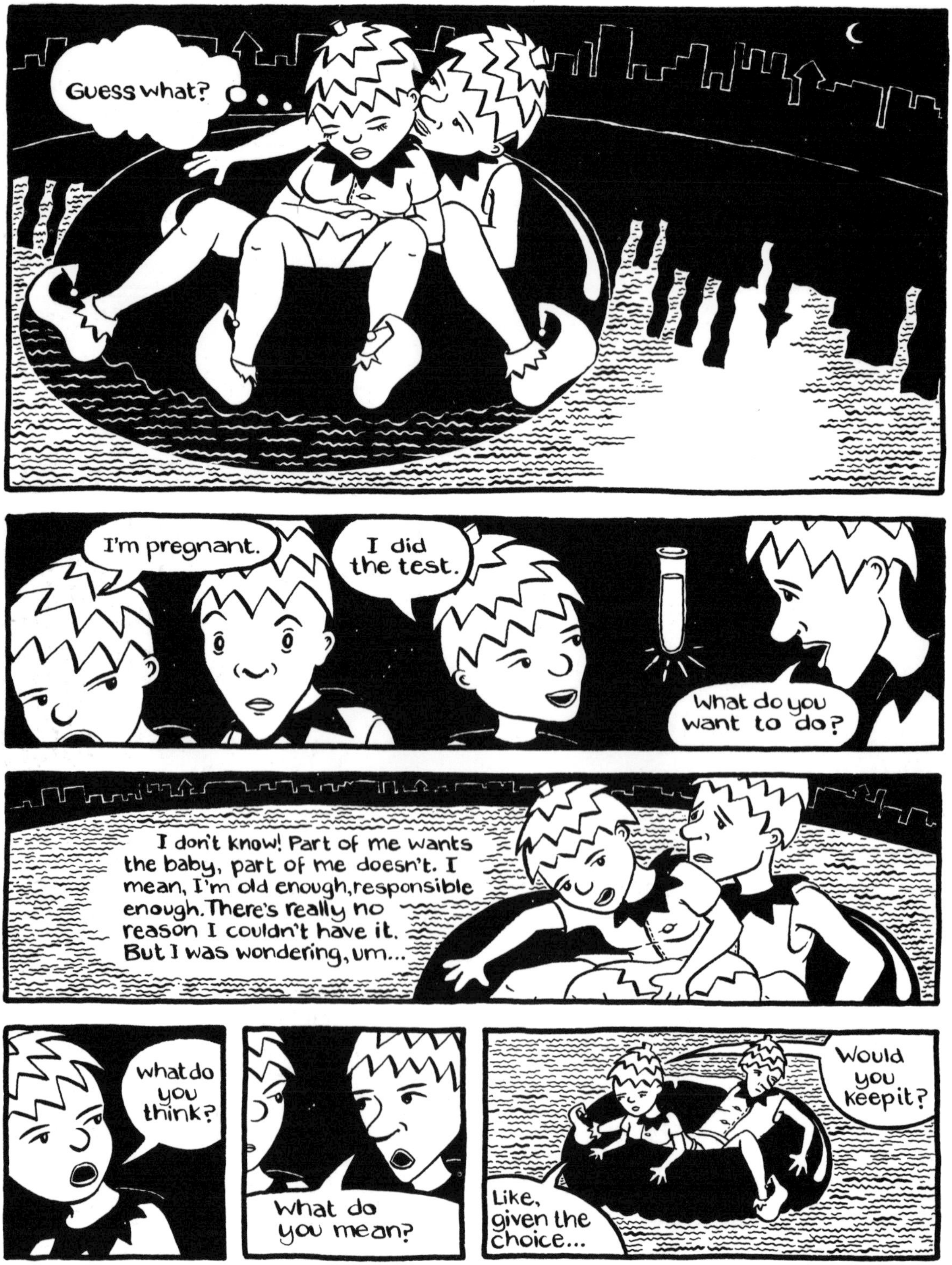
Guess what?
I'm pregnant.
I did the test.
What do you want to do?
I don't know! Part of me wants the baby, part of me doesn't. I mean, I'm old enough, responsible enough. There's really no reason I couldn't have it. But I was wondering, um...
what do you think?
What do you mean?
Would you keepit?
Like, given the choice...

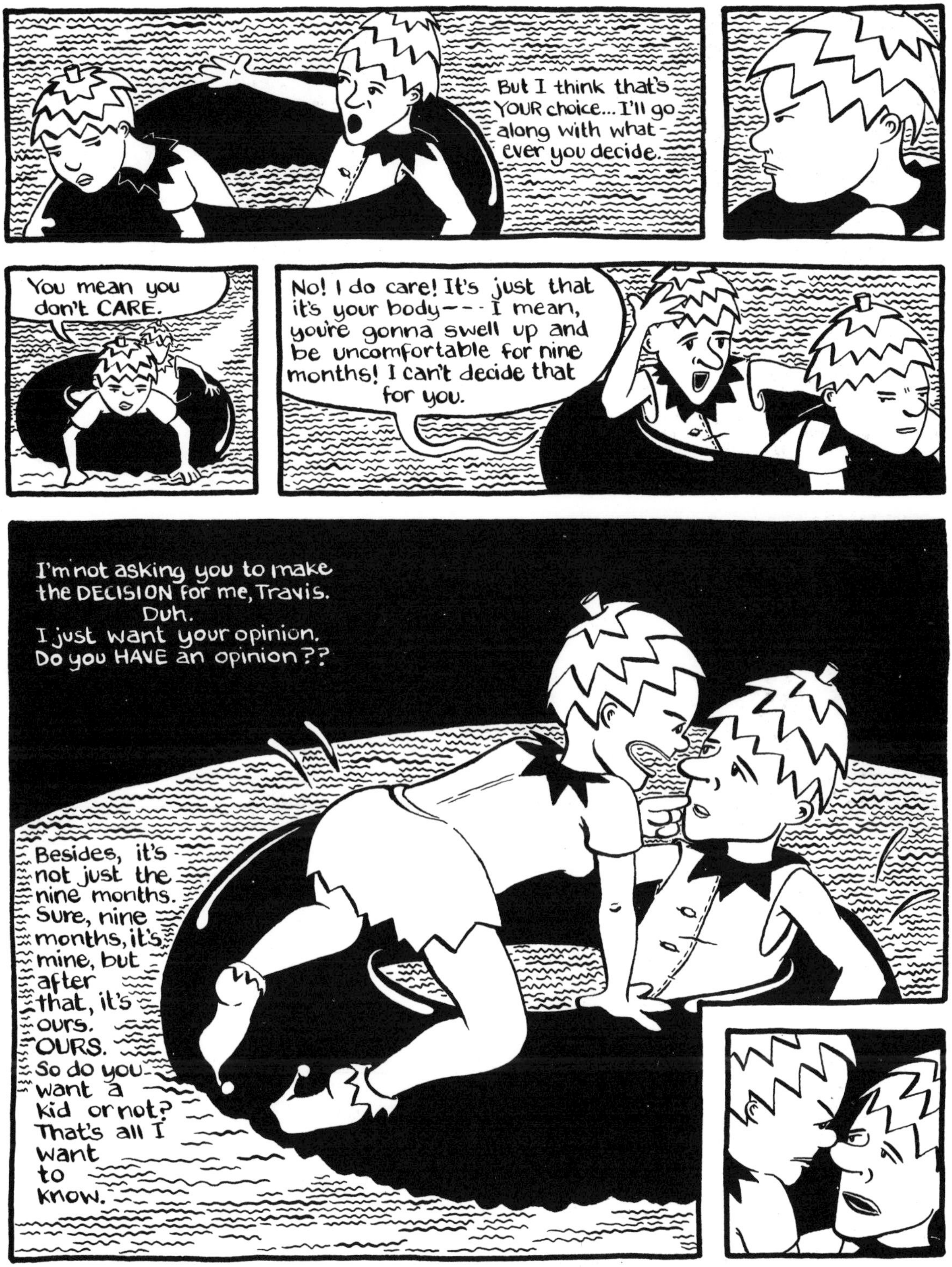
But I think that's YOUR choice... I'll go along with what-ever you decide.
You mean you don't CARE.
No! I do care! It's just that it's your body--- I mean, you're gonna swell up and be uncomfortable for nine months! I can't decide that for you.
I'm not asking you to make the DECISION for me, Travis. Duh.
I just want your opinion. Do you HAVE an opinion??
Besides, it's not just the nine months. Sure, nine months, it's mine, but after that, it's ours. OURS. So do you want a kid or not? That's all I want to know.

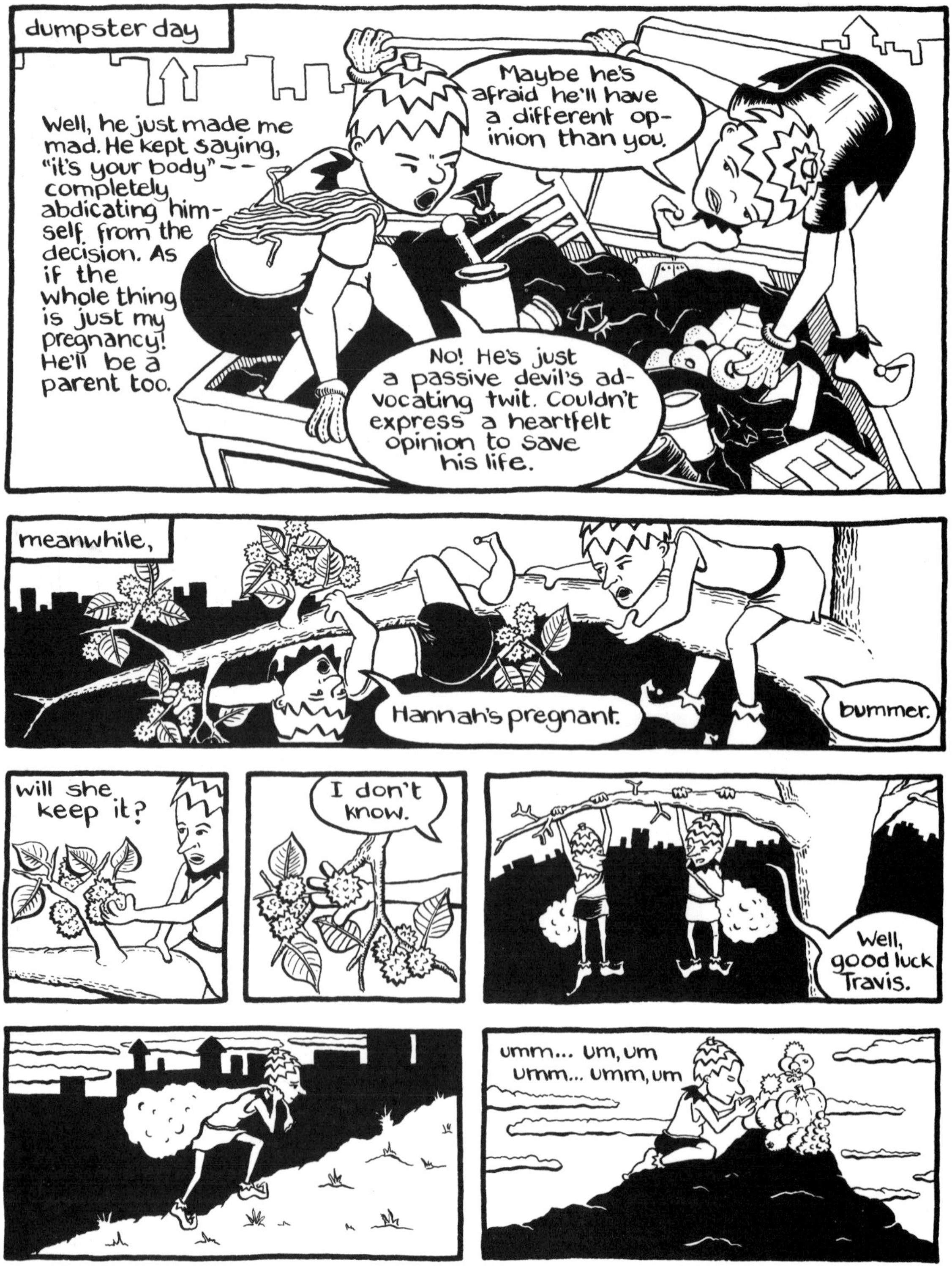
dumpster day
Well, he just made me mad. He kept saying, "it's your body"-- completely abdicating himself from the decision. As if the whole thing is just my pregnancy! He'll be a parent too.
Maybe he's afraid he'll have a different opinion than you.
No! He's just a passive devil's advocating twit. Couldn't express a heartfelt opinion to save his life.
meanwhile,
Hannah's pregnant.
bummer.
will she keep it?
I don't know.
Well, good luck Travis.
umm... um, um
umm... umm, um

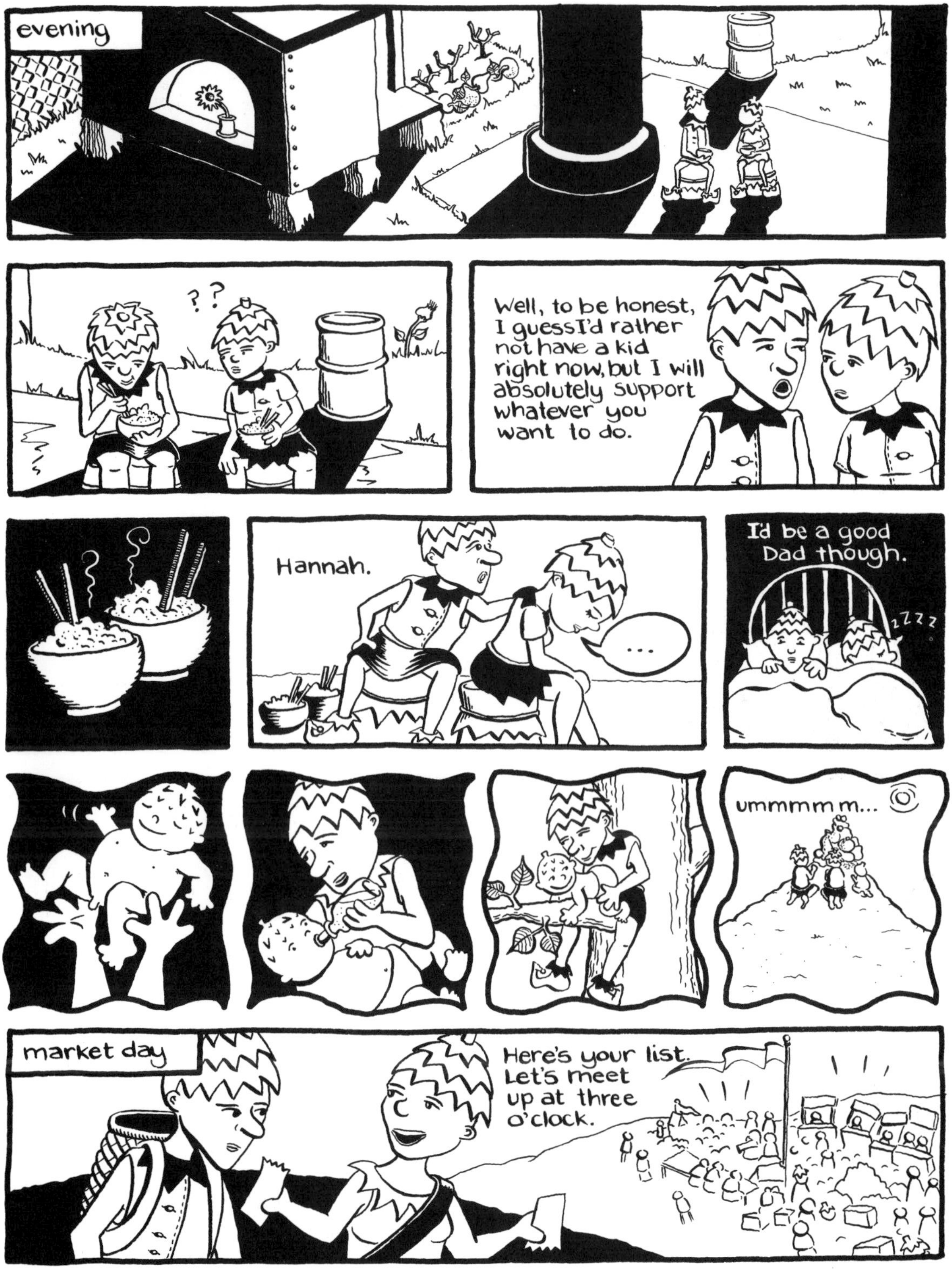
evening
? ?
Well, to be honest, I guess I'd rather not have a kid right now, but I will absolutely support whatever you want to do.
Hannah.
...
I'd be a good Dad though.
zzzz
ummmmm...
market day
Here's your list. Let's meet up at three o'clock.

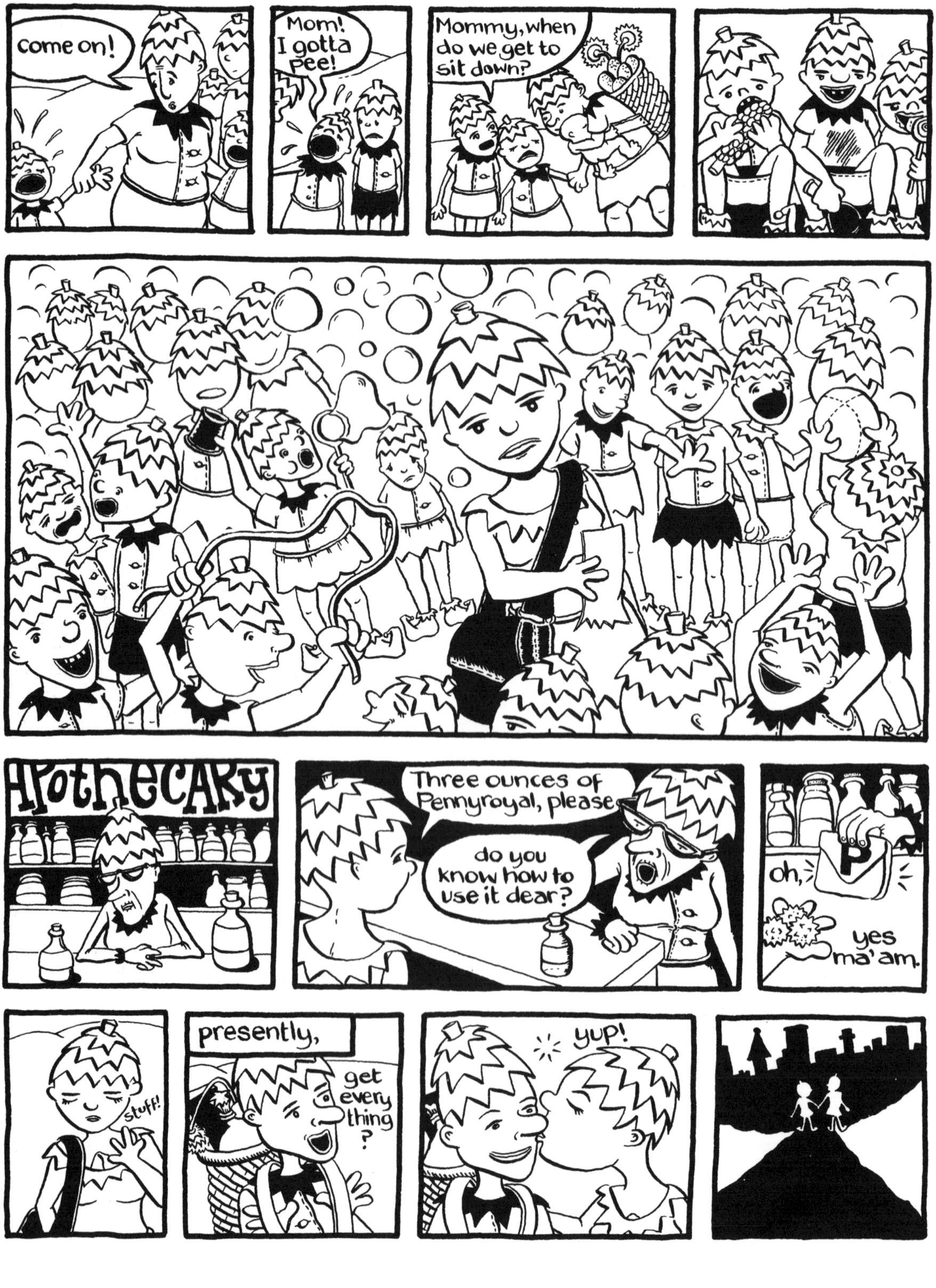
come on!
Mom! I gotta pee!
Mommy, when do we get to sit down?
Apothecary
Three ounces of Pennyroyal, please.
do you know how to use it dear?
oh,
yes ma'am.
stuff!
presently,
get every thing?
yup!

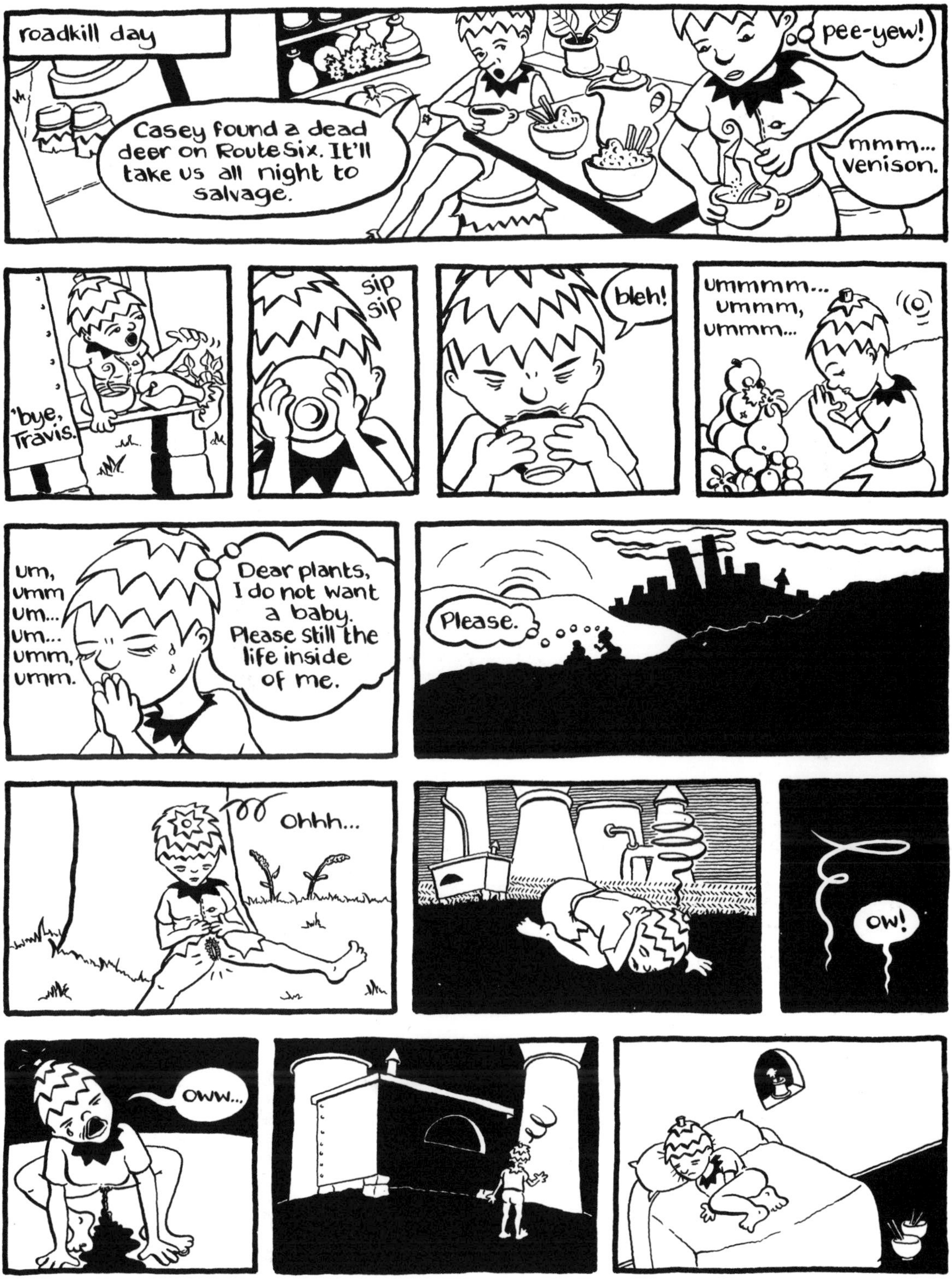
roadkill day
Casey found a dead deer on Route Six. It'll take us all night to salvage.
pee-yew!
mmm... venison.
'bye, Travis.
sip sip
bleh!
ummmm... ummm, ummm...
um, umm um... um... umm, umm.
Dear plants, I do not want a baby. Please still the life inside of me.
Please.
Ohhh...
ow!
oww...

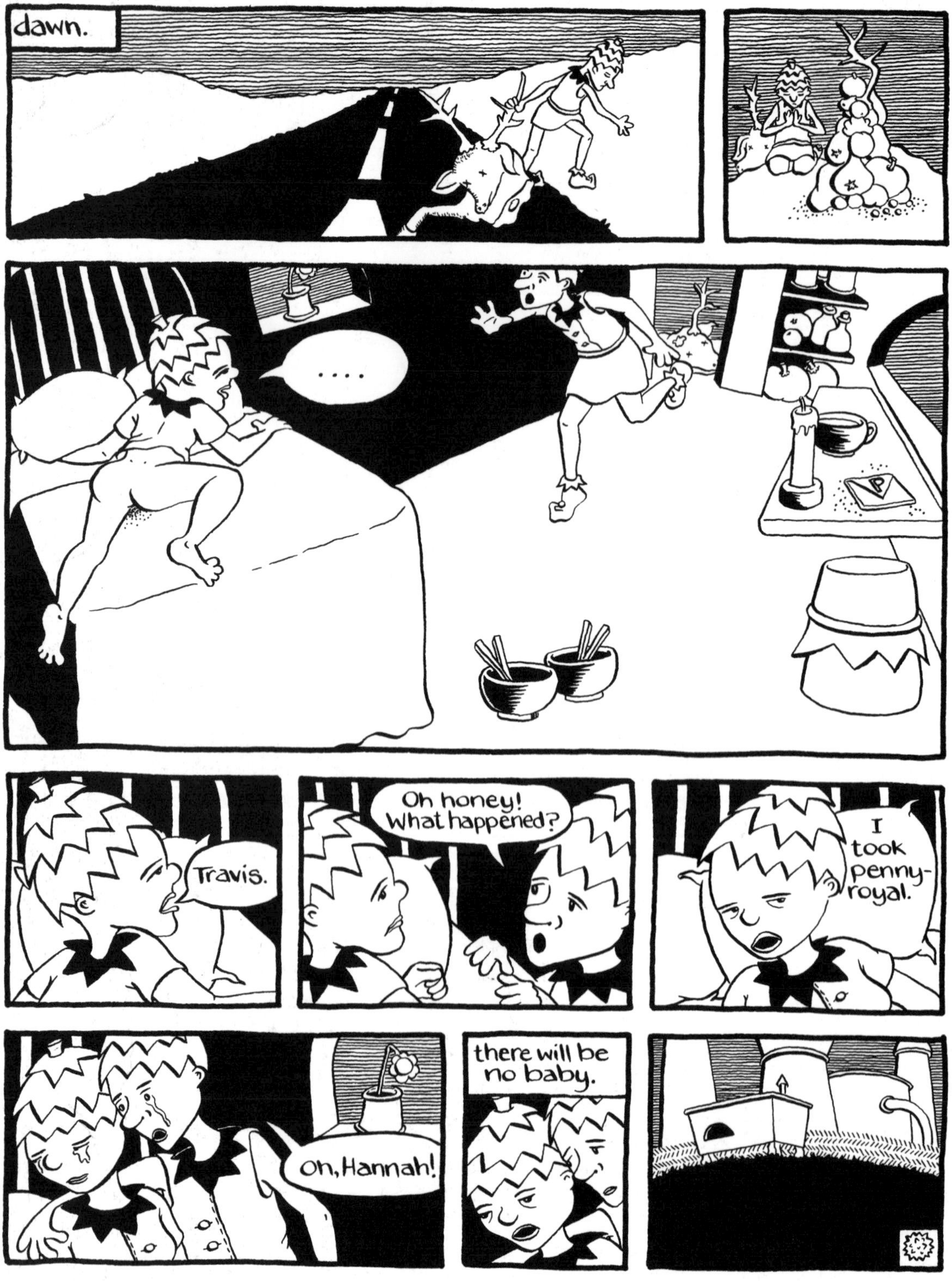
dawn.
....
Travis.
Oh honey! What happened?
I took penny-royal.
Oh, Hannah!
there will be no baby.

RESERVOIR

RESERVOIR

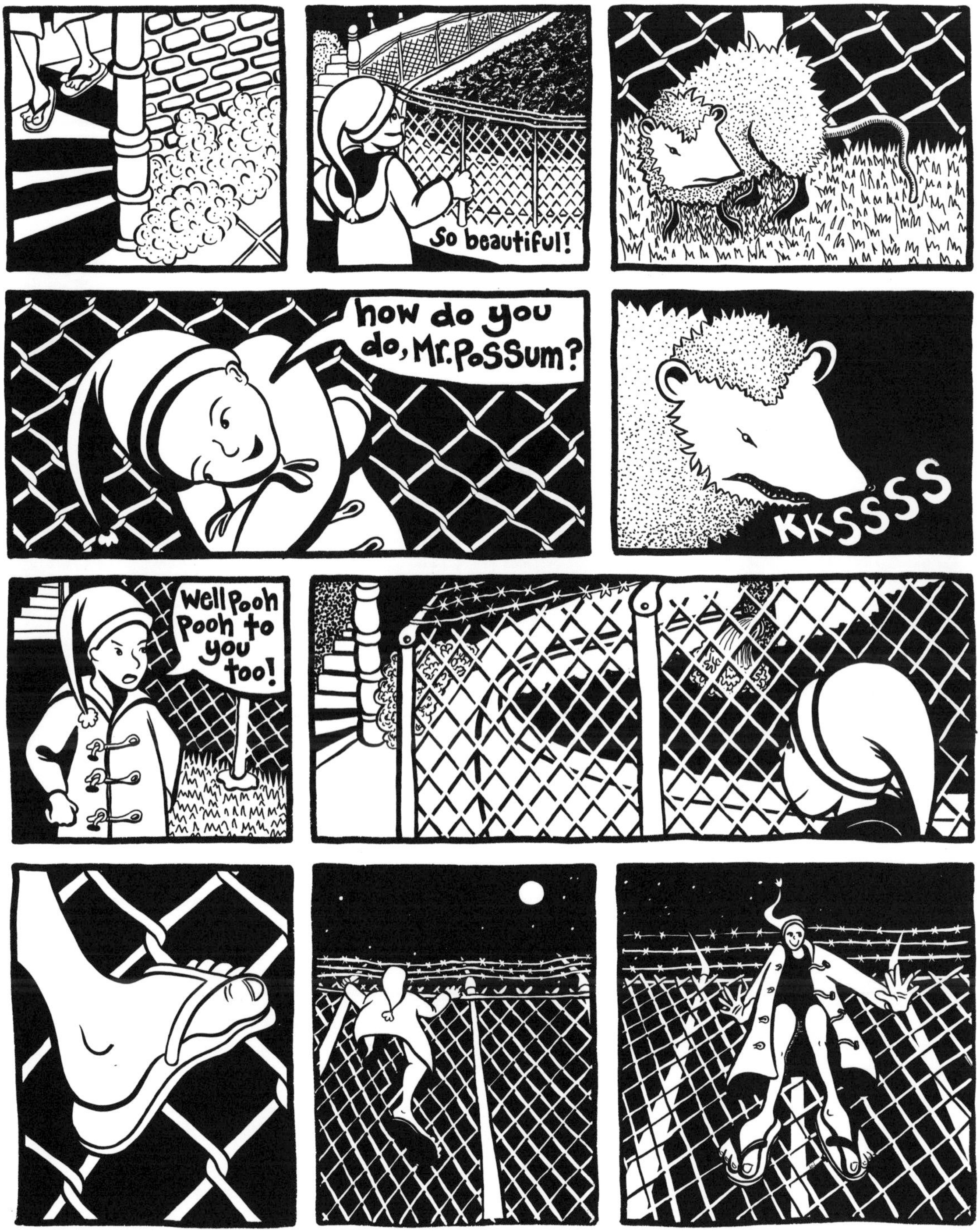
So beautiful!
how do you do, Mr. Possum?
KKSSSSS
Well Pooh Pooh to you too!

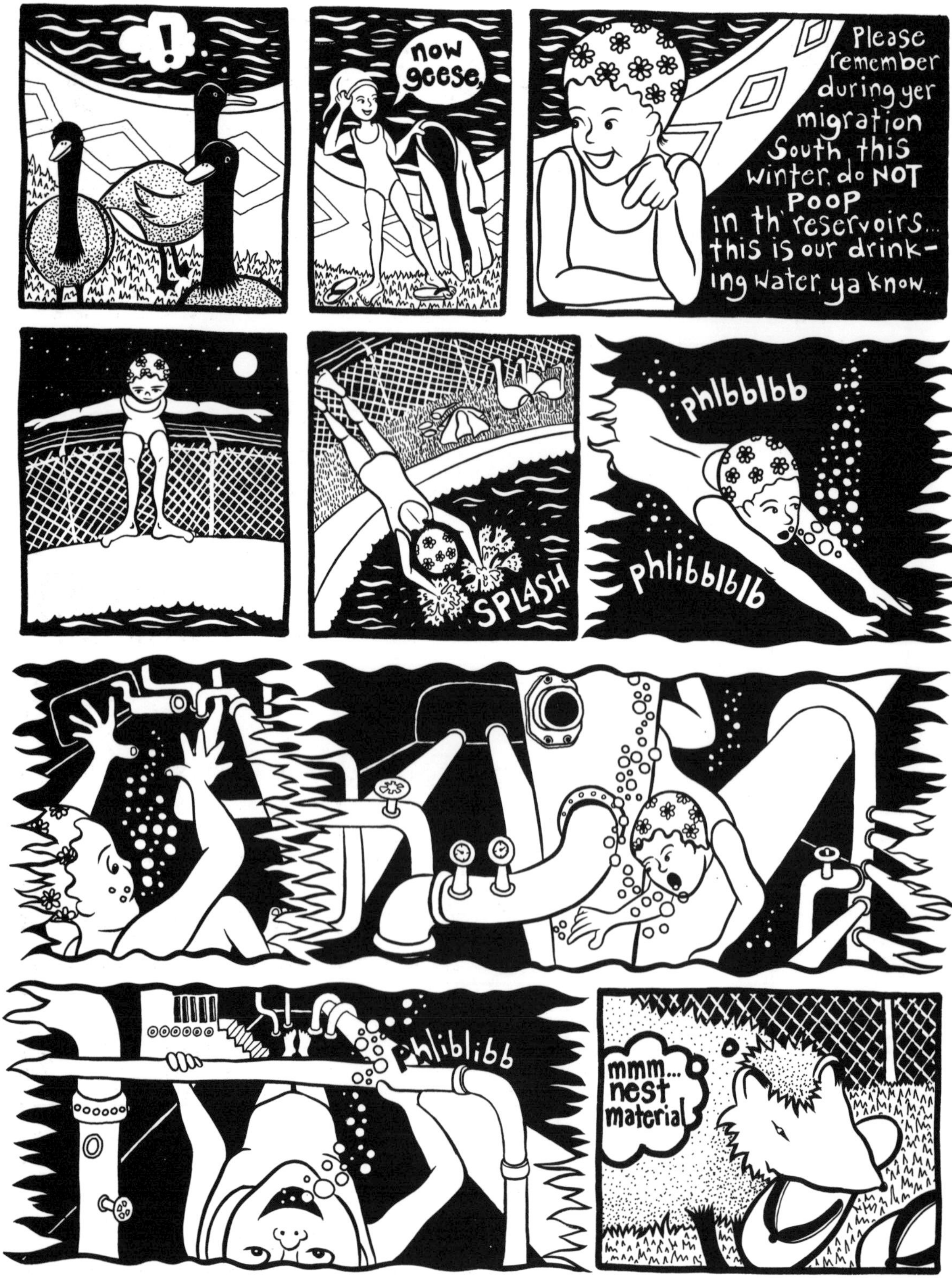
!
now geese,
Please remember during yer migration South this winter, do NOT POOP in th' reservoirs... this is our drinking water, ya know...
SPLASH
phlbblbb
phlibblblb
phliblibb
mmm... nest material

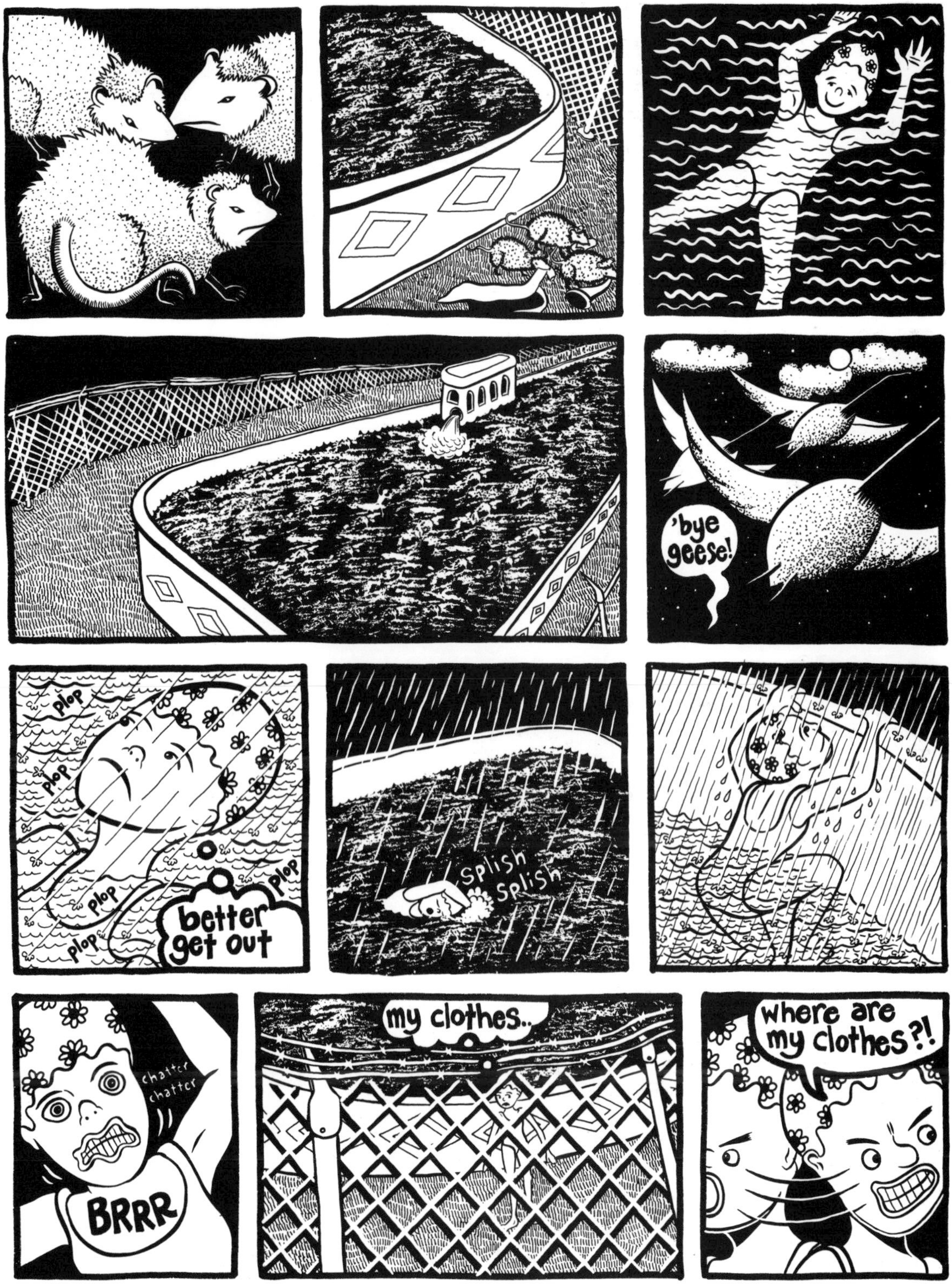
'bye geese!
plop
plop
plop
plop
plop
better get out
Splish Splish
chatter chatter
BRRR
my clothes..
where are my clothes?!

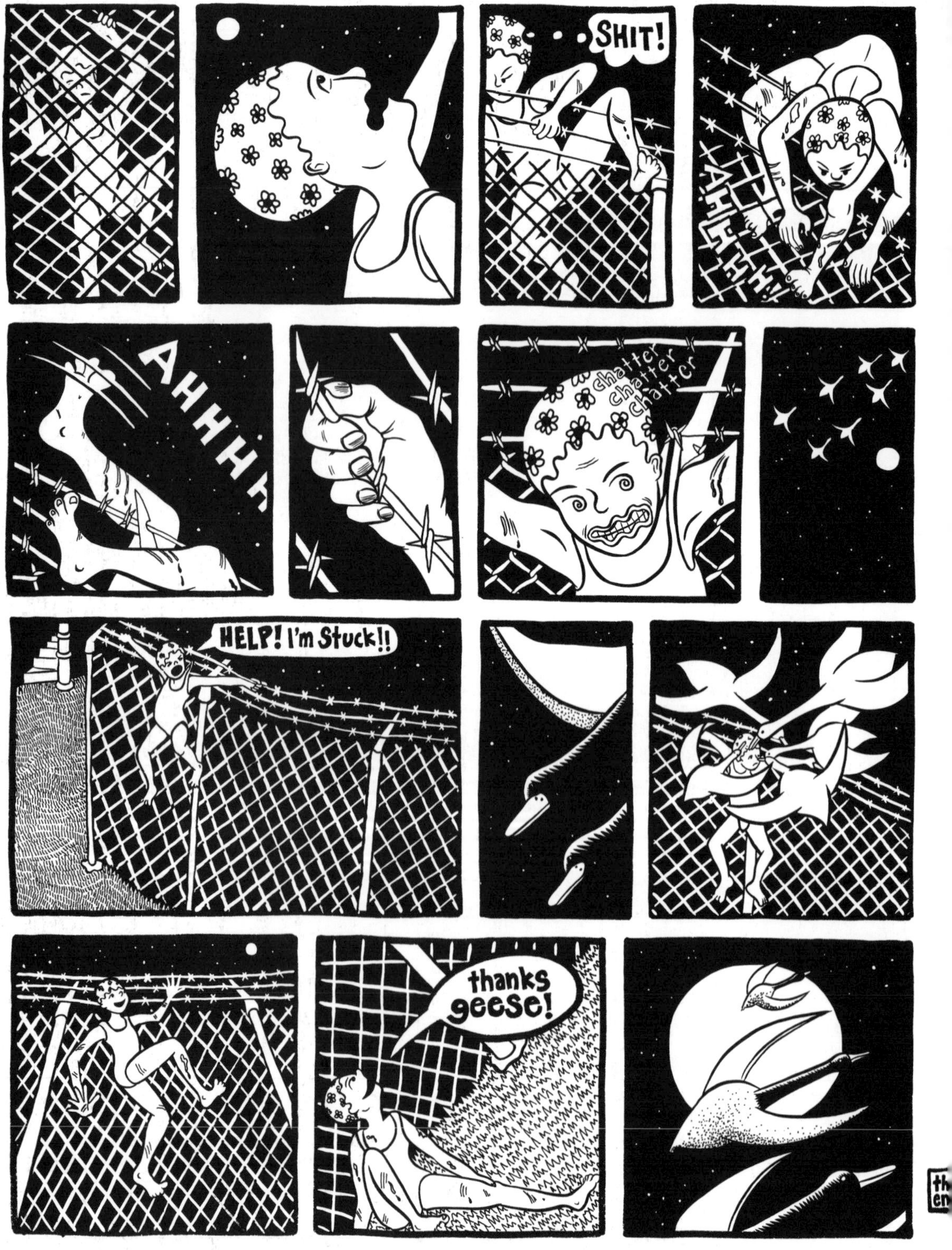
SHIT!
AHHHH
chatter chatter chatter
HELP! I'm Stuck!!
thanks geese!

FROZEN ANGEL

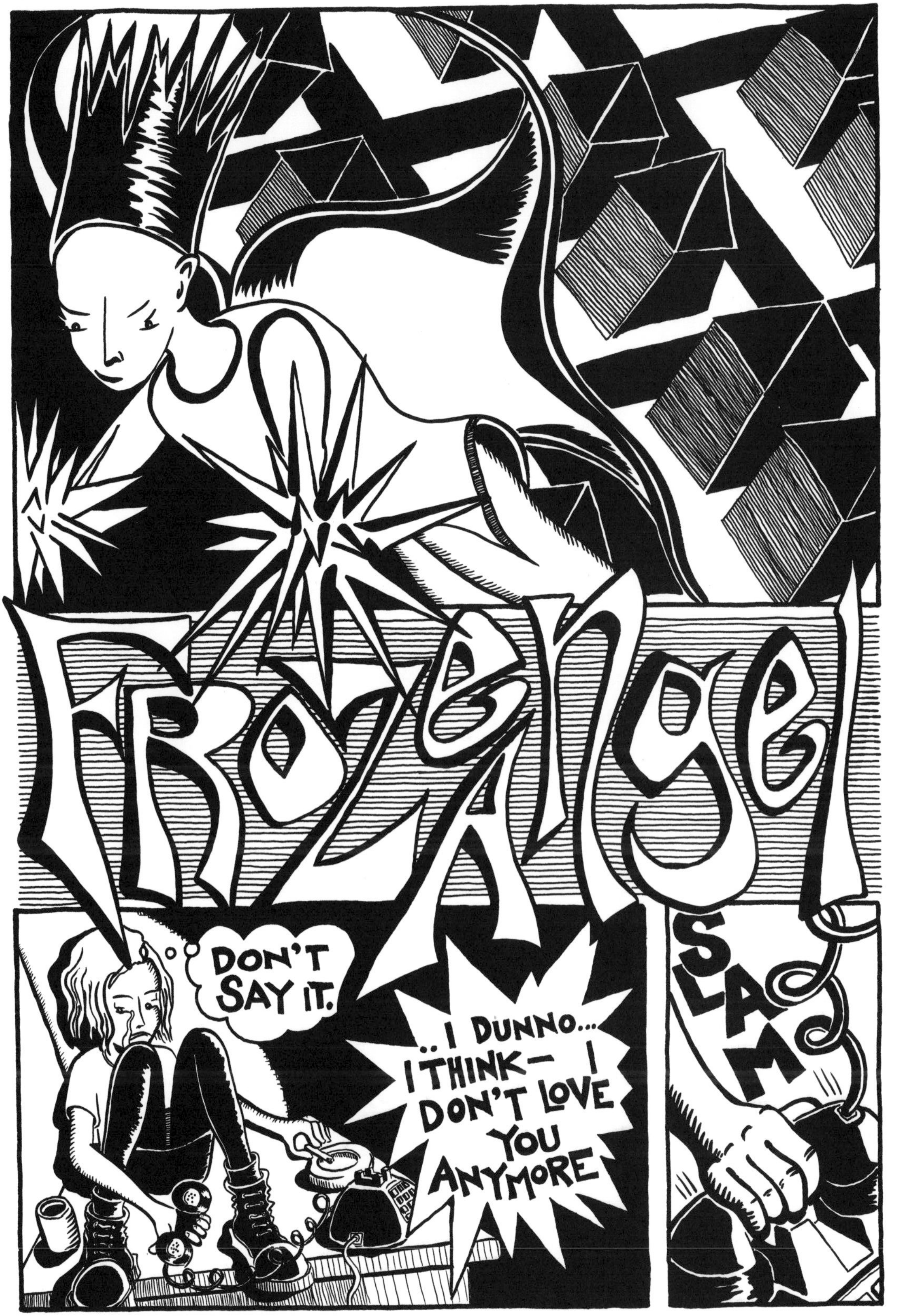
Frozen Angel
DON'T SAY IT.
..I DUNNO... I THINK— I DON'T LOVE YOU ANYMORE
SLAM

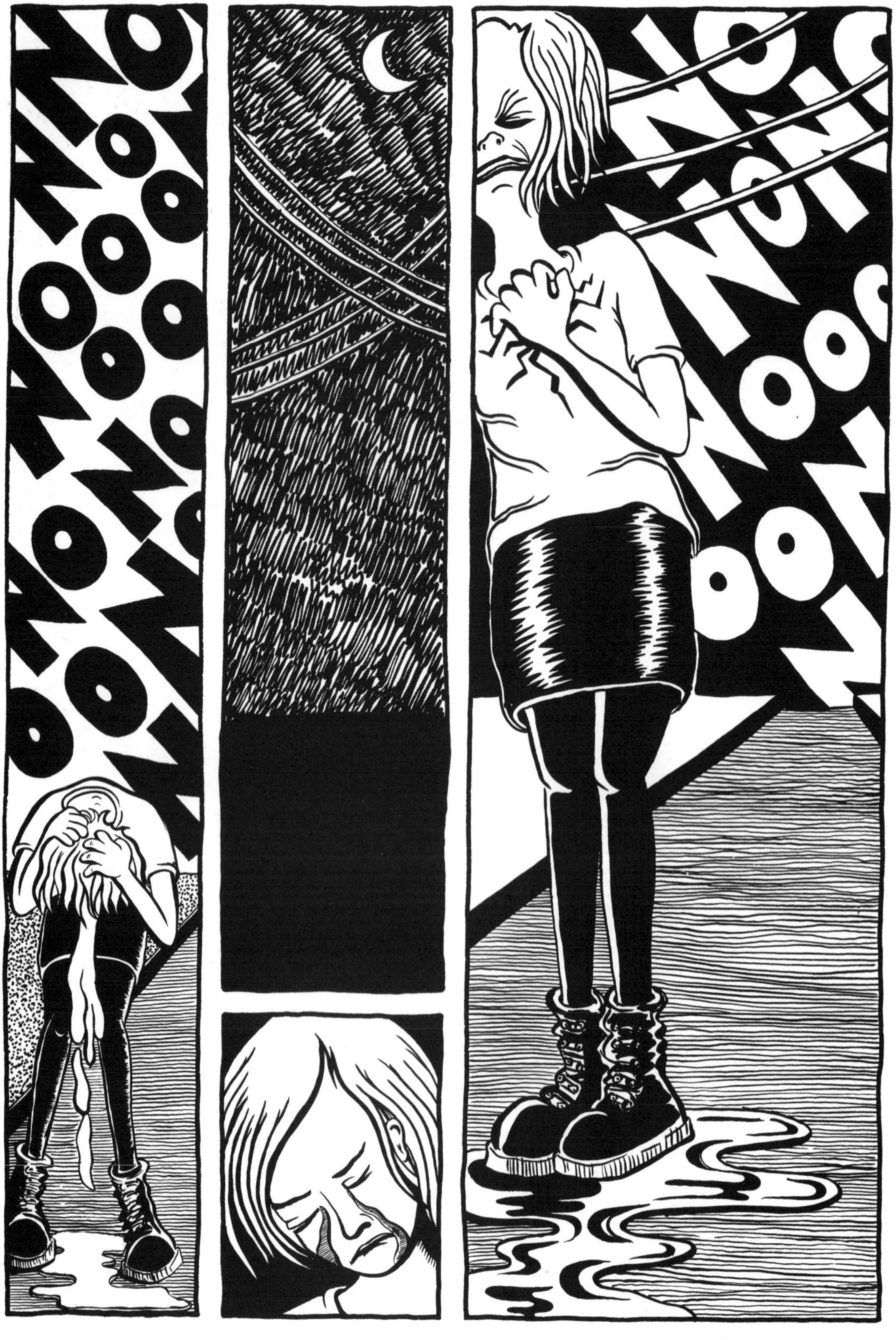

NO NO NO

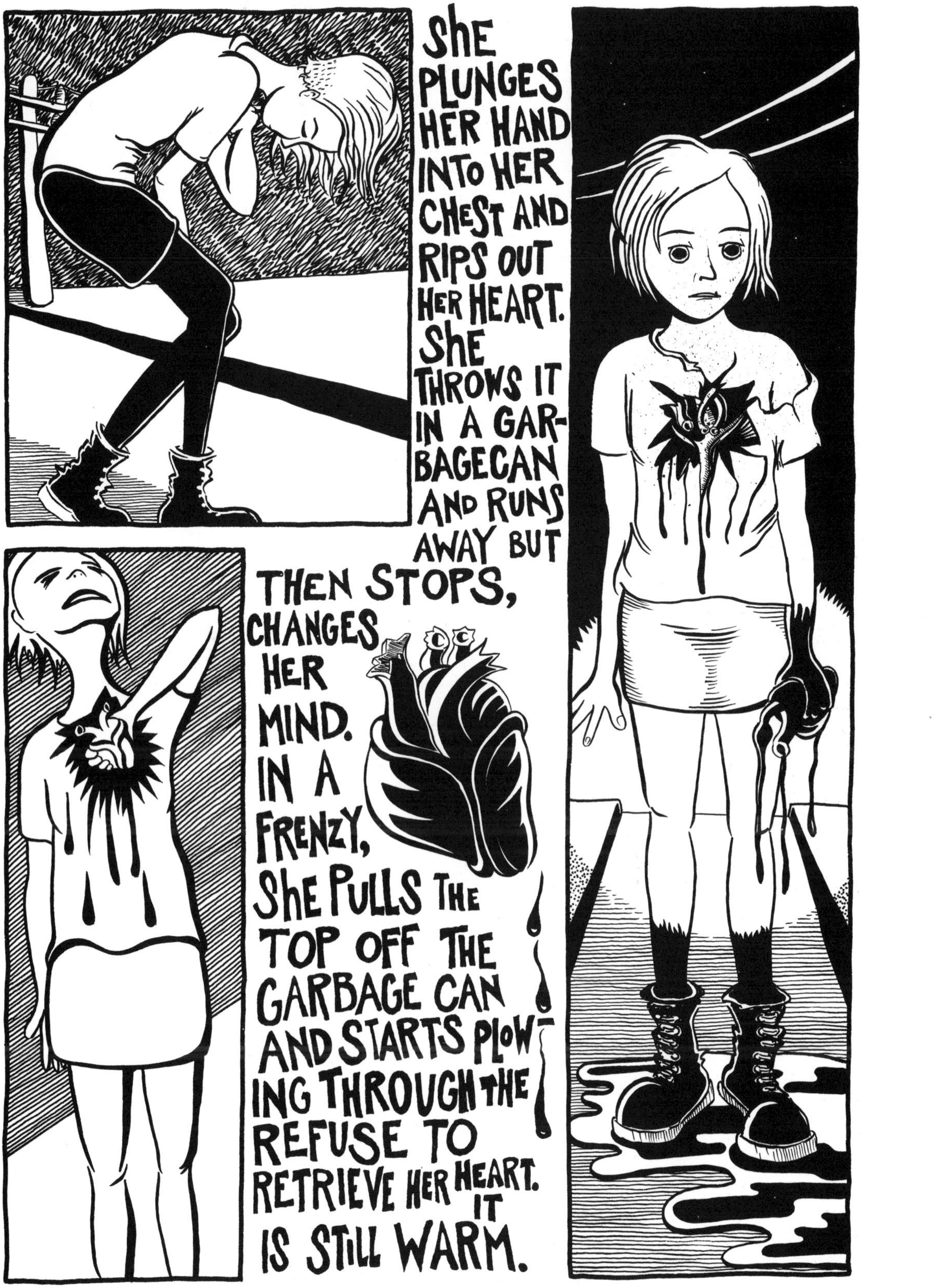
SHE PLUNGES HER HAND INTO HER CHEST AND RIPS OUT HER HEART. SHE THROWS IT IN A GAR-BAGE CAN AND RUNS AWAY BUT
THEN STOPS, CHANGES HER MIND. IN A FRENZY, SHE PULLS THE TOP OFF THE GARBAGE CAN AND STARTS PLOW-ING THROUGH THE REFUSE TO RETRIEVE HER HEART. IT IS STILL WARM.

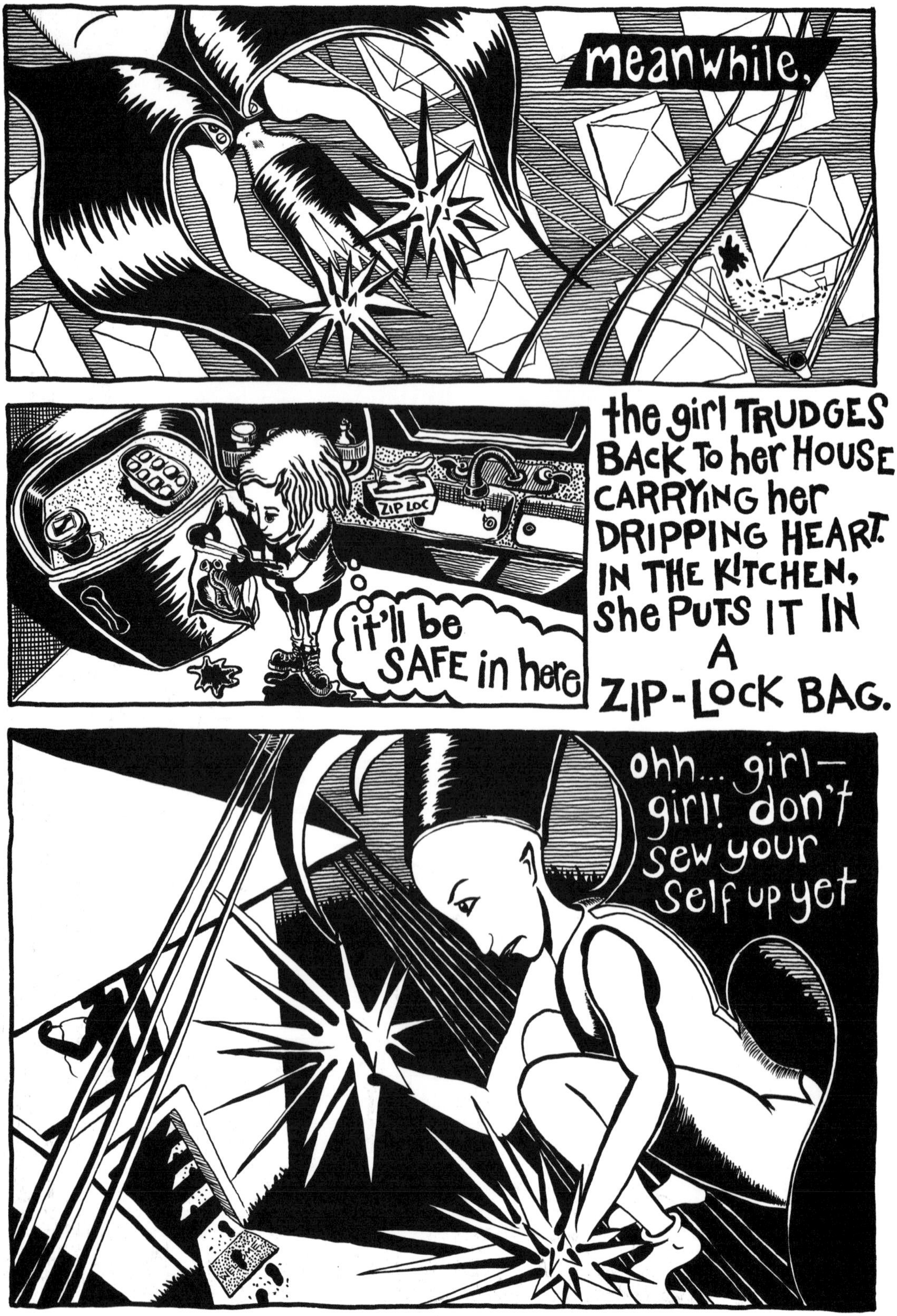
meanwhile,
the girl TRUDGES BACK To her HOUSE CARRYING her DRIPPING HEART. IN THE KITCHEN, she PUTS IT IN A ZIP-LOCK BAG.
ZIP LOC
it'll be SAFE in here
ohh... girl— girl! don't sew your self up yet

BEFORE SHE IS
FINISHED SEWING
HER CHEST UP, AN
ANGEL BLOWS IN
THROUGH THE
OPEN WINDOW.

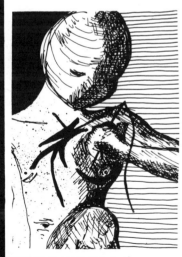

IT IS A FROZEN
ANGEL.

I WILL
LIVE IN YOU
WHERE YOUR
HEART
USED TO BE

I'LL
PROTECT
YOU!

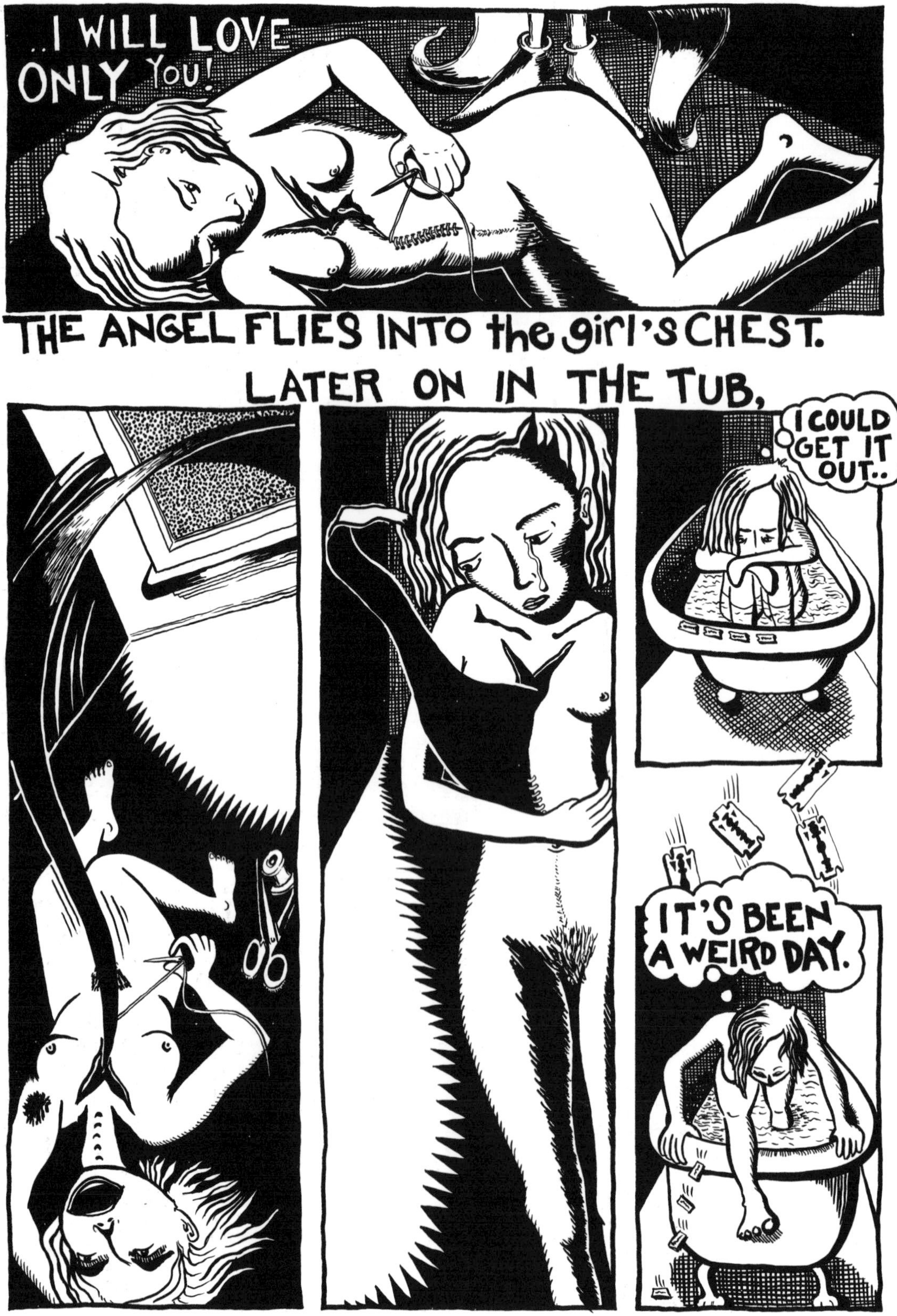
..I WILL LOVE ONLY YOU!
THE ANGEL FLIES INTO the girl's CHEST.
LATER ON IN THE TUB,
I COULD GET IT OUT..
IT'S BEEN A WEIRD DAY.

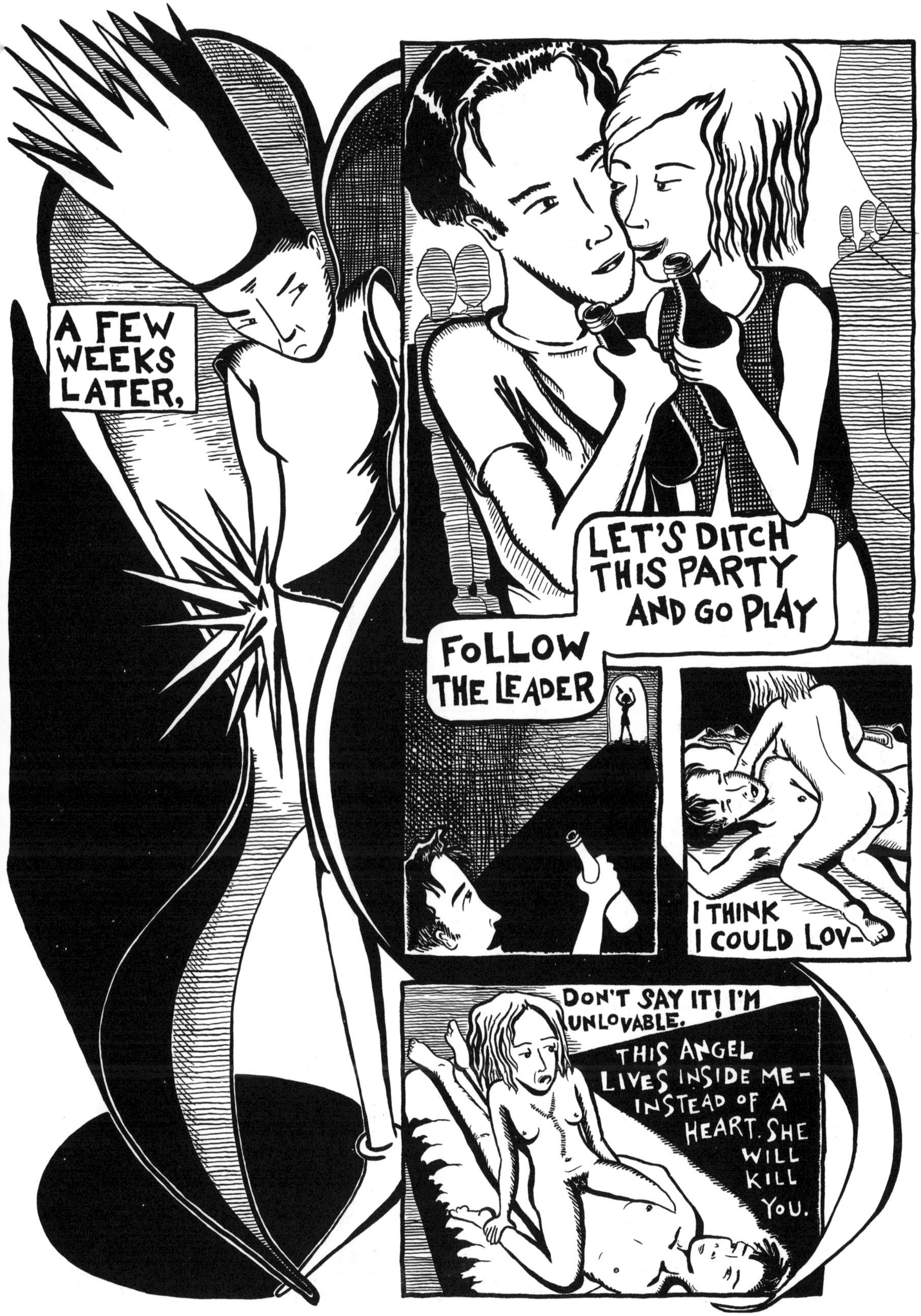
A FEW WEEKS LATER,
LET'S DITCH THIS PARTY AND GO PLAY
FOLLOW THE LEADER
I THINK I COULD LOV-
DON'T SAY IT! I'M UNLOVABLE.
THIS ANGEL LIVES INSIDE ME- INSTEAD OF A HEART. SHE WILL KILL YOU.

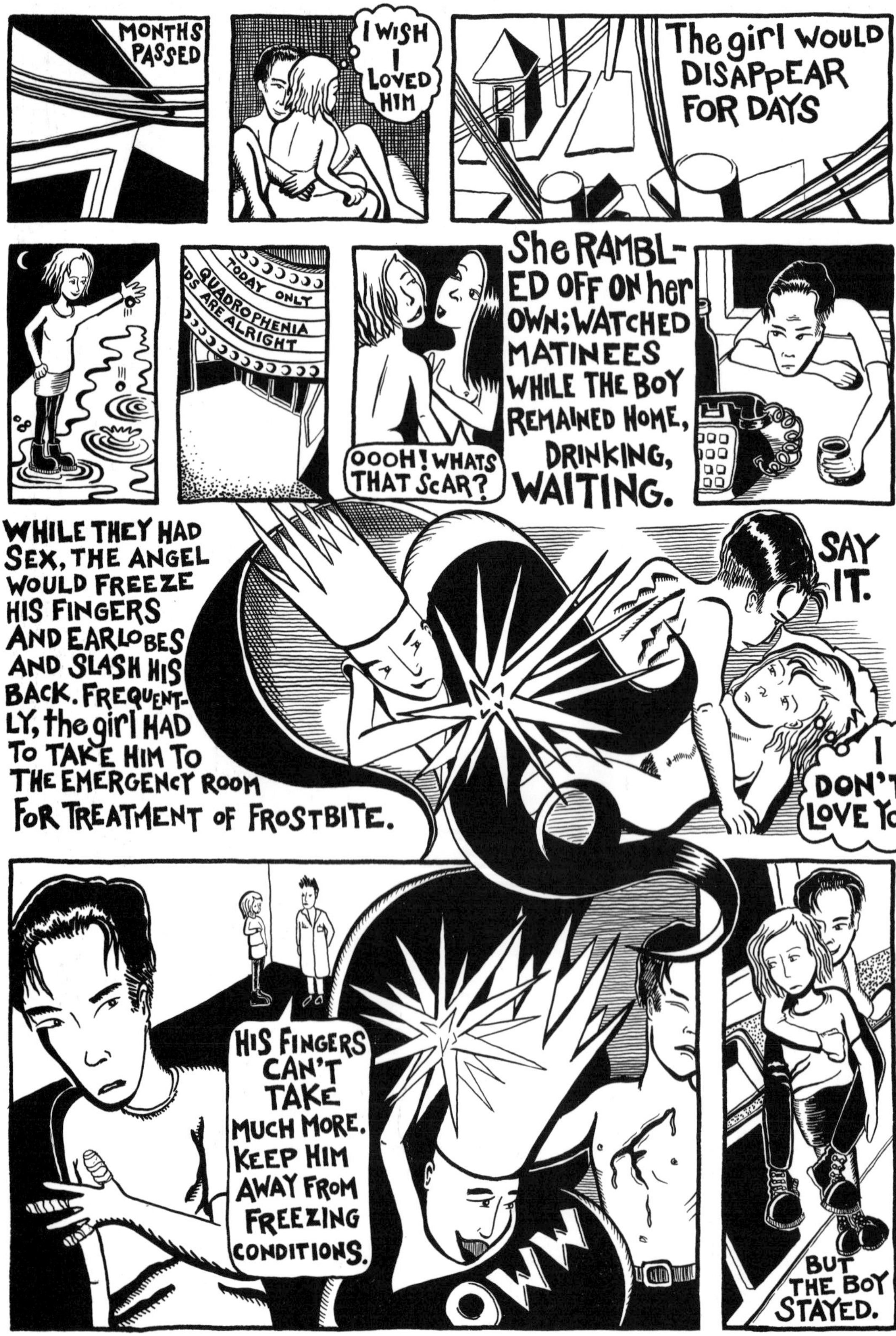

MONTHS PASSED
I WISH I LOVED HIM
The girl WOULD DISAPPEAR FOR DAYS
TODAY ONLY
QUADROPHENIA
DS ARE ALRIGHT
OOOH! WHATS THAT SCAR?
She RAMBLED OFF ON her OWN; WATCHED MATINEES WHILE THE BOY REMAINED HOME, DRINKING, WAITING.
WHILE THEY HAD SEX, THE ANGEL WOULD FREEZE HIS FINGERS AND EARLOBES AND SLASH HIS BACK. FREQUENTLY, the girl HAD TO TAKE HIM TO THE EMERGENCY ROOM FOR TREATMENT OF FROSTBITE.
SAY IT.
I DON'T LOVE YOU
HIS FINGERS CAN'T TAKE MUCH MORE. KEEP HIM AWAY FROM FREEZING CONDITIONS.
OWW
BUT THE BOY STAYED.

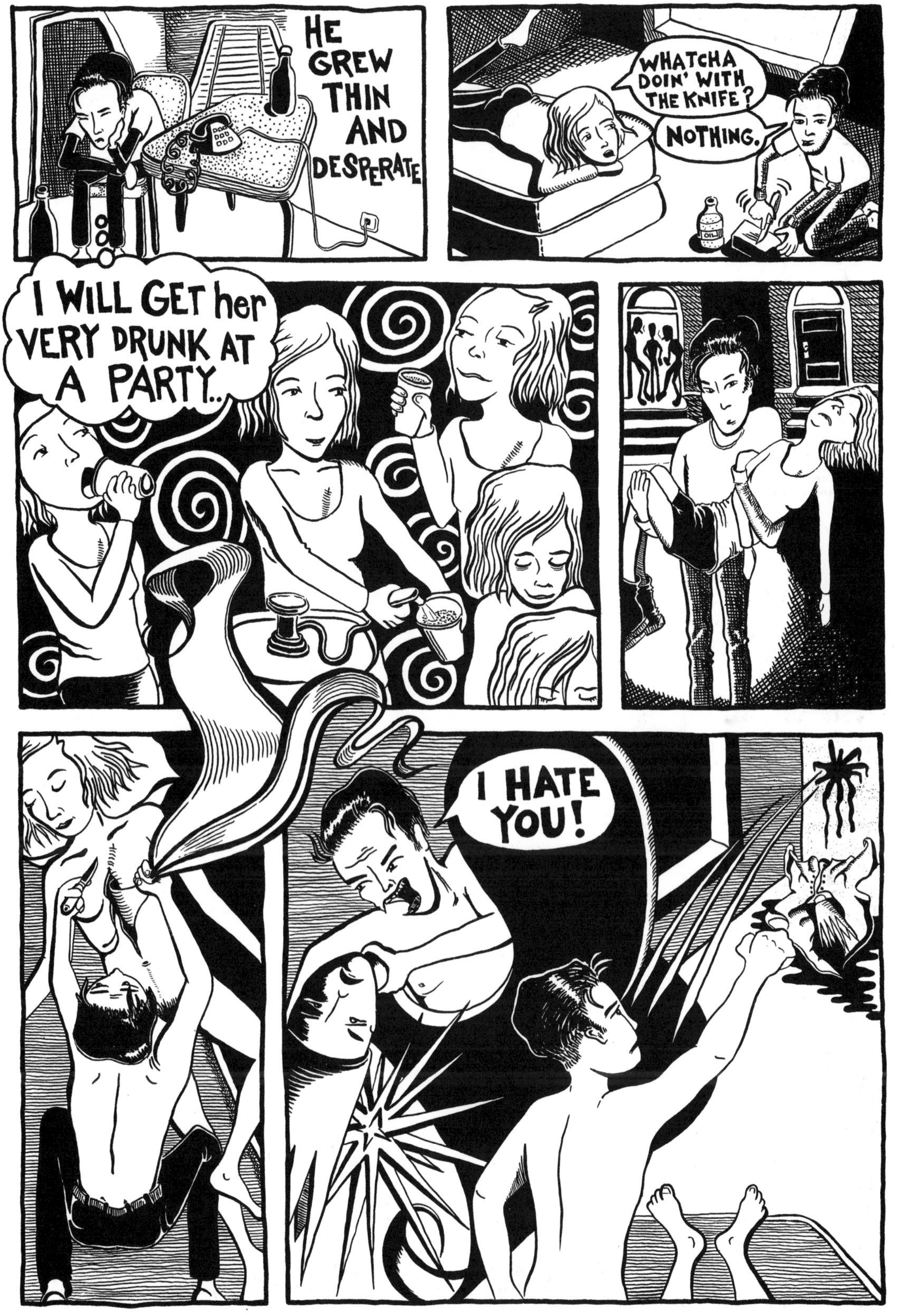
HE GREW THIN AND DESPERATE
WHATCHA DOIN' WITH THE KNIFE?
NOTHING.
OIL
I WILL GET her VERY DRUNK AT A PARTY..
I HATE YOU!

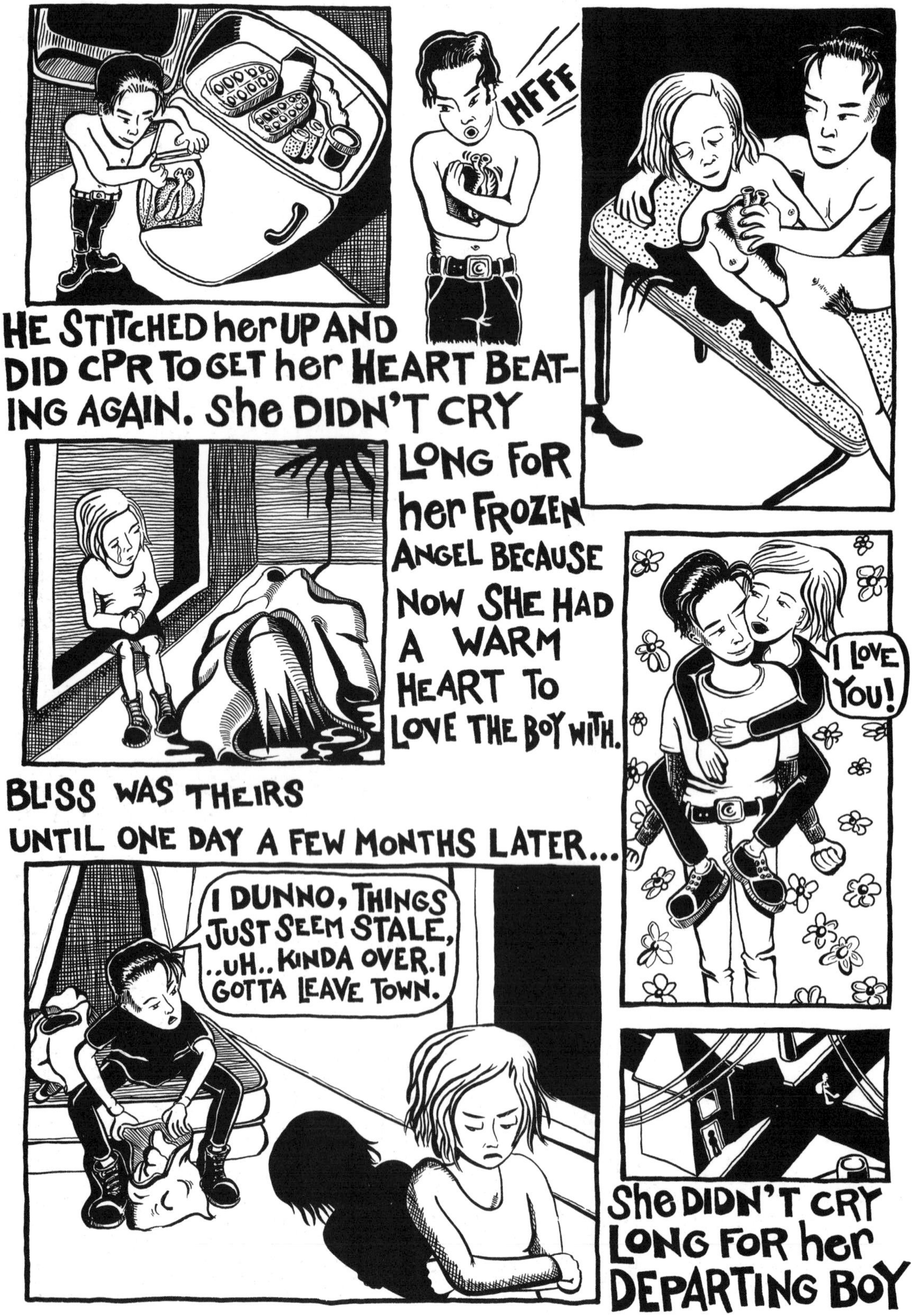
HFFF
HE STITCHED her UP AND DID CPR TO GET her HEART BEAT-ING AGAIN. She DIDN'T CRY
LONG FOR her FROZEN ANGEL BECAUSE NOW SHE HAD A WARM HEART TO LOVE THE BOY WITH.
I LOVE YOU!
BLISS WAS THEIRS
UNTIL ONE DAY A FEW MONTHS LATER...
I DUNNO, THINGS JUST SEEM STALE, ..UH.. KINDA OVER. I GOTTA LEAVE TOWN.
She DIDN'T CRY LONG FOR her DEPARTING BOY

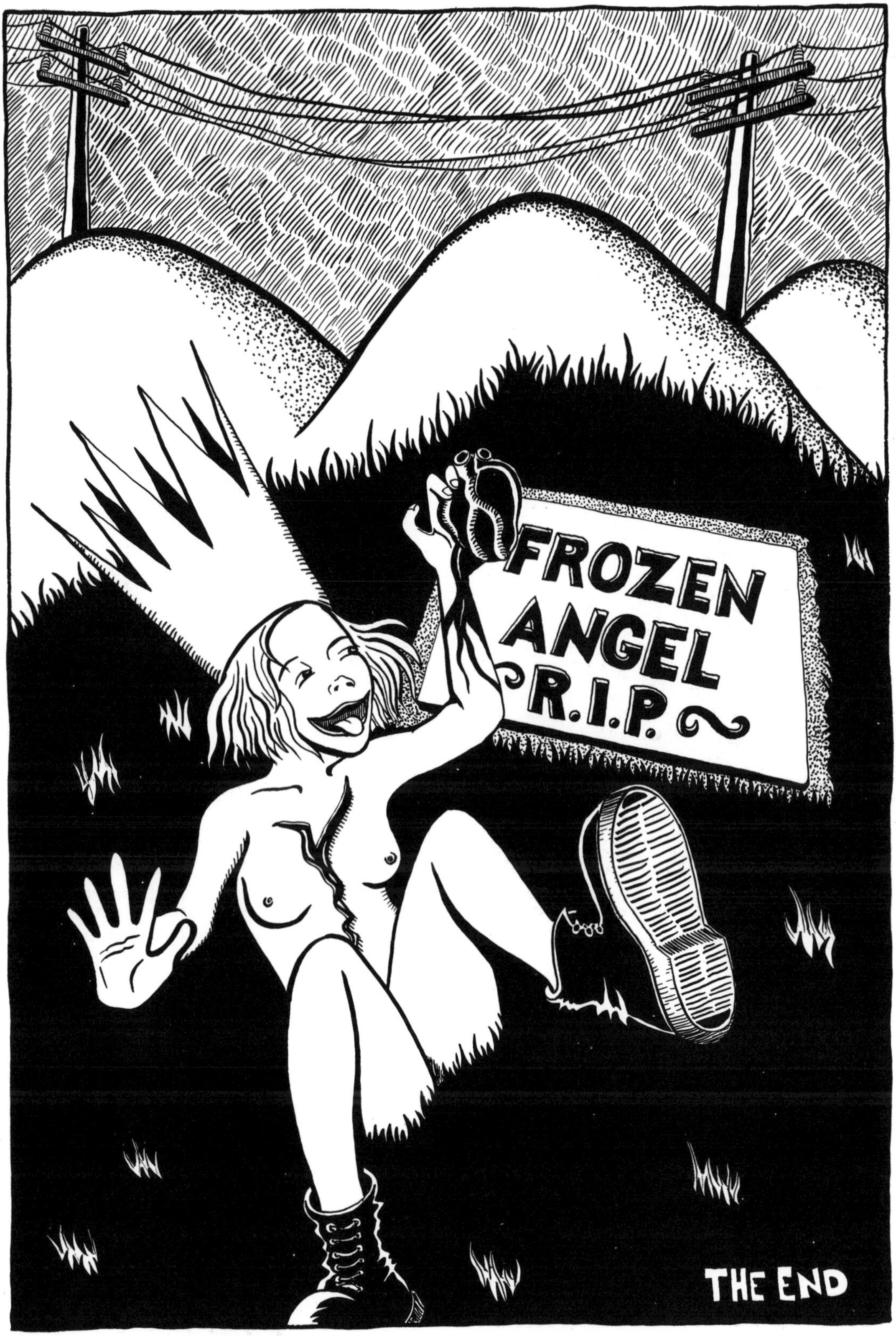
FROZEN
ANGEL
R.I.P.
THE END

WHISTLE AND QUEENIE

Whistle & Queenie

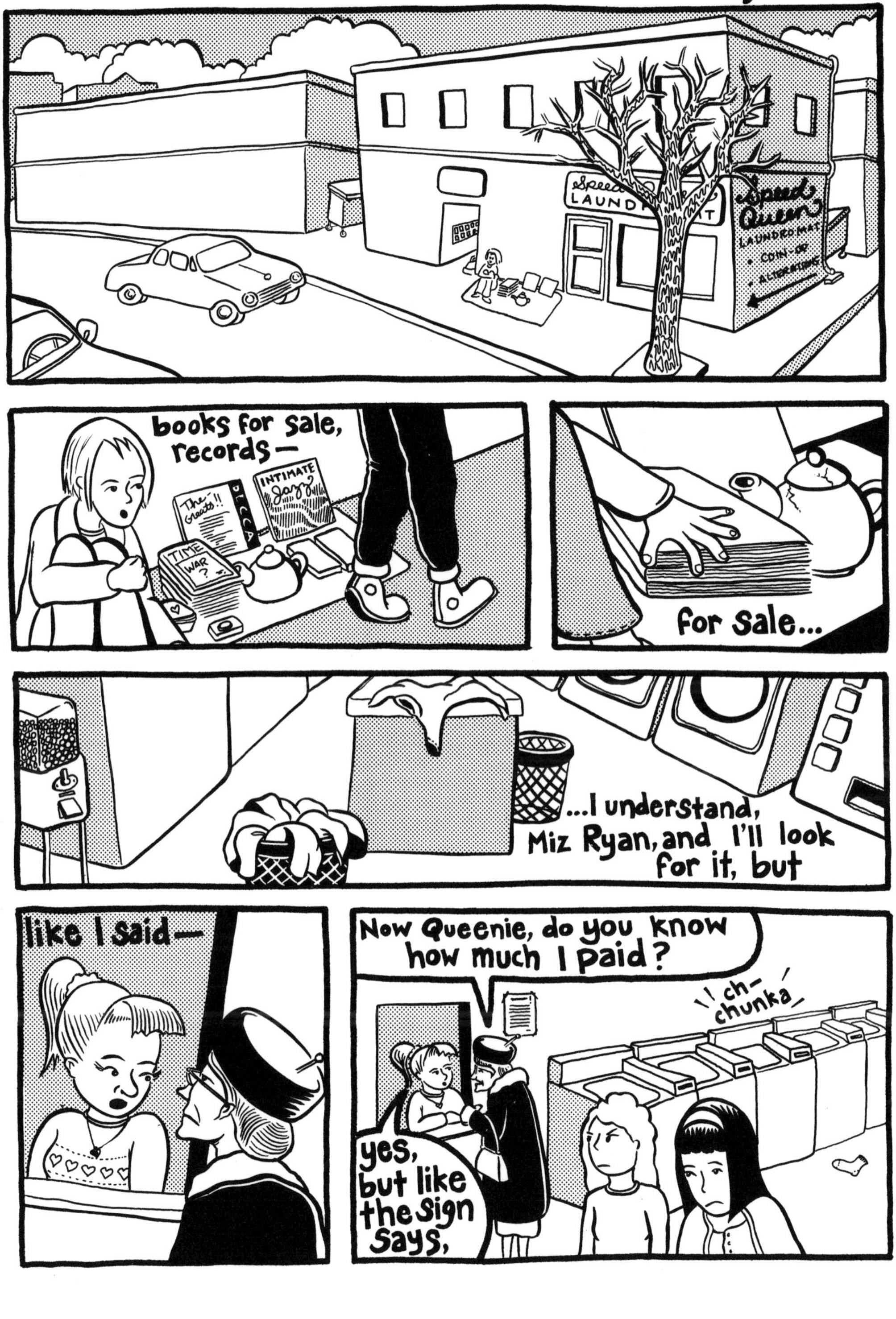
Speed Queen LAUNDROMAT
• COIN-OP
• ALTERATIONS
books for sale, records—
The Greats!!
DECCA
INTIMATE Jazz
TIME WAR ?
for sale...
...I understand, Miz Ryan, and I'll look for it, but
like I said—
Now Queenie, do you know how much I paid?
ch-chunka
yes, but like the sign says,

ATTENTION!
The Speed Queen Laundromat is not responsible for lost or stolen items. Please watch your belongings closely! —Mgmt

Sorry, Miz Ryan.

CLANG

CLOSED

?

CLANG

CLANG

rustle rustle

cool!

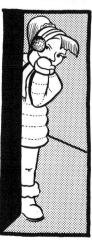

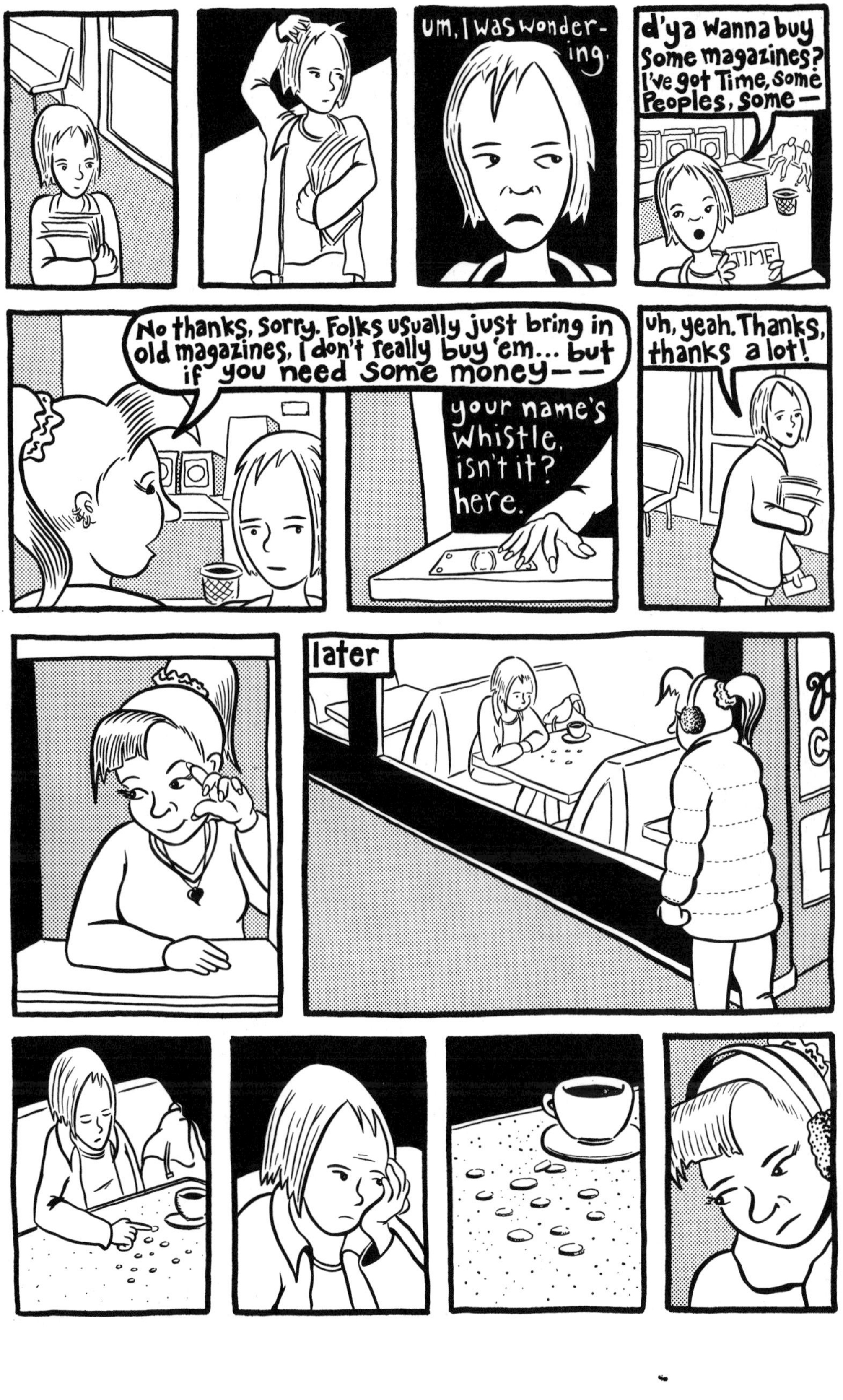
um, I was wonder-ing.
d'ya wanna buy some magazines? I've got Time, some Peoples, some—
TIME
No thanks, sorry. Folks usually just bring in old magazines, I don't really buy 'em... but if you need some money——
your name's Whistle, isn't it? here.
uh, yeah. Thanks, thanks a lot!
later

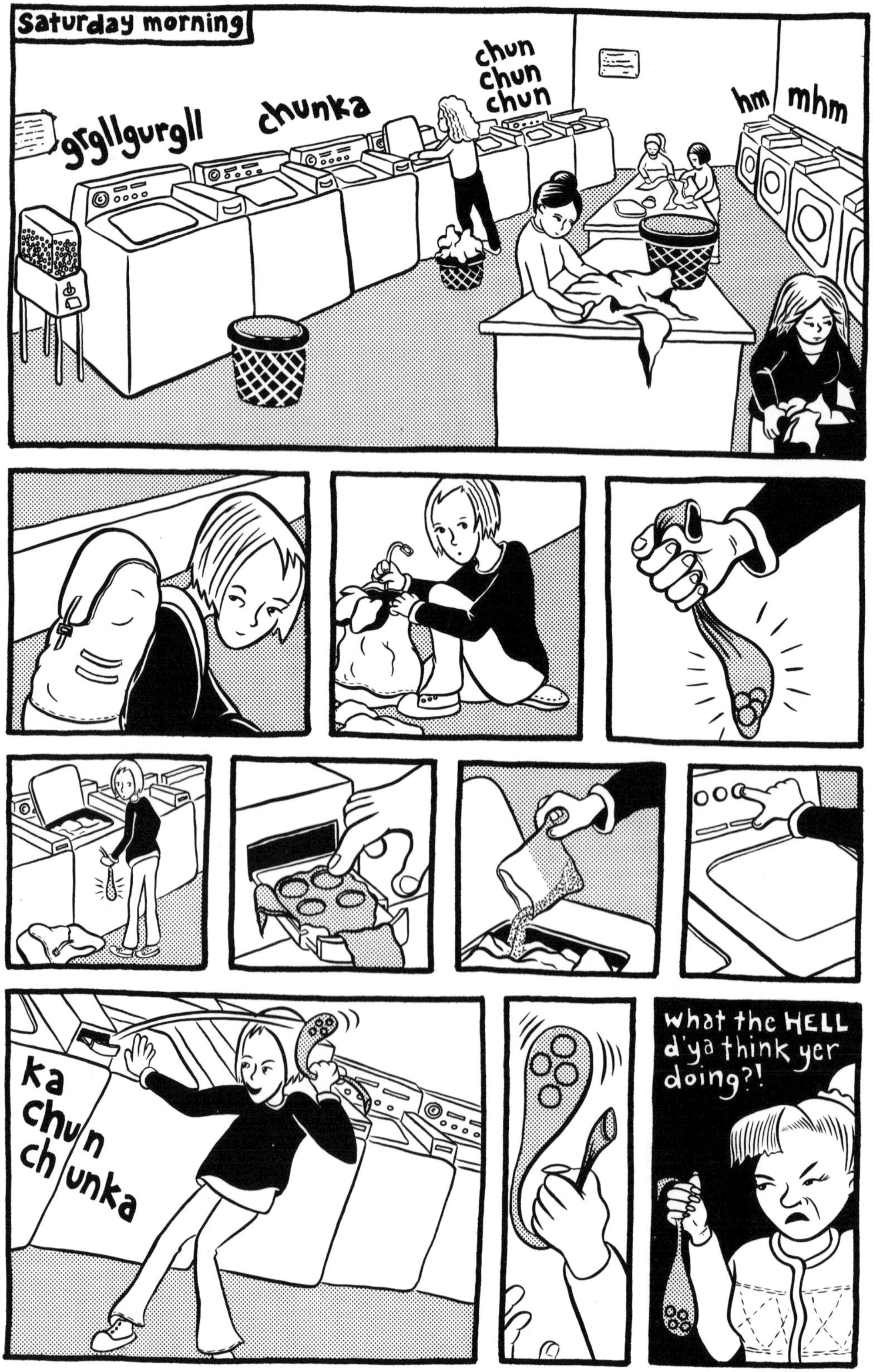
saturday morning
grgllgurgll
chunka
chun
chun
chun
hm
mhm
ka
chun
chunka
what the HELL d'ya think yer doing?!

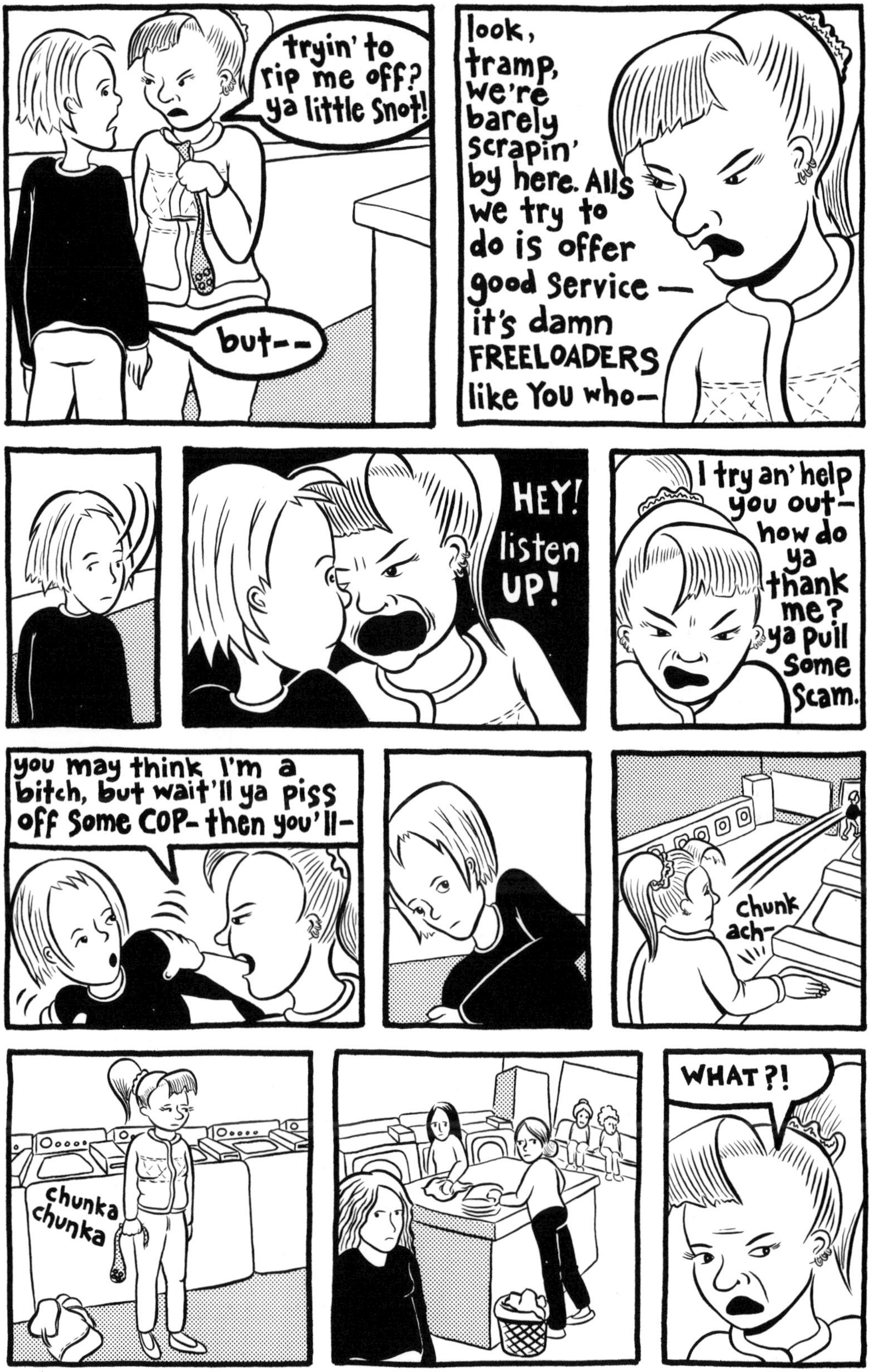
tryin' to rip me off? ya little Snot!
but--
look, tramp, we're barely scrapin' by here. Alls we try to do is offer good service — it's damn FREELOADERS like You who—
HEY! listen UP!
I try an' help you out— how do ya thank me? ya pull some Scam.
you may think I'm a bitch, but wait'll ya piss off some COP— then you'll—
chunk ach-
chunka chunka
WHAT?!

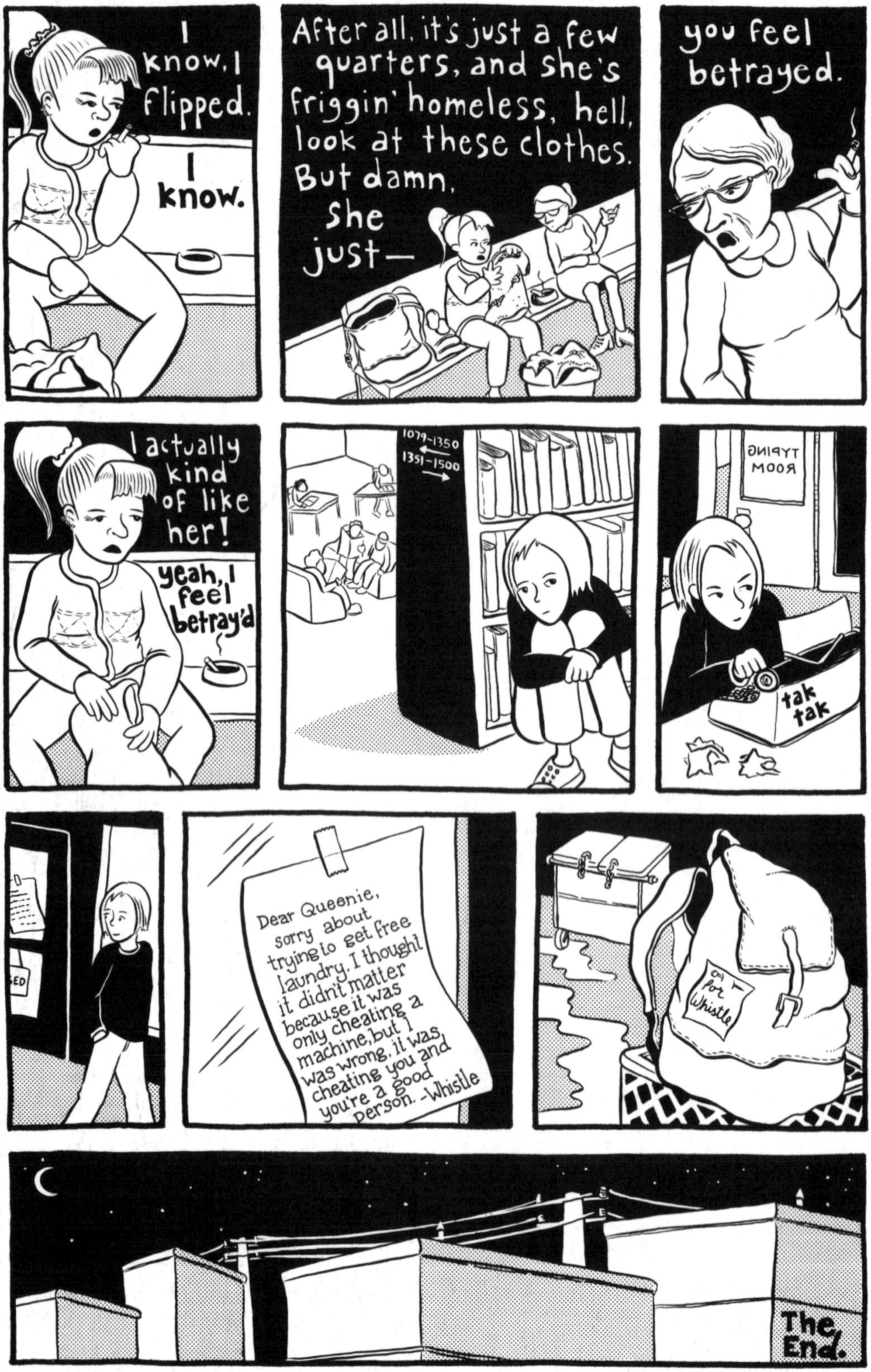
I know, I flipped.
I know.
After all, it's just a few quarters, and she's friggin' homeless, hell, look at these clothes. But damn, she just—
you feel betrayed.
I actually kind of like her!
yeah, I feel betray'd
1079–1350
1351–1500
TYPING ROOM
tak tak
Dear Queenie, sorry about trying to get free laundry. I thought it didn't matter because it was only cheating a machine, but I was wrong, it was cheating you and you're a good person. -Whistle
For Whistle
The End.

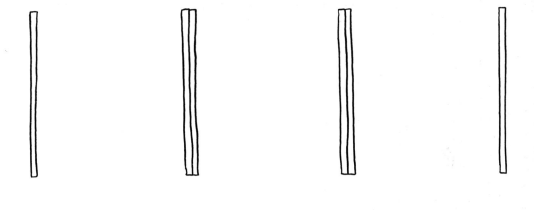

REUNION

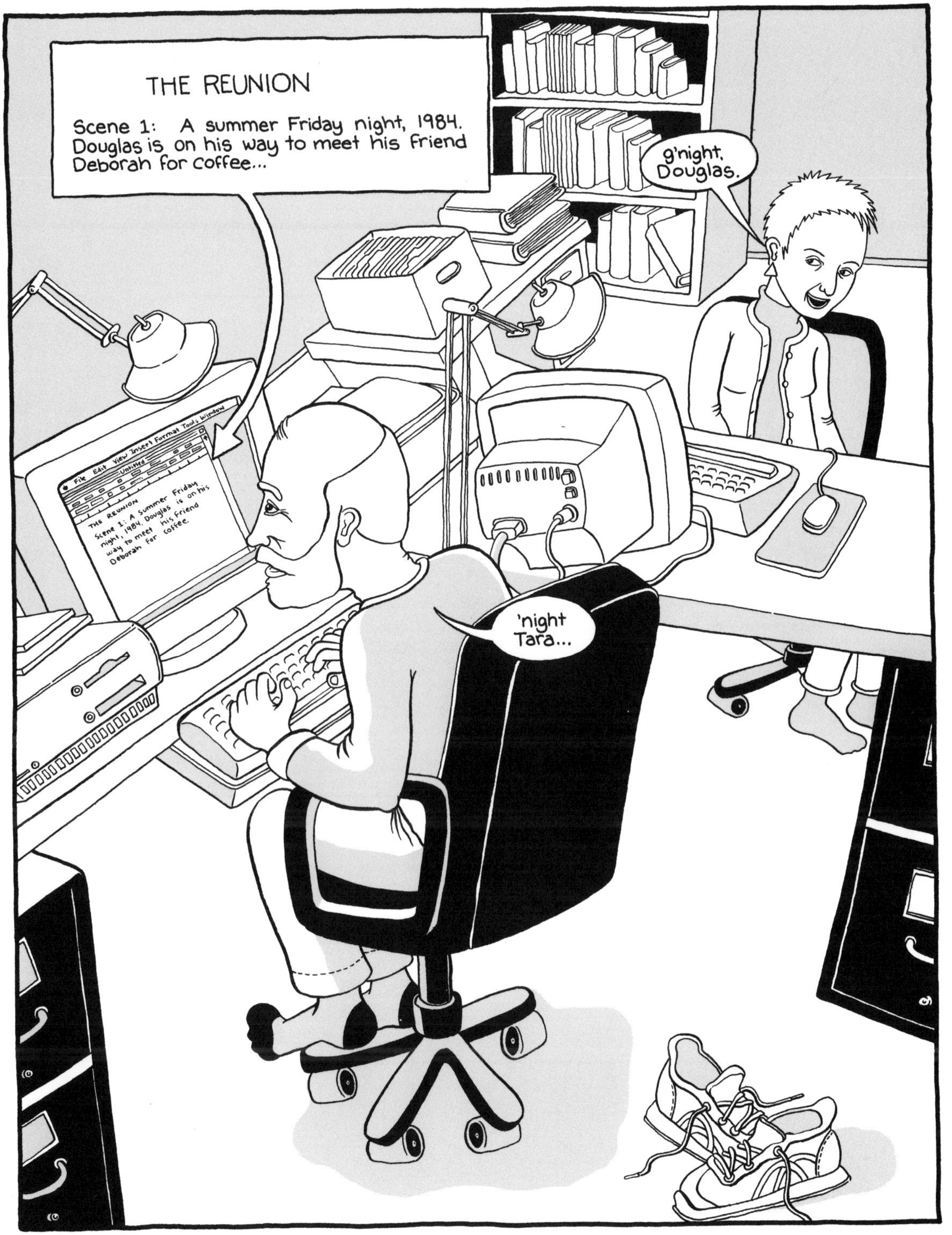
THE REUNION
Scene 1: A summer Friday night, 1984. Douglas is on his way to meet his friend Deborah for coffee...
File Edit View Insert Format Tools Window
Untitled
THE REUNION
Scene 1: A summer Friday night, 1984. Douglas is on his way to meet his friend Deborah for coffee.
g'night, Douglas.
'night Tara...

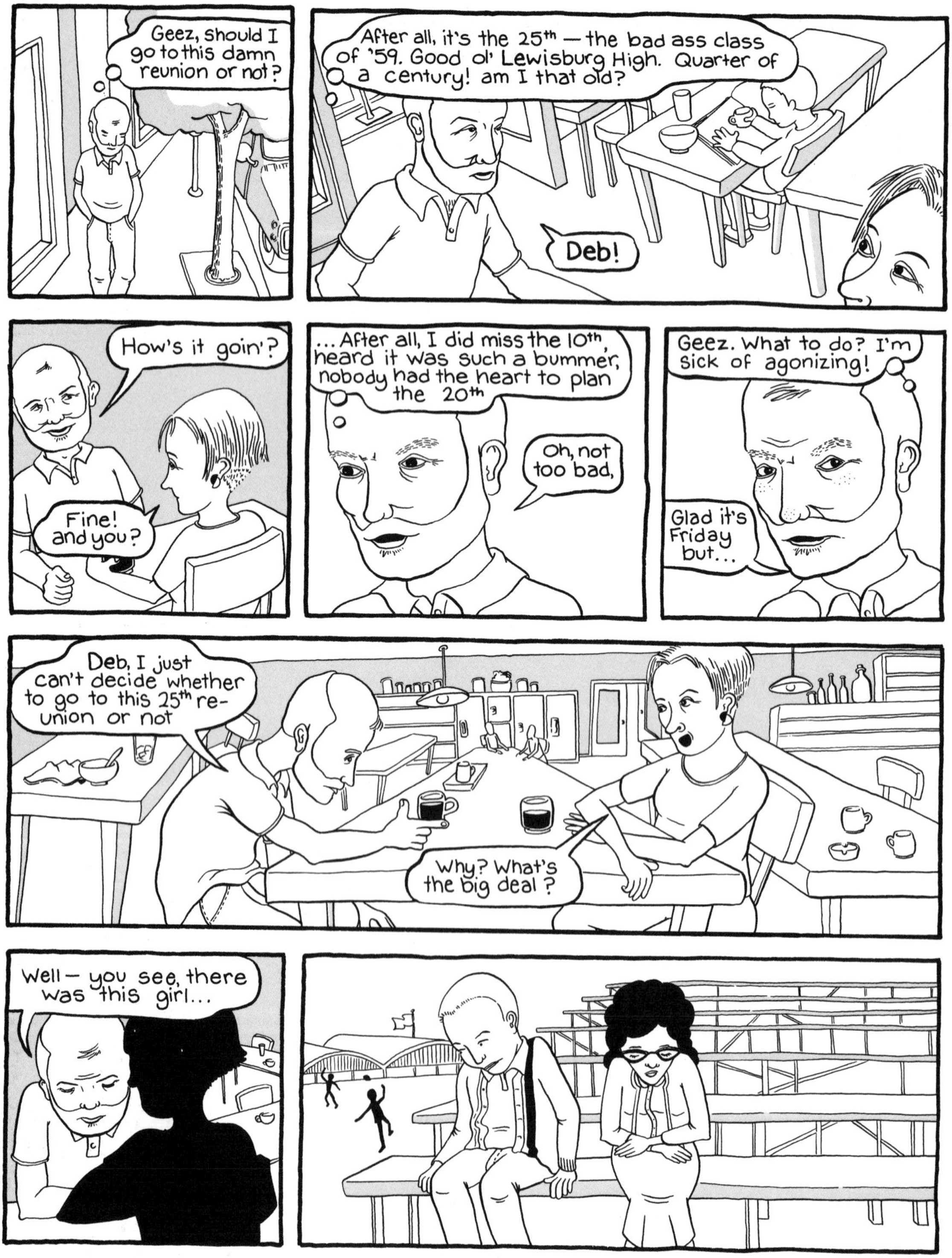
Geez, should I go to this damn reunion or not?
After all, it's the 25th — the bad ass class of '59. Good ol' Lewisburg High. Quarter of a century! am I that old?
Deb!
How's it goin'?
Fine! and you?
...After all, I did miss the 10th, heard it was such a bummer, nobody had the heart to plan the 20th
Oh, not too bad,
Geez. What to do? I'm sick of agonizing!
Glad it's Friday but...
Deb, I just can't decide whether to go to this 25th re-union or not
Why? What's the big deal?
Well— you see, there was this girl...

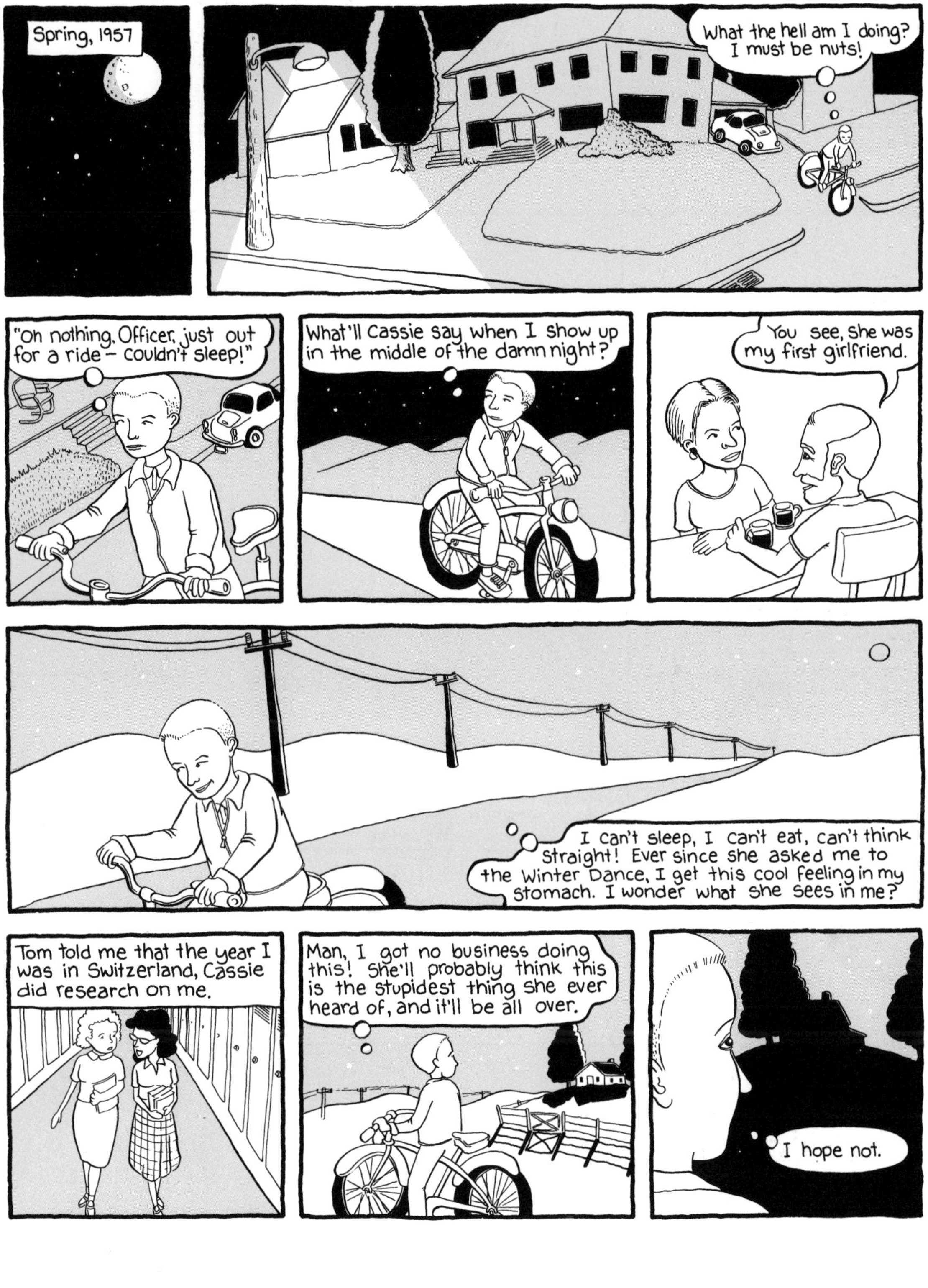
Spring, 1957
What the hell am I doing? I must be nuts!
"Oh nothing, Officer, just out for a ride – couldn't sleep!"
What'll Cassie say when I show up in the middle of the damn night?
You see, she was my first girlfriend.
I can't sleep, I can't eat, can't think straight! Ever since she asked me to the Winter Dance, I get this cool feeling in my stomach. I wonder what she sees in me?
Tom told me that the year I was in Switzerland, Cassie did research on me.
Man, I got no business doing this! She'll probably think this is the stupidest thing she ever heard of, and it'll be all over.
I hope not.

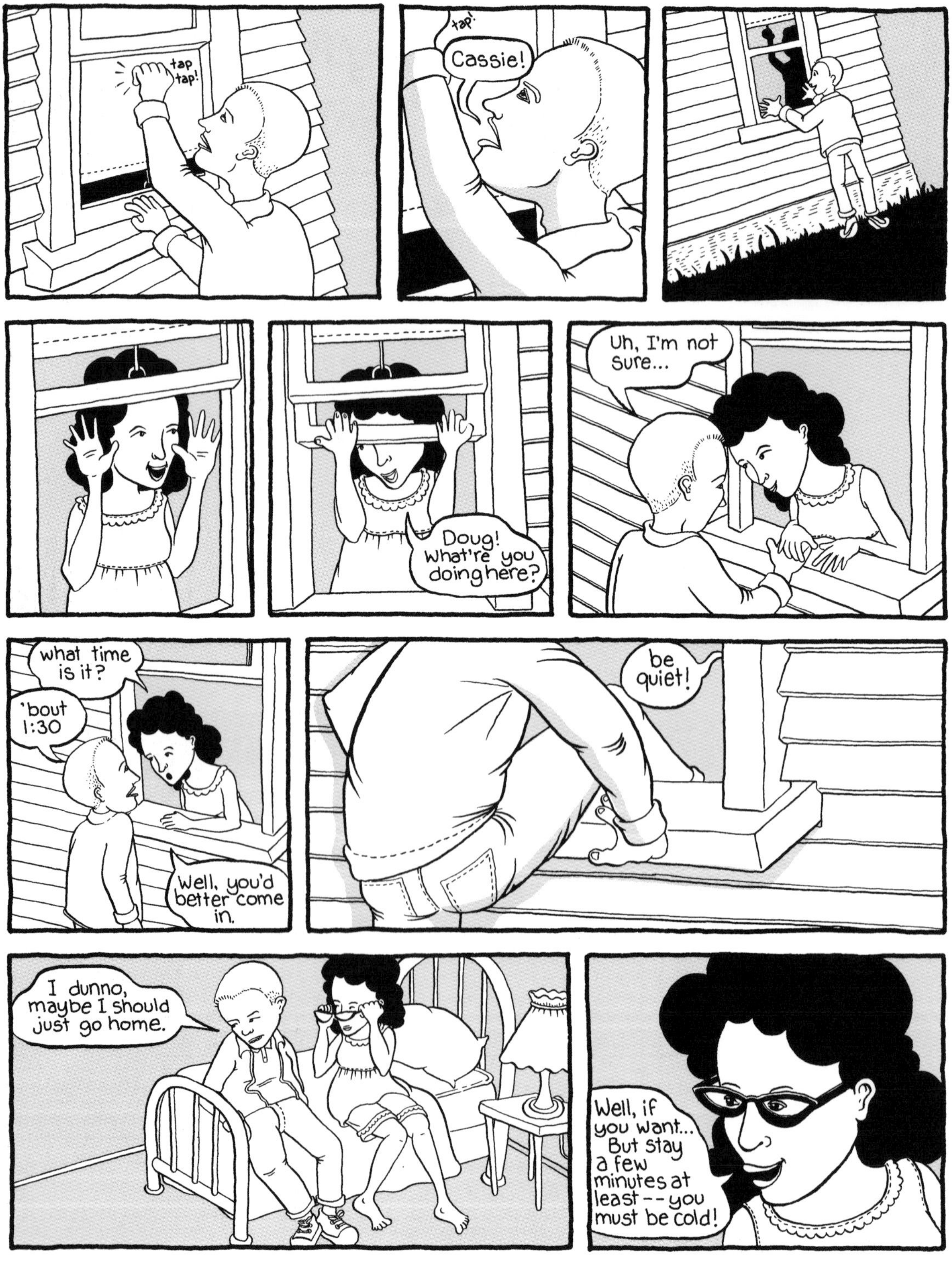
tap tap!
tap!
Cassie!
Doug! What're you doing here?
Uh, I'm not sure...
what time is it?
'bout 1:30
Well, you'd better come in.
be quiet!
I dunno, maybe I should just go home.
Well, if you want... But stay a few minutes at least -- you must be cold!

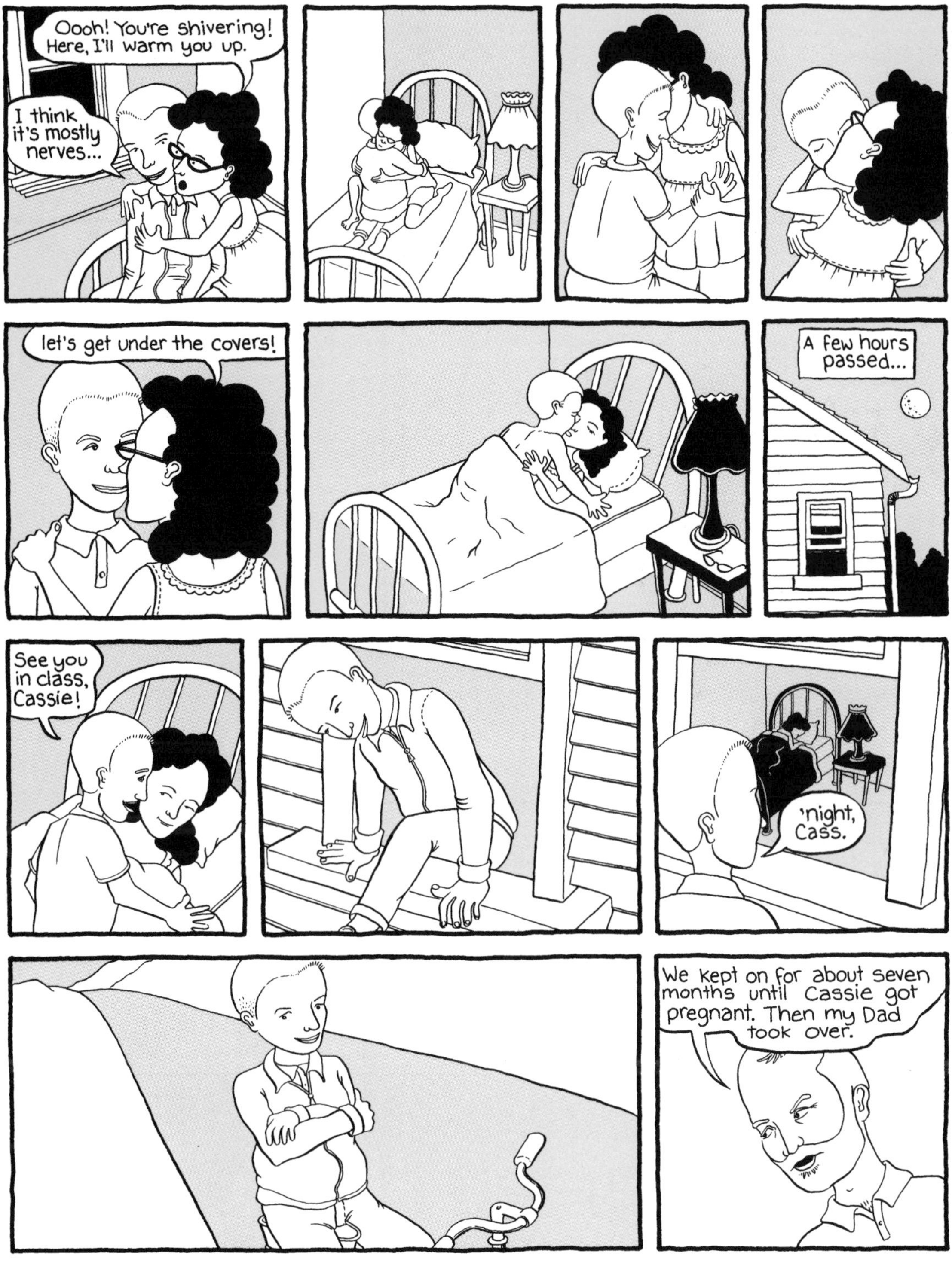
Oooh! You're shivering! Here, I'll warm you up.
I think it's mostly nerves...
let's get under the covers!
A few hours passed...
See you in class, Cassie!
'night, Cass.
We kept on for about seven months until Cassie got pregnant. Then my Dad took over.

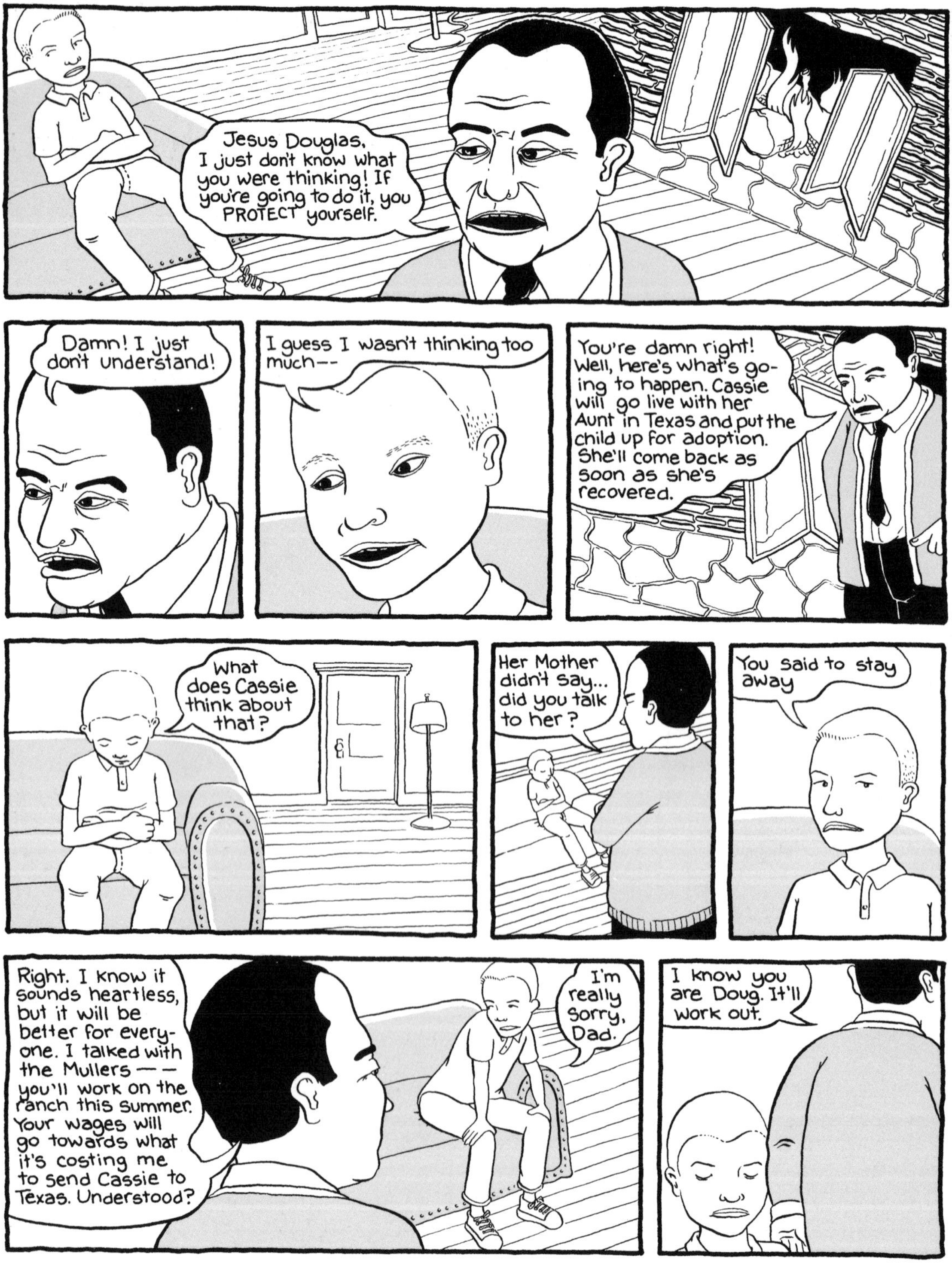
Jesus Douglas, I just don't know what you were thinking! If you're going to do it, you PROTECT yourself.
Damn! I just don't understand!
I guess I wasn't thinking too much--
You're damn right! Well, here's what's going to happen. Cassie will go live with her Aunt in Texas and put the child up for adoption. She'll come back as soon as she's recovered.
What does Cassie think about that?
Her Mother didn't say... did you talk to her?
You said to stay away
Right. I know it sounds heartless, but it will be better for everyone. I talked with the Mullers -- you'll work on the ranch this summer. Your wages will go towards what it's costing me to send Cassie to Texas. Understood?
I'm really sorry, Dad.
I know you are Doug. It'll work out.

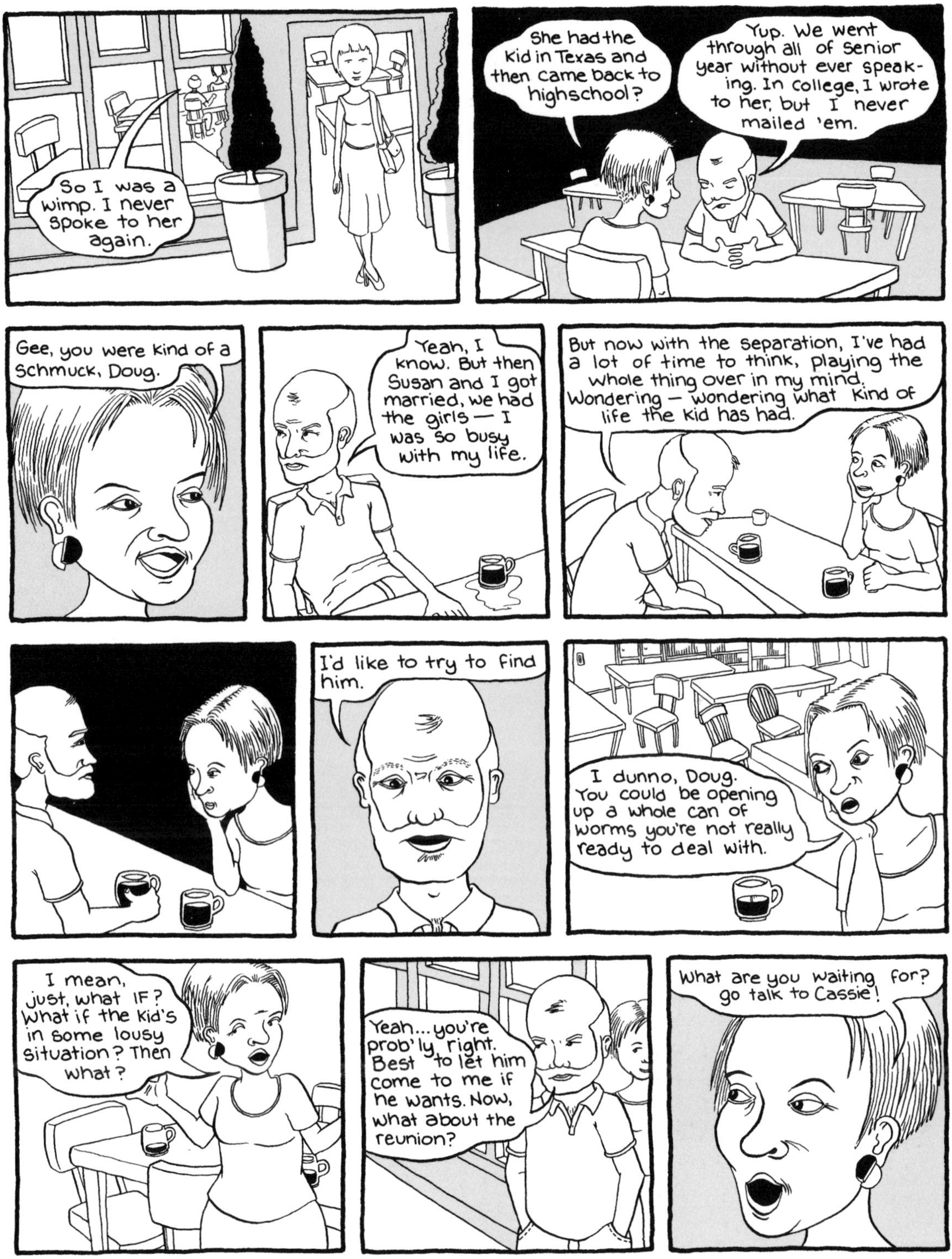

So I was a wimp. I never spoke to her again.
She had the kid in Texas and then came back to highschool?
Yup. We went through all of senior year without ever speak-ing. In college, I wrote to her, but I never mailed 'em.
Gee, you were kind of a schmuck, Doug.
Yeah, I know. But then Susan and I got married, we had the girls — I was so busy with my life.
But now with the separation, I've had a lot of time to think, playing the whole thing over in my mind. Wondering — wondering what kind of life the kid has had.
I'd like to try to find him.
I dunno, Doug. You could be opening up a whole can of worms you're not really ready to deal with.
I mean, just, what IF? What if the kid's in some lousy situation? Then what?
Yeah... you're prob'ly right. Best to let him come to me if he wants. Now, what about the reunion?
What are you waiting for? go talk to Cassie!

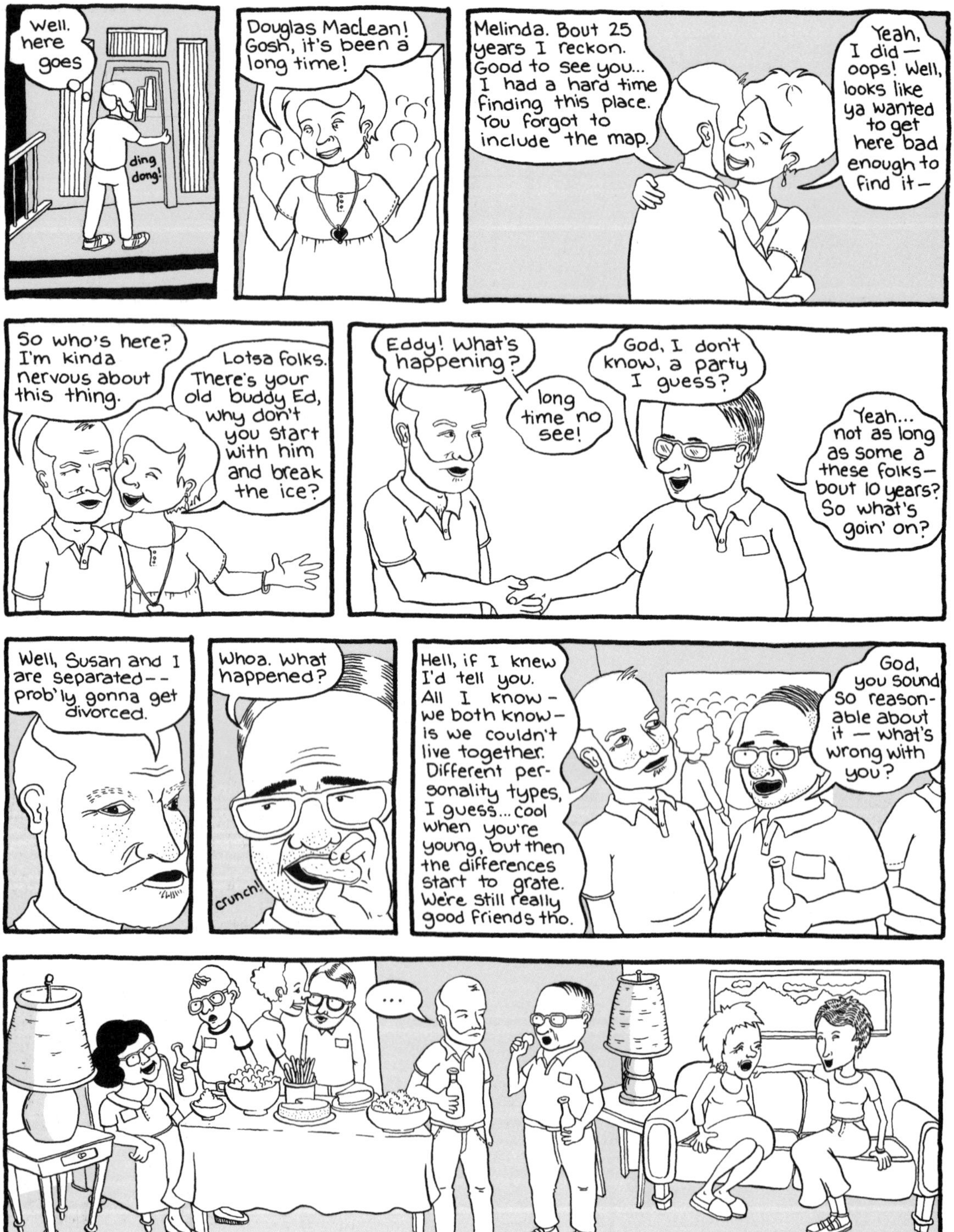
Well. here goes
ding dong!
Douglas MacLean! Gosh, it's been a long time!
Melinda. Bout 25 years I reckon. Good to see you... I had a hard time finding this place. You forgot to include the map.
Yeah, I did — oops! Well, looks like ya wanted to get here bad enough to find it —
So who's here? I'm kinda nervous about this thing.
Lotsa folks. There's your old buddy Ed, why don't you start with him and break the ice?
Eddy! What's happening?
long time no see!
God, I don't know, a party I guess?
Yeah... not as long as some a these folks — bout 10 years? So what's goin' on?
Well, Susan and I are separated-- prob'ly gonna get divorced.
Whoa. What happened?
crunch!
Hell, if I knew I'd tell you. All I know - we both know - is we couldn't live together. Different personality types, I guess... cool when you're young, but then the differences start to grate. We're still really good friends tho.
God, you sound so reasonable about it — what's wrong with you?
...

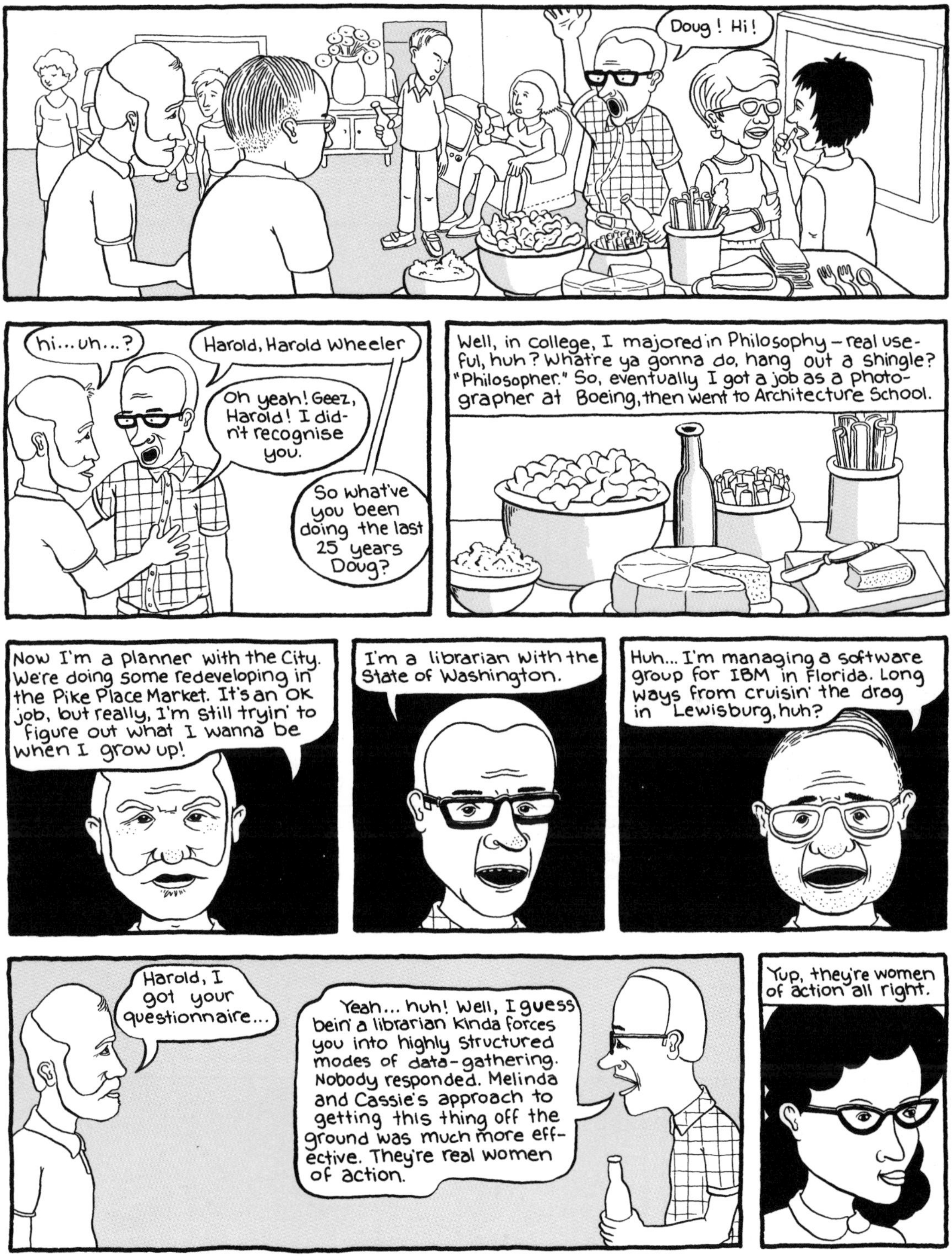
Doug! Hi!
hi...uh...?
Harold, Harold Wheeler
Oh yeah! Geez, Harold! I didn't recognise you.
So what've you been doing the last 25 years Doug?
Well, in college, I majored in Philosophy – real useful, huh? Whatre ya gonna do, hang out a shingle? "Philosopher." So, eventually I got a job as a photographer at Boeing, then went to Architecture School.
Now I'm a planner with the City. We're doing some redeveloping in the Pike Place Market. It's an OK job, but really, I'm still tryin' to figure out what I wanna be when I grow up!
I'm a librarian with the State of Washington.
Huh... I'm managing a software group for IBM in Florida. Long ways from cruisin' the drag in Lewisburg, huh?
Harold, I got your questionnaire...
Yeah... huh! Well, I guess bein' a librarian kinda forces you into highly structured modes of data-gathering. Nobody responded. Melinda and Cassie's approach to getting this thing off the ground was much more effective. They're real women of action.
Yup, they're women of action all right.

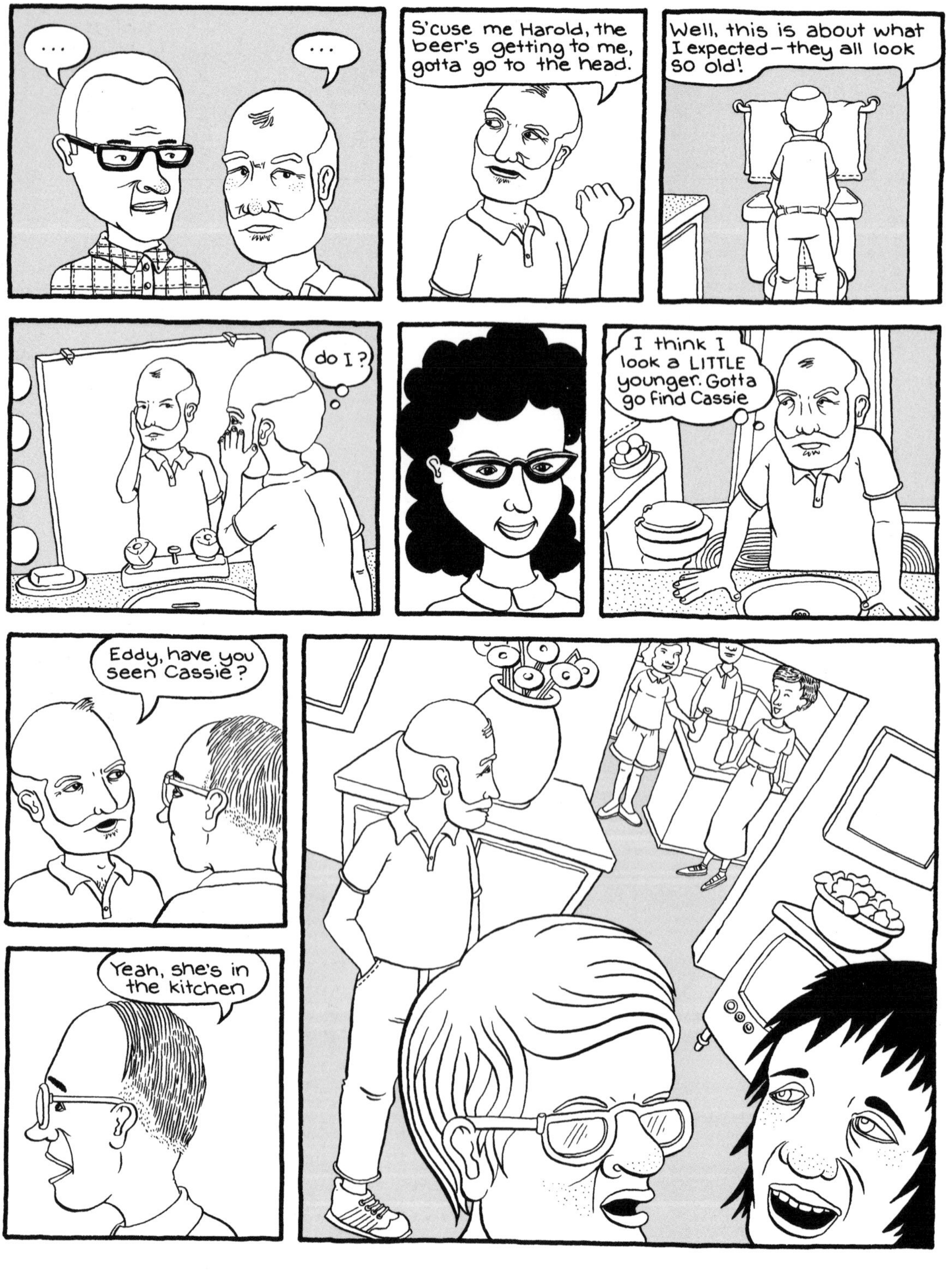
...
...
S'cuse me Harold, the beer's getting to me, gotta go to the head.
Well, this is about what I expected—they all look so old!
do I?
I think I look a LITTLE younger. Gotta go find Cassie
Eddy, have you seen Cassie?
Yeah, she's in the kitchen

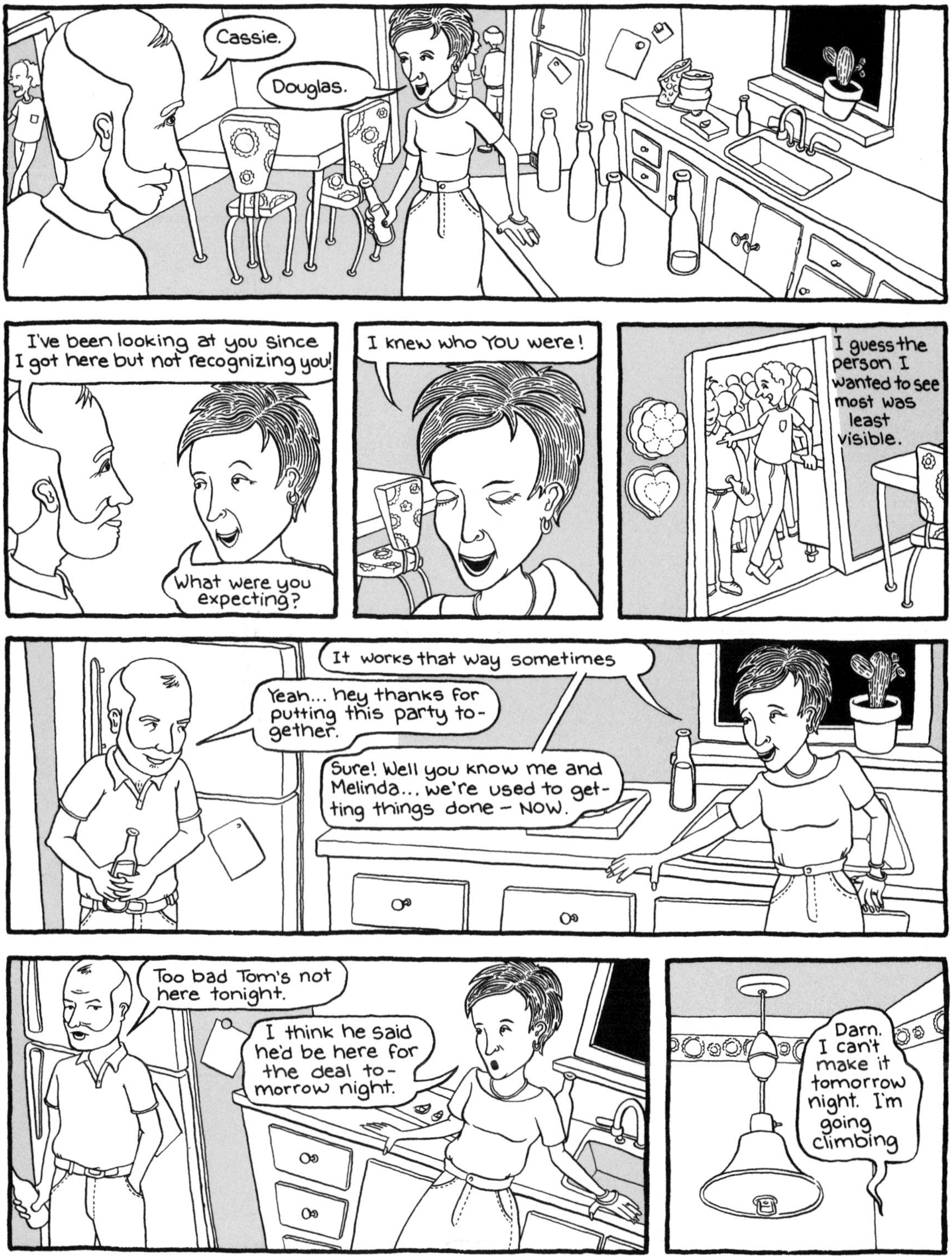
Cassie.
Douglas.
I've been looking at you since I got here but not recognizing you!
What were you expecting?
I knew who YOU were!
I guess the person I wanted to see most was least visible.
Yeah... hey thanks for putting this party together.
It works that way sometimes
Sure! Well you know me and Melinda... we're used to getting things done – NOW.
Too bad Tom's not here tonight.
I think he said he'd be here for the deal tomorrow night.
Darn. I can't make it tomorrow night. I'm going climbing

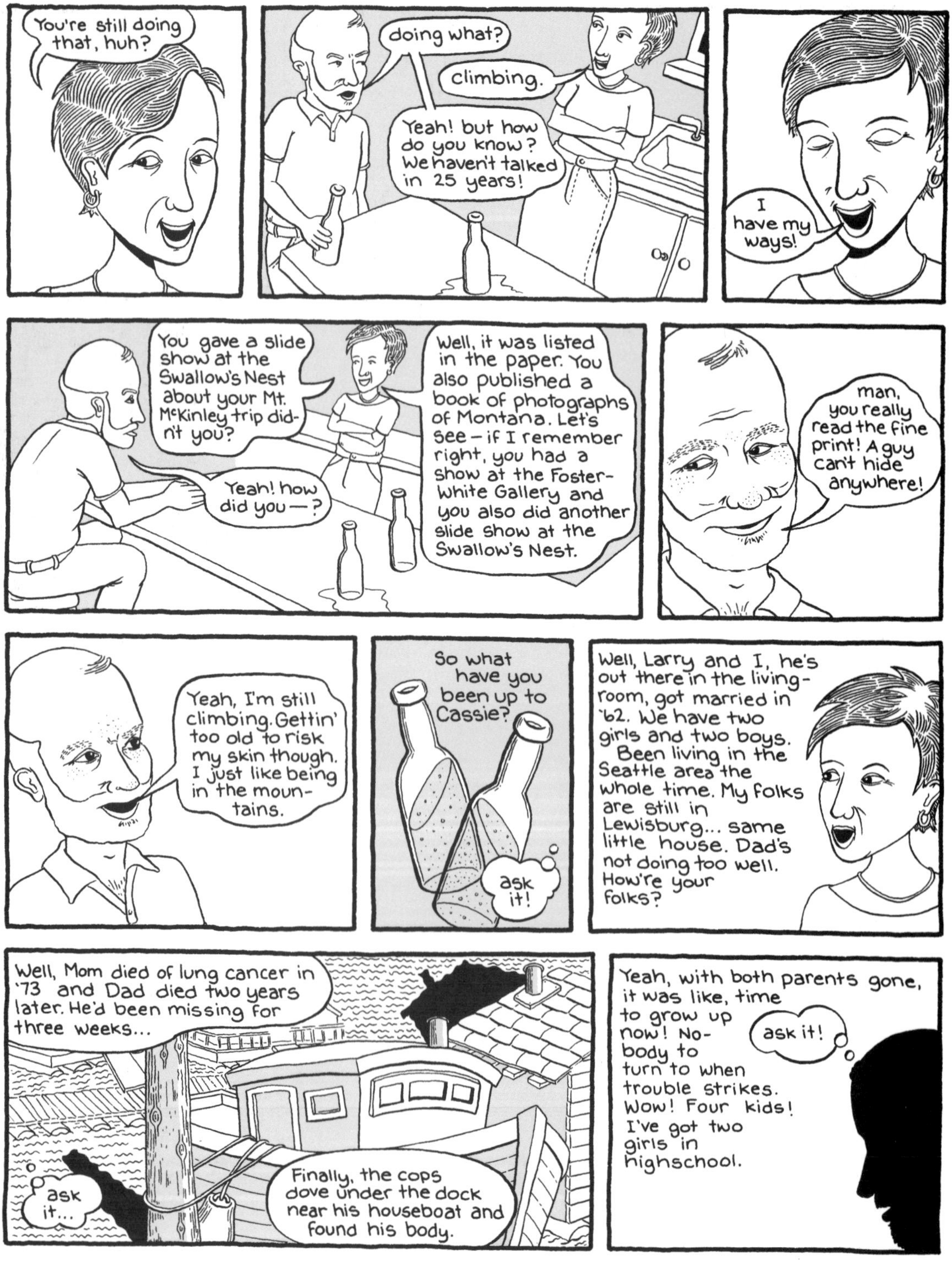
You're still doing that, huh?
doing what?
climbing.
Yeah! but how do you know? We haven't talked in 25 years!
I have my ways!
You gave a slide show at the Swallow's Nest about your Mt. McKinley trip didn't you?
Yeah! how did you—?
Well, it was listed in the paper. You also published a book of photographs of Montana. Let's see – if I remember right, you had a show at the Foster-White Gallery and you also did another slide show at the Swallow's Nest.
man, you really read the fine print! A guy can't hide anywhere!
Yeah, I'm still climbing. Gettin' too old to risk my skin though. I just like being in the mountains.
So what have you been up to Cassie?
ask it!
Well, Larry and I, he's out there in the living-room, got married in '62. We have two girls and two boys. Been living in the Seattle area the whole time. My folks are still in Lewisburg... same little house. Dad's not doing too well. How're your folks?
Well, Mom died of lung cancer in '73 and Dad died two years later. He'd been missing for three weeks...
ask it...
Finally, the cops dove under the dock near his houseboat and found his body.
Yeah, with both parents gone, it was like, time to grow up now! Nobody to turn to when trouble strikes. Wow! Four kids! I've got two girls in highschool.
ask it!

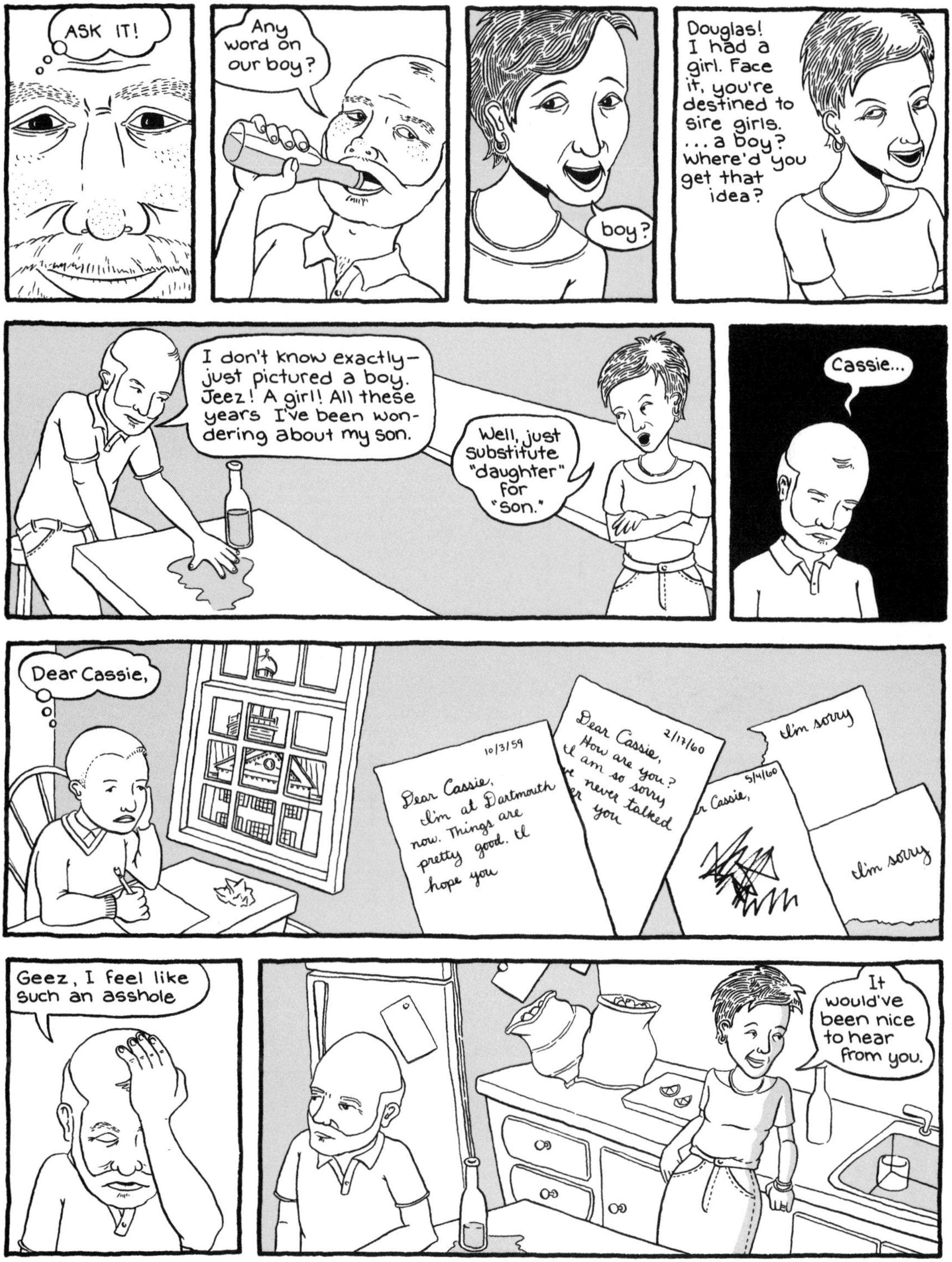
ASK IT!
Any word on our boy?
boy?
Douglas! I had a girl. Face it, you're destined to sire girls. ... a boy? where'd you get that idea?
I don't know exactly—just pictured a boy. Jeez! A girl! All these years I've been wondering about my son.
Well, just substitute "daughter" for "son."
Cassie...
Dear Cassie,
10/3/59
Dear Cassie, I'm at Dartmouth now. Things are pretty good. I hope you
2/17/60
Dear Cassie, How are you? I am so sorry
e never talked
r you
5/4/60
r Cassie,
I'm sorry
I'm sorry
Geez, I feel like such an asshole
It would've been nice to hear from you.

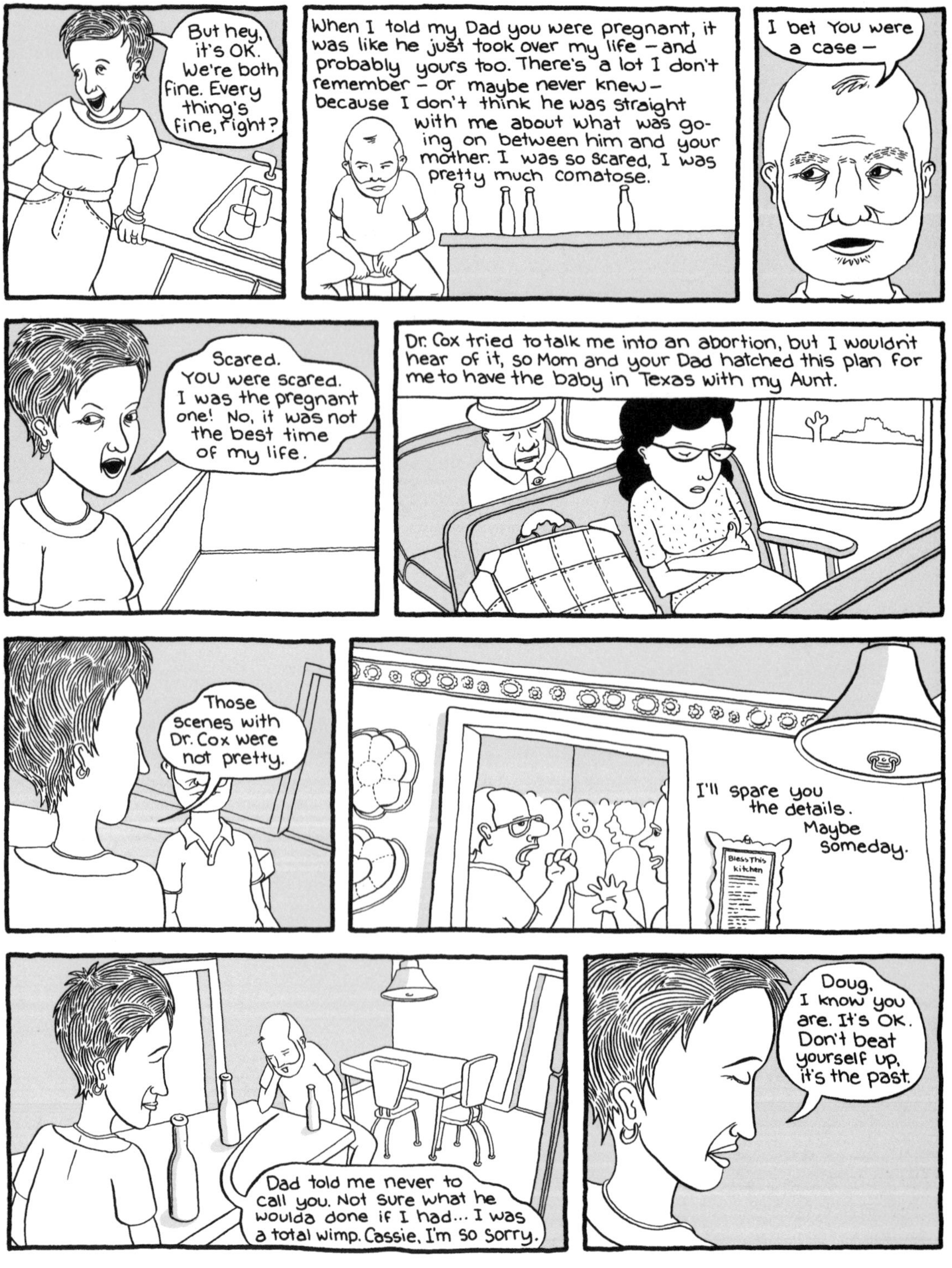
But hey, it's OK. We're both fine. Every thing's fine, right?
When I told my Dad you were pregnant, it was like he just took over my life – and probably yours too. There's a lot I don't remember – or maybe never knew – because I don't think he was straight with me about what was going on between him and your mother. I was so scared, I was pretty much comatose.
I bet You were a case –
Scared. YOU were scared. I was the pregnant one! No, it was not the best time of my life.
Dr. Cox tried to talk me into an abortion, but I wouldn't hear of it, so Mom and your Dad hatched this plan for me to have the baby in Texas with my Aunt.
Those scenes with Dr. Cox were not pretty.
I'll spare you the details. Maybe someday.
Bless This kitchen
Dad told me never to call you. Not sure what he woulda done if I had... I was a total wimp. Cassie, I'm so sorry.
Doug, I know you are. It's OK. Don't beat yourself up, it's the past.

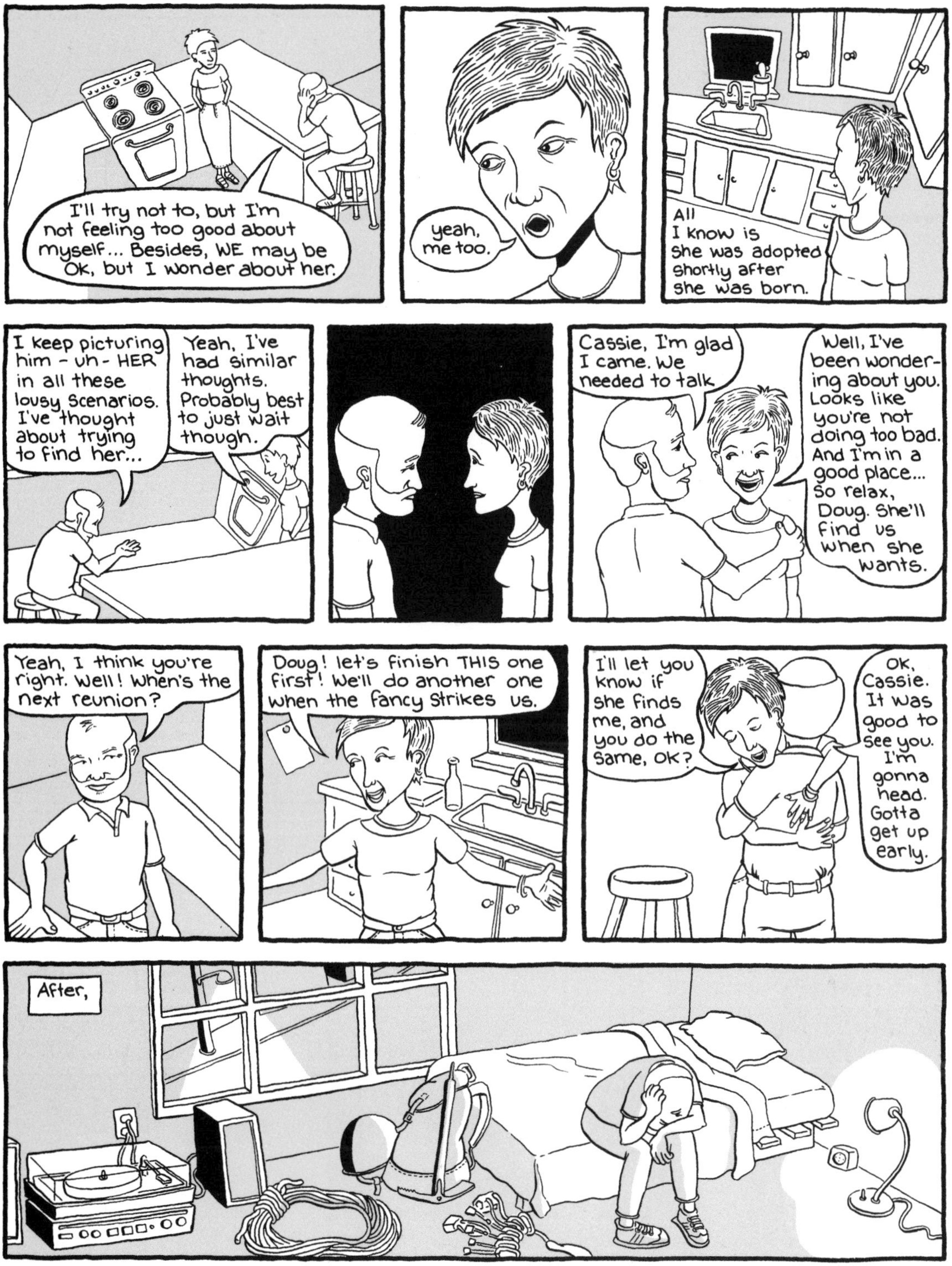
I'll try not to, but I'm not feeling too good about myself... Besides, WE may be Ok, but I wonder about her.
yeah, me too.
All I know is she was adopted shortly after she was born.
I keep picturing him - uh - HER in all these lousy scenarios. I've thought about trying to find her...
Yeah, I've had similar thoughts. Probably best to just wait though.
Cassie, I'm glad I came. We needed to talk.
Well, I've been wondering about you. Looks like you're not doing too bad. And I'm in a good place... So relax, Doug. She'll find us when she wants.
Yeah, I think you're right. Well! When's the next reunion?
Doug! let's finish THIS one first! We'll do another one when the fancy strikes us.
I'll let you know if she finds me, and you do the same, OK?
OK, Cassie. It was good to see you. I'm gonna head. Gotta get up early.
After,

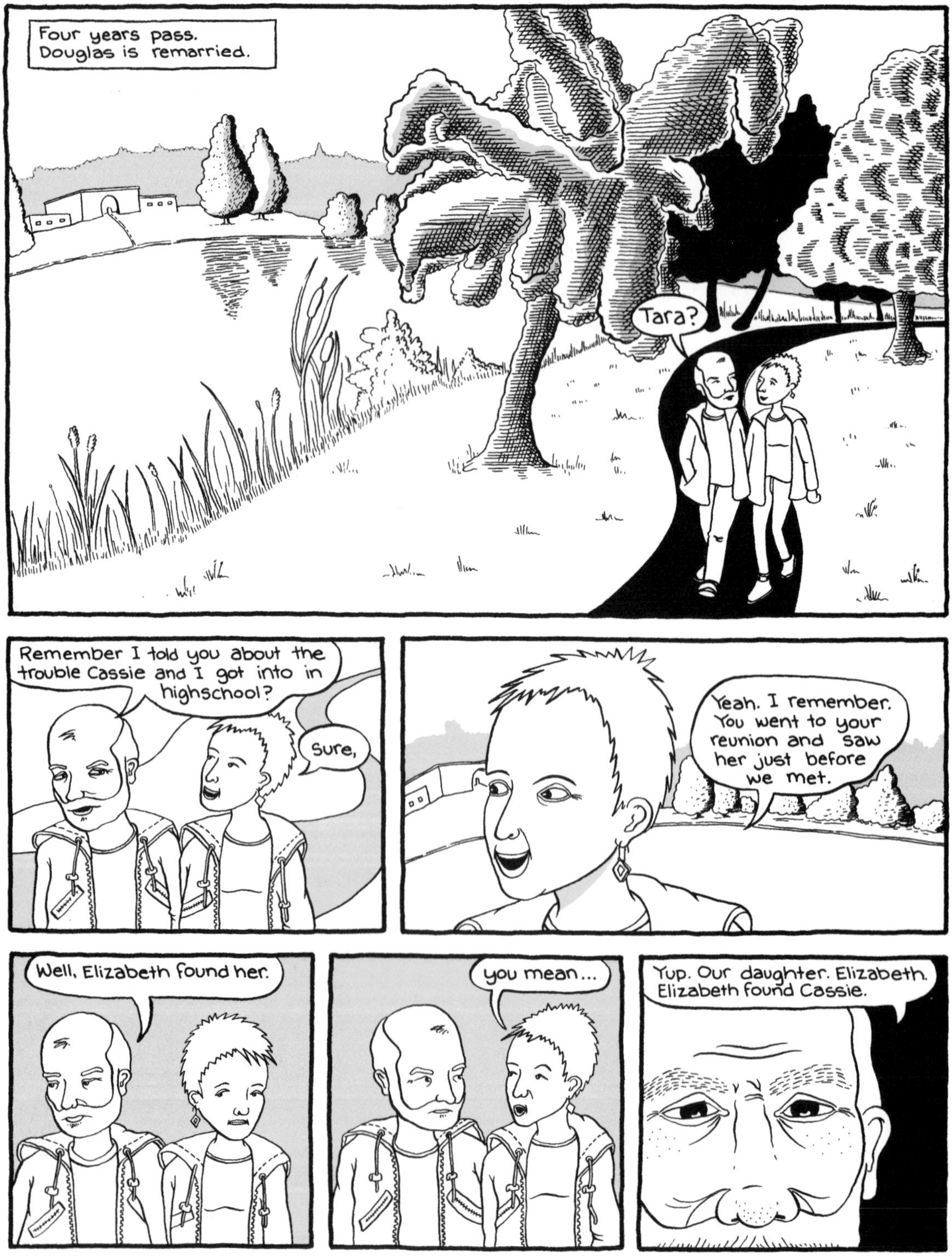
Four years pass.
Douglas is remarried.
Tara?
Remember I told you about the trouble Cassie and I got into in highschool?
Sure,
Yeah. I remember. You went to your reunion and saw her just before we met.
Well, Elizabeth found her.
you mean...
Yup. Our daughter. Elizabeth. Elizabeth found Cassie.

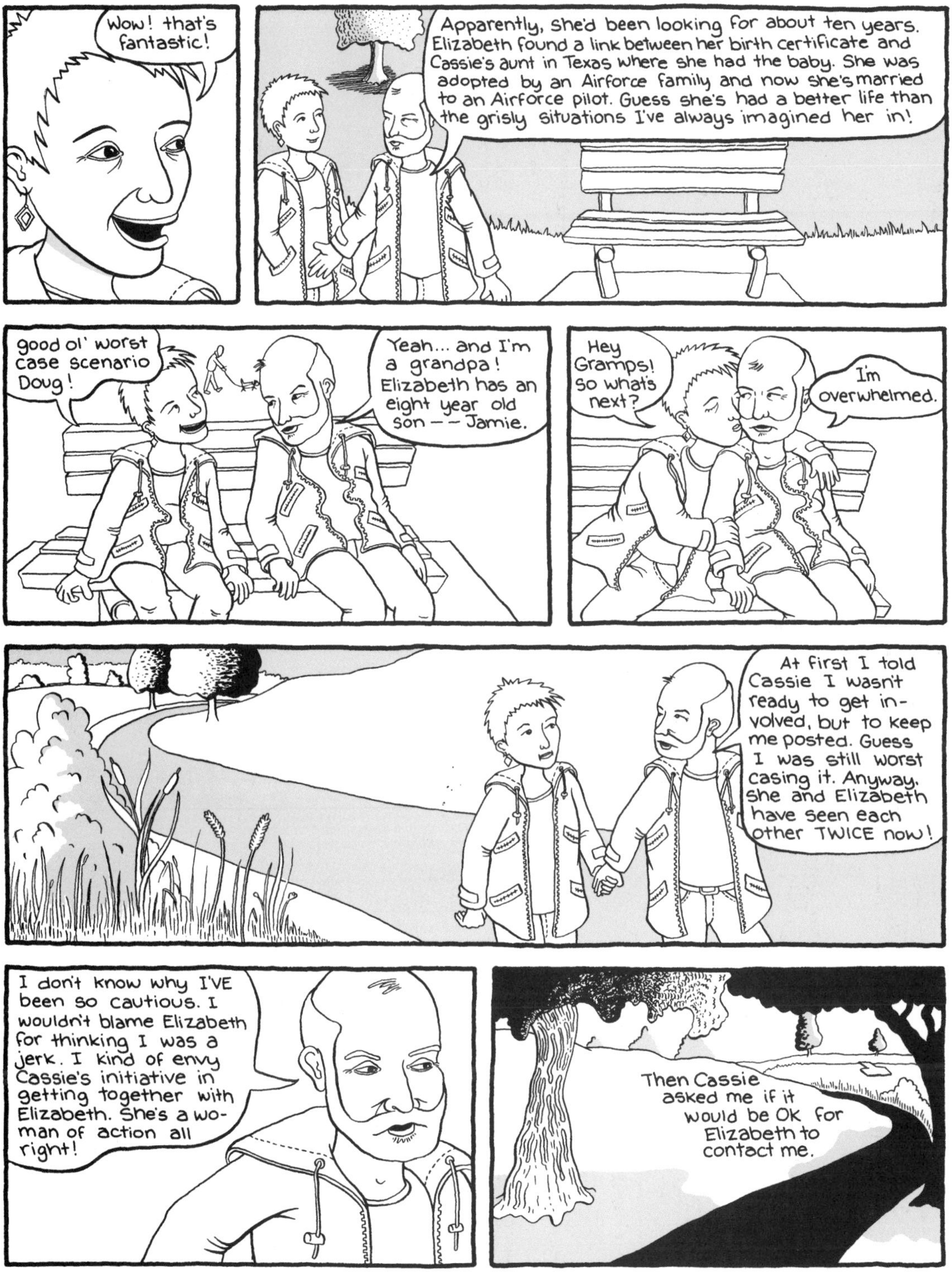

Wow! that's fantastic!
Apparently, she'd been looking for about ten years. Elizabeth found a link between her birth certificate and Cassie's aunt in Texas where she had the baby. She was adopted by an Airforce family and now she's married to an Airforce pilot. Guess she's had a better life than the grisly situations I've always imagined her in!
good ol' worst case scenario Doug!
Yeah... and I'm a grandpa! Elizabeth has an eight year old son -- Jamie.
Hey Gramps! so what's next?
I'm overwhelmed.
At first I told Cassie I wasn't ready to get in-volved, but to keep me posted. Guess I was still worst casing it. Anyway, she and Elizabeth have seen each other TWICE now!
I don't know why I'VE been so cautious. I wouldn't blame Elizabeth for thinking I was a jerk. I kind of envy Cassie's initiative in getting together with Elizabeth. She's a wo-man of action all right!
Then Cassie asked me if it would be OK for Elizabeth to contact me.

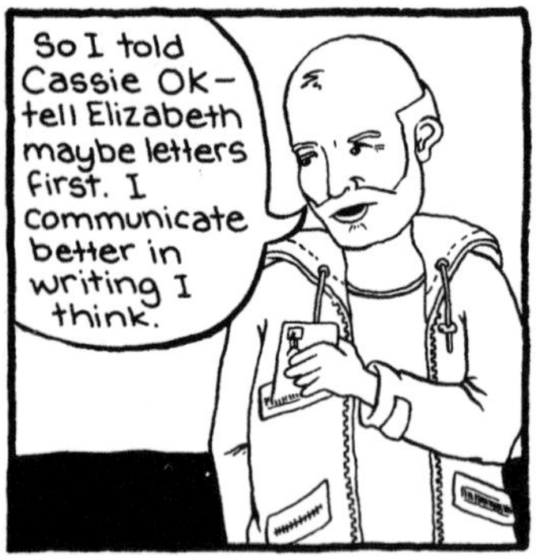
So I told Cassie Ok– tell Elizabeth maybe letters first. I communicate better in writing I think.

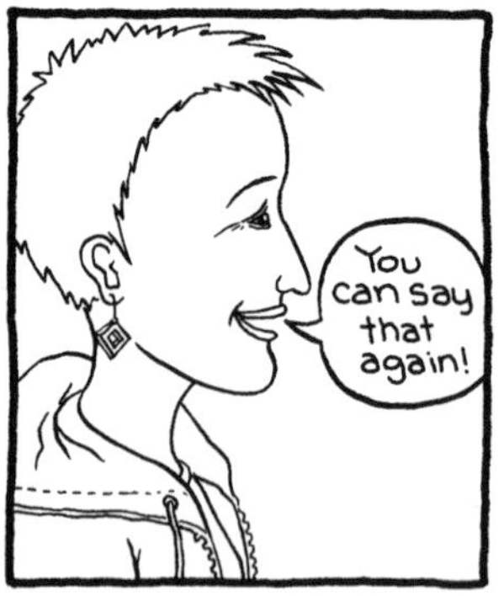
You can say that again!

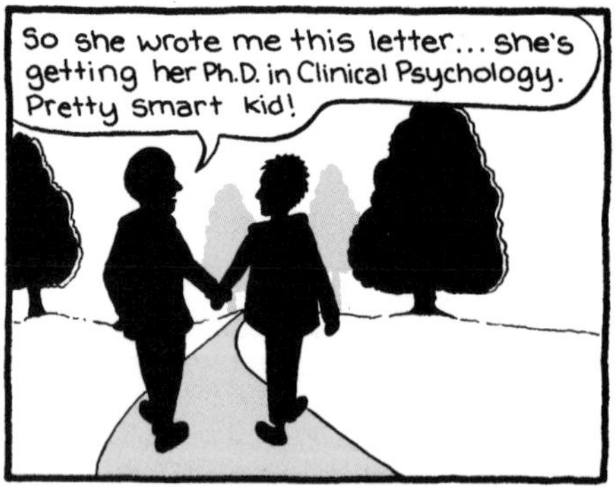
So she wrote me this letter... she's getting her Ph.D. in Clinical Psychology. Pretty smart kid!

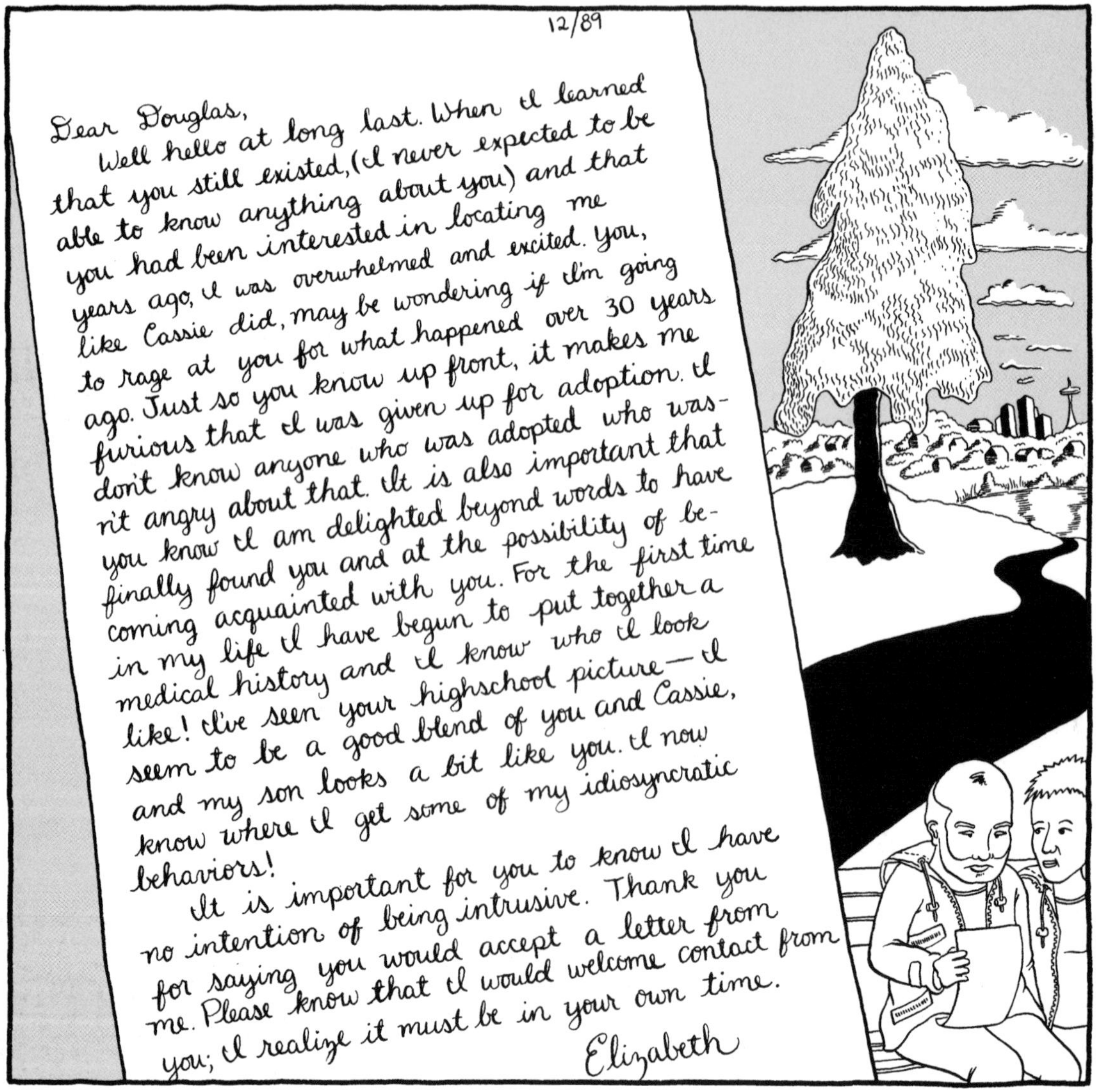
12/89
Dear Douglas,
Well hello at long last. When I learned
that you still existed, (I never expected to be
able to know anything about you) and that
you had been interested in locating me
years ago, I was overwhelmed and excited. You,
like Cassie did, may be wondering if I'm going
to rage at you for what happened over 30 years
ago. Just so you know up front, it makes me
furious that I was given up for adoption. I
don't know anyone who was adopted who was-
n't angry about that. It is also important that
you know I am delighted beyond words to have
finally found you and at the possibility of be-
coming acquainted with you. For the first time
in my life I have begun to put together a
medical history and I know who I look
like! I've seen your highschool picture— I
seem to be a good blend of you and Cassie,
and my son looks a bit like you. I now
know where I get some of my idiosyncratic
behaviors!
It is important for you to know I have
no intention of being intrusive. Thank you
for saying you would accept a letter from
me. Please know that I would welcome contact from
you; I realize it must be in your own time.
Elizabeth

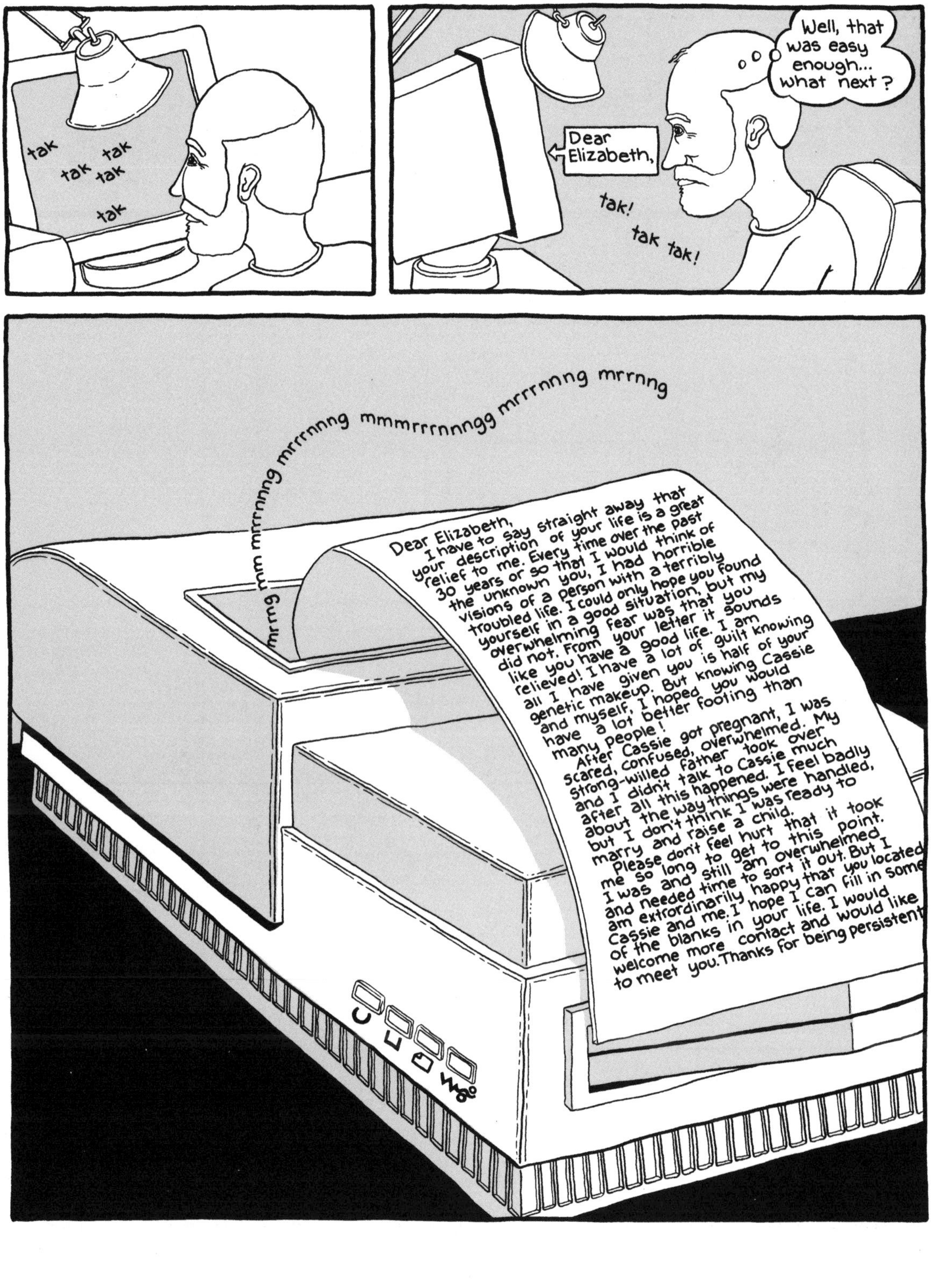
tak tak tak tak tak tak
Dear Elizabeth,
tak! tak tak!
Well, that was easy enough... what next?
mrrng mm mrrrnnng mrrrnnng mrrrnnng mmmrrrnnngg mrrrnnng mrrnng
Dear Elizabeth,
I have to say straight away that
your description of your life is a great
relief to me. Every time over the past
30 years or so that I would think of
the unknown you, I had horrible
visions of a person with a terribly
troubled life. I could only hope you found
yourself in a good situation, but my
overwhelming fear was that you
did not. From your letter it sounds
like you have a good life. I am
relieved! I have a lot of guilt knowing
all I have given you is half of your
genetic makeup. But knowing Cassie
and myself, I hoped you would
have a lot better footing than
many people!
After Cassie got pregnant, I was
scared, confused, overwhelmed. My
strong-willed father took over
and I didn't talk to Cassie much
after all this happened. I feel badly
about the way things were handled,
but I don't think I was ready to
marry and raise a child.
Please don't feel hurt that it took
me so long to get to this point.
I was and still am overwhelmed
and needed time to sort it out. But I
am extrordinarily happy that you located
Cassie and me. I hope I can fill in some
of the blanks in your life. I would
welcome more contact and would like
to meet you. Thanks for being persistent

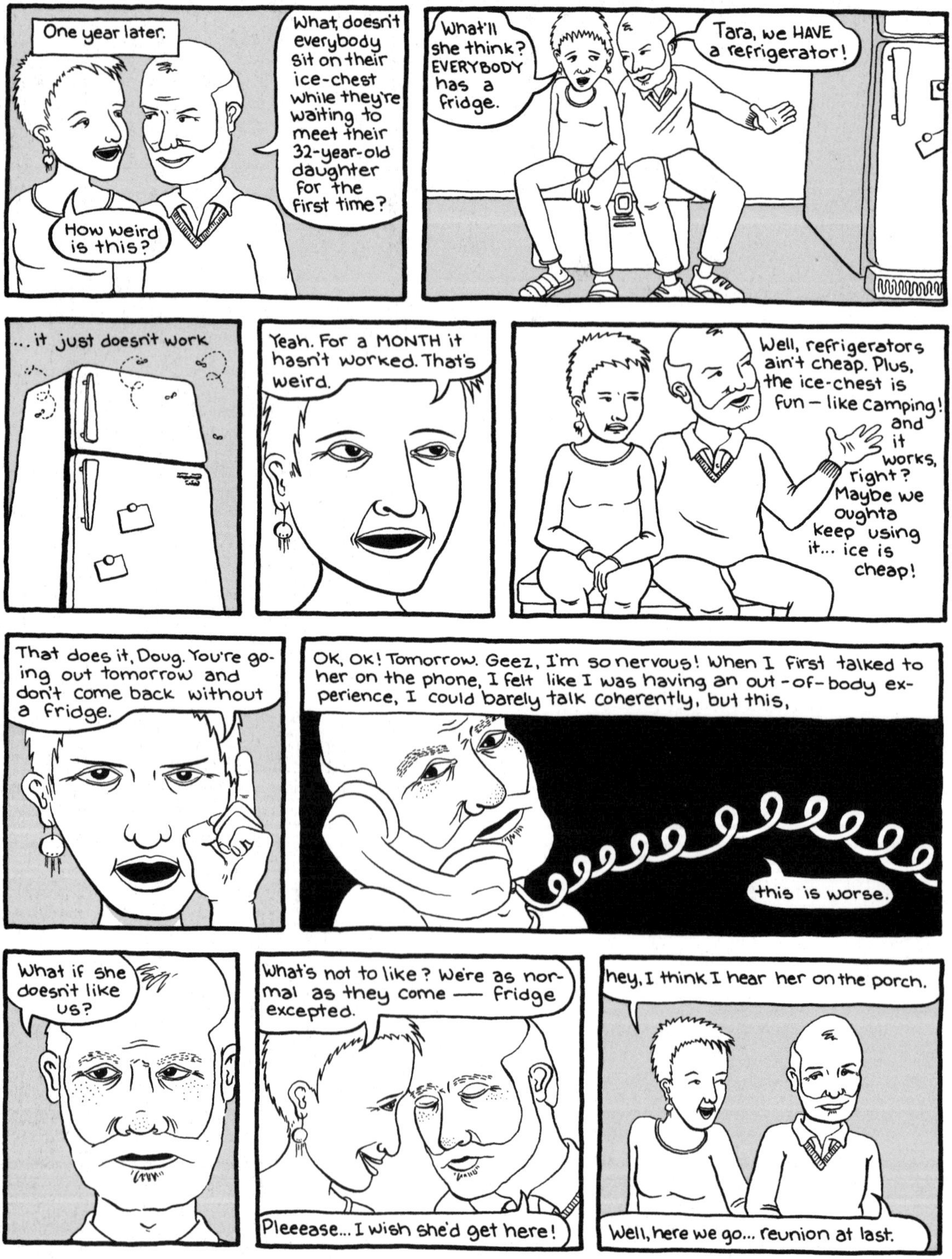

One year later.
How weird is this?
What, doesn't everybody sit on their ice-chest while they're waiting to meet their 32-year-old daughter for the first time?
What'll she think? EVERYBODY has a fridge.
Tara, we HAVE a refrigerator!
... it just doesn't work
Yeah. For a MONTH it hasn't worked. That's weird.
Well, refrigerators ain't cheap. Plus, the ice-chest is fun — like camping! and it works, right? Maybe we oughta keep using it... ice is cheap!
That does it, Doug. You're going out tomorrow and don't come back without a fridge.
OK, OK! Tomorrow. Geez, I'm so nervous! When I first talked to her on the phone, I felt like I was having an out-of-body experience, I could barely talk coherently, but this,
this is worse.
What if she doesn't like us?
What's not to like? We're as normal as they come — fridge excepted.
Pleeease... I wish she'd get here!
hey, I think I hear her on the porch.
Well, here we go... reunion at last.

NOTES

(Originally written in 1998 for the first edition of this book.)

FROZEN ANGEL
Girlhero #1, July 1993

————

I self-published the first *Girlhero* with Xeric Grant money. Though this story is not autobiographical, the girl's apartment resembles the one I lived in during my final year of college in 1991. This was the first work I did with a brush, after realizing the limits of inking with a Rapidograph pen.

HER PEAS AND QUEUES
Girlhero #2, February 1992

————

This was my first dialogue-heavy story and I learned a lot about word balloon placement. I also began to question my labor intensive, large, block-lettering method when I almost got carpal tunnel syndrome lettering this story. Unwisely, I stuck with it for two more issues! I think I feared my own ineffable "style" would be lost if I changed it.

RESERVOIR
Girlhero #3, July 1994, Action Girl, 1994

————

This is another story where the central idea was based on a dream—probably generated by the fact that I lived across the screet from a reservoir.

THE ART OF BEING A SUCCESSFUL BUSINESS GIRL
Girlhero #3

————

The initial idea was a time-travelling office temp. In my research I came across a secretarial manual from the 1920s and that helped me flesh out the story. It never really came together, though, and I think "interesting failure" would be the kindest way to describe this story.

WHISTLE & QUEENIE
Dark Horse Presents #100, 1995

————

"W&Q" is special to me because it marks the point at which I had enough of a handle on the rudiments of making a comic that I was able to start thinking soberly and analytically about such things as panel order, transitions, and manipulating time.

COMPOSITION
Action Girl #3, 1995

————

This is the first story I inked with a dip-pen. My main concern was how to represent music without resorting to cartoony musical notes or written-out song lyrics. I wanted the music to be a physical part of the story and to be literally a visual translation of sound. This has become an obsession of mine in comics.

THE MARRIED MAN

Girlhero #4, April 1995

The only autobiographical element in this story is that I am, in fact, a janitor and the story takes place in Olympia, Washington where I went to college.

PENNYROYAL TEA

Girlhero #5, May 1996

Finally, I give up the labor-intensive block lettering! During the summer of 1995, I started doodling little people with artichoke hats. I drew them constantly; I couldn't stop drawing them. It was not the first time in my artistic life that a single image took hold of me and wouldn't let go. This story did not, however, cure me of my artichoke jag. I am planning to do a whole book of artichoke tales in the future.

IN ZANANA

Girlhero #5

This is the first story where I made all the panels exactly the same size. It was nice to remove one of the many decisions required in making comics. It freed me to concentrate on other things such as how to draw fabric. My boyfriend had recently given me as a birthday present *Dynamic Wrinkles & Drapery* by Burne Hogarth.

THE REUNION

Girlhero #6, November 1997

I'd mentioned to my Dad numerous times that I'd like to collaborate with him on a comic, but I figured he'd give me some sweet tale from childhood. What I got was one of the pivotal experiences of his life. I learned from this story that when I write a comic, I'm also semi-consciously visualizing it in my head. When my Dad handed me his script, I drew a total visual blank. I thought it was going to be weird drawing my Dad having sex, but once I got going, it was just like drawing any other character.

QUEEN OF THE BLACK BLACK

1997

This story is inspired by the work of the sculptor, Louise Nevelson. It is not in *any* way biographical though. The story has nothing to do with Nevelson's life. However, the poem at the beginning of the story starting with "I am…" was written by her. I'd been planning to do this story since *Girlhero #4*, but I kept putting it off. I agonized about how ro draw the Queen's artwork and finally decided to paint it with gouache because I didn't think I could pull off the density I wanted with just black and white. So the paint was, essentially, a crutch.

THE DADDY MASK

1998

For the third time, I try to draw music. I am still not satisfied!